HOLT
Social Studies

North Carolina Constitution
Study Guide

★ ★ ★ ★ ★ ★ ★ ★

- **Establishes connections with North Carolina Civics and Economics Competency Goals and Objectives**

- **Examines the history and development of the U.S. Constitution**

- **Illustrates connections between the North Carolina and U.S. Constitutions**

- **Discusses the North Carolina and U.S. Constitutions in a modern context**

- **Encourages critical thinking**

AMERICAN BAR ASSOCIATION
Defending Liberty
Pursuing Justice

1866

HOLT, RINEHART AND WINSTON

A Harcourt Education Company

Orlando • **Austin** • New York • San Diego • London

To the Teacher

The chapters of this Constitution Study Guide examine the sources, development, and application of the U.S. Constitution. In addition, constitutional parallels and similarities to the North Carolina Constitution are noted in the margin next to the relevant discussion. The texts of the U.S. Constitution and the North Carolina Constitution, both with annotations, follow the chapters. Answers to all assessment items, including the Section Reviews, Going to the Source and Constitutional Challenge exercises, and Constitutional Analysis Questions, can be found in the *Civics in Practice: Principles of Government and Economics, North Carolina Edition,* Teacher Support System.

Written by the American Bar Association Division for Public Education:
Standing Committee Chair Alan Kopit; Division Director Mabel McKinney-Browning; Contributing Writers James Landman, Katie Fraser, and Michelle Parrini.

ISBN 10: 0-03-096295-1

ISBN 13: 978-0-03-096295-0

4 5 6 7 032 10 09 08

Education for Democracy

At the time the Constitution was signed, America had just survived a war of independence with Britain, only white men could vote, and the vast majority of black men and women were enslaved. In the two centuries since then, the United States has survived a civil war, two world wars, and a revolution in civil rights. Today, the United States is the largest democracy in the world. It is a country in which all citizens over the age of eighteen can vote regardless of race or gender. And the U.S. Constitution is still the supreme law of the land, the oldest written constitution in the world that is still in force.

Why has the U.S. Constitution endured through the wars, crises, and social changes of two hundred years? One reason is that the Constitution is a flexible document that can be changed and interpreted. It has been amended twenty-seven times since it was signed in 1787. Another is that the American people have continued to learn about the U.S. Constitution, support it, and participate in our dynamic democracy.

A constitution begins as words on paper. But a constitution must be lived, not just read. Every generation must learn about the Constitution. Every citizen must understand it in order to be able to respond to changing circumstances, appreciate the significance of our liberties, and engage in civil discourse about our nation's future.

This book was written by the American Bar Association Division for Public Education. The Division's programs, publications and resources are intended to educate and inform people about law and the justice system. The Division's work reaches millions of people every year.

Public education about the Constitution and the law is crucial to maintaining and improving our constitutional democracy. The ABA is committed to making it a more integral part of the education that all citizens receive.

There is an old saying that the course of civilization is a race between catastrophe and education. In a democracy such as ours, we must make sure that education wins the race.

-President John F. Kennedy

www.abanet.org/publiced

DIVISION FOR
PUBLIC
EDUCATION
AMERICAN BAR ASSOCIATION

TABLE OF CONTENTS

TABLE OF CONTENTS

CHAPTER 3

THE BILL OF RIGHTS 46

North Carolina Civics and Economics Objectives

1.07 Evaluate the extent to which the Bill of Rights extended the Constitution.

2.06 Analyze court cases that demonstrate how the United States Constitution and the Bill of Rights protect the rights of individuals.

CHAPTER 4

THE LIFE OF THE CONSTITUTION:
HISTORICAL MILESTONES 71

North Carolina Civics and Economics Objectives

3.06 Analyze how the Fourteenth Amendment extends the Bill of Rights' protection to citizens of a state.

TABLE OF CONTENTS

SOURCES OF THE CONSTITUTION

✦ This illustration depicts the signing of the Declaration of Independence. The Declaration expresses many defining American constitutional principles.

What You Will Learn

In this chapter you will learn about the influences on our constitutional principles and government structure. These influences included

★ The political ideas of ancient Greek and Roman writers
★ The political ideas of seventeenth and eighteenth century writers
★ Ancient Greek and Roman governments
★ The trends of European and English governments during the seventeenth and eighteenth centuries
★ The colonial experience of self-government
★ The colonial struggle with the British for power after the French and Indian War, and
★ The weakness of Britain's unwritten constitution.

Ancient Sources of the Constitution

Introduction

The writers of the U.S. Constitution studied different types of ancient governments. They learned about democracy from books about ancient Greece. They drew lessons from the experiences of the ancient governments of Athens and Rome. Likewise, the political theories of ancient Greek and Roman writers such as Plato, Aristotle, and Cicero affected American thinking about constitutional principles.

Ancient Greek Democracy

The United States is a democracy. **Democracy** is a form of government that allows people to participate in governing. A democracy may be a **direct** or an **indirect democracy**. In a **direct democracy**, people participate in government directly by voting. In an **indirect democracy**, people participate in government indirectly by electing other people to represent them and vote on laws for them. Democracy in the United States is indirect. We elect people to represent and govern for us. Our representatives write and vote on laws for us. You will learn more about our system of representation in Chapter Two. You will also learn more about modern democracies in Chapter Five.

Many cities called **city-states** existed in ancient Greece. Greece was not united under one ruler. Each city-state had its own independent government and government leader. Some of the city-states had monarchies. A **monarchy** is a government ruled by one person for life. Many monarchies are hereditary. The ruler of a monarchy receives his position by birth. **Monarch** is the term for the ruler of a monarchy.

Some city-states in ancient Greece had democracies. The city-state of Athens experimented with democracy from 505–322 BC. In the fifth century, as many as 60,000 men participated directly in government in Athens by voting on laws. But not everyone participated in government. Athens established qualifications for citizenship. Only citizens had rights such as voting on laws. Only men born in Athens who owned land met the citizenship qualifications. This meant that only landowners could vote to accept laws. For the first time in history in ancient Athens, more than a very few people participated directly in governing.

ANCIENT DEMOCRACY: 505–322 BC

Ancient Athens had three branches of government

- an Assembly of Citizens
- a Council of 500 Citizens
- a People's Court

The Assembly and the Council made laws. The Council of 500 included 50 men from each of the 10 tribes of Athens. Anyone who was a citizen could attend the Assembly to vote on laws. During the Peloponnesian War (431–404 BC), some 5,000 men attended each Assembly meeting!

✦ Plato ran a famous Academy, or school, in Athens and was Aristotle's teacher. They both wrote about ideal governments.

Ancient Greek Writers

Common Good

Plato (c. 428–348 BC) wrote about his views on the ideal, or best, government in an essay called *The Republic* (360 BC). During Plato's lifetime, people believed that rulers often made decisions to serve their own self-interest. They did not do what was best for the country. Critics believed these leaders weakened the structure of government. They believed a strong government required leaders who put aside their own individual or private interests. Plato expressed the idea that self-interest should be kept separate from political power.

According to Plato, the ideal **state**, or government, should not just make the ruler happy. It should not just make one group of people happy. The goal of the ideal state was to create good for all collectively. Individuals, Plato believed, needed to give up certain things for the good of all citizens. In some instances, people might seek their own individual happiness in Plato's ideal state. They could act on their own behalf as long as their actions hurt no one else.

In his book *Politics* (350 BC), Aristotle (384–322 BC) also expressed the opinion that ideal governments should be concerned with the common good, or common interest.

Likewise, the men who wrote the U.S. Constitution believed that government should create a common good. They also thought that individuals should be free to seek their happiness as individuals. When they wrote the Constitution, Americans combined these two ideas. Under our Constitution, individuals are free to act as long as their actions do not restrict the freedom of another person or harm a greater common good.

Constitutions

During his lifetime Aristotle also wrote about constitutions. A constitution was not just a written document for Aristotle. It was the way of life of a society. By constitution, Aristotle meant the laws, customs, and institutions that create order for people.

FOCUS ON NORTH CAROLINA CONSTITUTION

The idea that government should benefit all citizens goes back to Ancient Greece. So does the idea of a constitution, which is a blueprint for a government. The Preamble to the North Carolina Constitution includes both ideas. It states that "this Constitution" is established to secure the people's civil, political, and religious liberties, and "for the better government of this State."

★ ★ ★ ★ ★ ★

JOBS FOR ANCIENT WOMEN

In *The Republic*, Plato wrote that in the ideal state, jobs as rulers and soldiers should be open to women. He believed girls should receive the same kind of education as boys so they might become future rulers and soldiers. Plato wrote *The Republic* in 360 BC. Yet in the United States, women were only given the legal right to vote in 1920 with the passage of the Nineteenth Amendment to the U.S. Constitution.

England based its constitution on Aristotle's ideas. England's constitution has many sources. Some of the sources are written. Some sources are not written. Aristotle's list of sources for a constitution are all sources of laws and rights for the English constitution.

As you will learn in Section III, Americans wanted a written constitution. Based on their experience, the American colonists came to believe that England's unwritten constitution allowed government to abuse its power.

Republics

In addition to writing about the qualities of ideal governments, many ancient Greek writers described types of government. One type they described is a **republic**. To the ancient Greeks, a republic was a **representative democracy**. Another term for representative democracy is indirect democracy. In ancient times in a republic,

- People elected representatives to act and govern in their general interests,
- Different parts of society participated in governing, and
- An elected leader served for a limited period of time.

The American colonists understood a republic to have these three qualities.

The Roman Republic

The Greek experience in Athens influenced the founding of a Roman republic. Greek writers also influenced its founding principles. Established in 509 BC, in the Roman Republic, elected representatives acted and governed in the common interests of Rome's people. Different parts of society participated in governing, and the leader served for a limited period of time.

REVOLUTIONARY AMERICANS AND ANCIENT HEROES

Many colonial Americans admired Athenian democracy and the Roman Republic so much that they took nicknames, or pen names, for themselves from ancient heroes. Writers John Trenchard and Thomas Gordon used the pen name Cato. Cato supported the Roman Republic. He led campaigns against the establishment of a hereditary emperor in Rome.

◆ Aristotle was from Macedonia, also the home of Alexander the Great, whom he tutored. After Alexander conquered Athens, Aristotle created an Athenian school called the Lyceum.

The Roman Republic was a **mixed government**. A mixed government has characteristics of a monarchy, aristocracy, and democracy. **Aristocracy** is a type of government ruled by the individuals born into a country's noble class. Aristocracy also refers to the group of individuals born into nobility in a country. An **aristocrat** is a person who inherits or is born into the noble, high-ranking class of society. For much of history, and as late as the nineteenth century, people often viewed aristocrats as the best individuals to govern.

In his nonfiction essay "On the Republic," Cicero (106–43 BC) wrote that a mixed government was the most desirable form of government. Plato and Aristotle agreed. In general, ancient Greek and Roman writers believed that a mixed government was ideal.

Ancient writers thought that a republic was the most desirable government because it was balanced. In a **balanced government**, no single interest, group of people, or branch of government dominates the governing. A republic's mixed-government structure allowed different parts of society to participate in governing.

In addition, the Roman Republic was a **limited government**. No single person held complete governing authority. The head of the Roman Republic included two leaders who shared a position called a consul. The other branches of government checked the power of the consuls. The government structure included a Senate composed of the aristocracy, also known as the **patricians**. The Senate created laws. It also watched over the two consuls.

✦ Cicero was a successful Roman lawyer. He was elected to each of the major Roman offices, including consul, and supported the Roman Republic.

The third government branch was called the **council of plebes**. The council of plebes included people called **plebeians**. Plebeians held citizenship rights but were not aristocrats.

Wars between 133–31 BC increased the size of the Roman Republic. In 31 BC the republic ended. A hereditary monarch called an emperor became the ruler. The Senate and council of plebes lost their power.

FOCUS ON NORTH CAROLINA CONSTITUTION

The North Carolina Constitution places limits on the state government. For example, Article I, Sections 7 and 8, prohibit state government from taking certain actions without the consent of the people. Article I also lists the rights of the people that are protected by the constitution against the power of the state.

✦ As consul, Cicero ordered the execution without trial of five people for their role in a plot to take over Rome. Later, he was exiled for it. When Caesar became the first emperor of Rome, he pardoned Cicero.

The Beginning of the American Republic

Before they wrote the Constitution, some Americans idealized the golden age of the Roman Republic with its balanced and mixed government. They wanted to create a representative (indirect) democracy. Others wanted to create a more direct democracy, like the democracy of ancient Athens.

Many Americans believed that the geographic conquests of Rome weakened its republican government structure. They believed a republic could only work in a small geographic area. After declaring independence from Britain, Americans considered the Roman experience when they set up their first state governments. They thought of each state as a republic. You will learn more about early state governments in Chapter Two.

Americans also considered the Roman experience when they wrote the federal Constitution. Some people reasoned that a republic covering a large territory would prevent factions, or groups of people united by particular interests, from dominating government. They believed that a republic's balanced government framework would be more easily sustained under a federal system. A federal system of government is one in which two or more states agree to unite and grant control of common matters to a central authority created by and with the consent of the members. In fact, in a newspaper article called *The Federalist No. 10* (1787), James Madison argued that if particular groups sought dominance within a state or among various states, their power would be lessened by the many other groups within a federal system. Madison wrote that an extensive geographic area offered ideal conditions for a republic.

In the end, the word *democracy* did not appear in the U.S. Constitution. Article IV, Section 4 provides "The United States shall guarantee to every state in this Union a Republican Form of Government." Our government became more democratic over time. At first, very few people participated in government in the United States. You will learn more about the expansion of democracy in our country in Chapter Four.

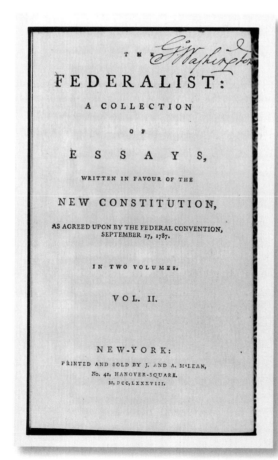

✦ *The Federalist* essays, also known as *The Federalist Papers*, were originally published individually as a series of newspaper articles. In *The Federalist No. 10*, James Madison advocated for a federal republic for the United States.

THE G⁰ Washington
FEDERALIST:

A COLLECTION

OF

E S S A Y S,

WRITTEN IN FAVOUR OF THE

NEW CONSTITUTION,

AS AGREED UPON BY THE FEDERAL CONVENTION, SEPTEMBER 17, 1787.

IN TWO VOLUMES.

VOL. II.

NEW-YORK:

PRINTED AND SOLD BY J. AND A. M'LEAN, No. 41, HANOVER-SQUARE. M,DCC,LXXXVIII.

SECTION 1 REVIEW

IMPORTANT TERMS

1 Match the terms in the right column with the definition in the left column.

A. A government allowing people to participate in governing — **Balanced**

B. A government ruled by the noble class, or individuals belonging to nobility — **Aristocracy**

C. A government with qualities of monarchy, aristocracy, and democracy — **Athens**

D. A government in which no one interest, group, or government branch dominates — **Mixed**

E. A government in which complete authority belongs to no single person — **State**

F. A democratic Greek city-state — **Democracy**

G. A word for government — **Limited**

2 Pick the two words in the following group of words or phrases that represent two different types of government. Write each of the words at the top of a separate column. In each column, list the words that describe that type of government.

- monarchy
- elected
- hereditary
- governs for life
- governs for set time
- republic

REVIEWING FACTS

3 What type of government did Plato, Aristotle, and Cicero believe was the best?

4 List the two criteria for citizenship in the city-state of Athens.

5 To the American colonists and the ancient Greeks and Romans, a republic had three characteristics. List the characteristics.

REVIEWING MAIN IDEAS

Use complete sentences to answer the following questions.

6 What is a direct democracy? Give an example.

7 What is an indirect democracy? Give an example.

8 What is the goal of Plato's ideal state?

9 What did *constitution* mean for Aristotle?

10 What ancient sources influenced our constitutional principles?

UNDERSTANDING CONCEPTS

11 Societies have rules or laws for our common good. For example, we drive on the right-hand side of the street. The common good achieved is safety. List three laws. Next, write a paragraph answering the question, What common good is achieved by each law?

Enlightenment Political Thought and Experience

Introduction

The **Enlightenment** was a period of great changes in worldviews in Europe, England, and the colonies. It lasted from the 1650s to the 1750s. During the Enlightenment, people began to believe that learning came from experience. People observed and wrote about the world. It was an age of science.

The American colonists considered the ideas of Enlightenment thinkers. Like the ancient Greeks, Enlightenment thinkers wrote about the best types of government. The ideas of these Enlightenment thinkers can be seen in our constitutional principles.

Absolute and Limited Monarchy

Enlightenment thinkers wrote about two trends of their age. These trends influenced their theories about governments and politics. They wrote about the development of

1. Absolute monarchies in Europe from 1660–1789
2. A limited monarchy in England between 1642–1688.

Before 1660, monarchs and aristocrats shared governing in Europe. Then the monarchs took important jobs from the aristocrats. Aristocrats lost the jobs of overseeing the military, collecting taxes, and running the courts.

✦ Jacob Leisler led a revolt in 1689 against colonial officials in New York who supported King James II, and headed the provisional government until 1691.

Without responsibilities important to the monarch, aristocrats had no way to influence a king. Monarchs then held absolute governing power. Aristocrats could not check the monarch's power. For example, aristocrats could no longer threaten to keep tax money from a king if a monarch abused his power. These monarchies existed from 1660–1798.

England followed a different path. Today, the English Parliament is the representative assembly of England. It has two chambers—the House of Lords and the House of Commons. The modern Parliament makes laws. Before 1642, the Parliament's job was to collect taxes. Sometimes Parliament advised the king. It was not a representative assembly. Before 1642, the aristocrats belonging to Parliament did not make laws, but they wanted a greater role in government. After 1642, they fought for power with the monarch.

Finally, in 1688 in a bloodless struggle called the Glorious Revolution, Parliament won. King James II left the country. Then Parliament invited William and Mary of Orange to become the English monarchs. They agreed to terms listed in a bill of rights. Under the English Bill of Rights (1689), a monarch could no longer make or end laws without Parliamentary approval. Without permission from Parliament, a monarch could not collect taxes. Also, the king could not keep an army during peacetime.

The Glorious Revolution permanently limited the monarch's power. In the 50 years after the Glorious Revolution, the prime minister, the leader of Parliament, and Parliament shared governing with the monarch. They checked the power of the crown. Most important, England became a limited government.

◆ Through the Glorious Revolution, the English Parliament secured a greater role in government. Today, Parliament makes laws and is the representative assembly of England.

Did You KNOW?

The period of world history from 1660–1789 is called the Age of Absolutism because European monarchs held absolute governing power.

The Social Contract, Natural Rights, and Popular Sovereignty

Did You KNOW?

Leviathan is a word that comes from Hebrew. It can mean something unusually large or overawing. Why do you think Thomas Hobbes chose the word *leviathan* as the name of his book?

Enlightenment thinkers sought explanations for the world that were not religious or centered around God. Before the Enlightenment, people thought God or religion could explain everything. They believed in the divine right of kings. The **divine right of kings** meant that God chose a monarch. Likewise, God gave the monarch authority to rule. The monarch then was only answerable to God. During the Enlightenment, writers questioned the idea that a king's sovereignty came from God. **Sovereignty** means "supreme," *or the highest degree of political authority.* No longer believing in the divine right of kings freed thinkers to express new theories about the origin or source of sovereignty. Two of these thinkers included the Englishmen Thomas Hobbes (1588–1679) and John Locke (1632–1704). Hobbes and Locke also wrote about their opinions on the best relationship between people and their government.

The Social Contract

Thomas Hobbes thought that people were selfish. He thought they would always place their own private interests before common, public interests. In his book *Leviathan* (1651), Hobbes wrote that in nature, before people formed a society, pre-existing principles arose. He called the principles **natural laws**. According to Hobbes, because of the conflicts that resulted when people pursued their own interests, people formed a society. They also agreed to follow laws and rules for behavior. Hobbes called the agreement a **social contract**. People agreed to the social contract because otherwise wars would be constant.

◆ Thomas Hobbes thought that without a strong central government to keep people in check, they would wage constant wars "of every man against every man."

To enforce the social contract, people granted sovereignty to a political authority. It was the job of a political authority or ruler to enforce natural laws. The ruler needed to keep peace. Hobbes believed since people were selfish, only a strong ruler could keep peace. Hobbes viewed human nature negatively.

In contrast, John Locke viewed human nature positively. He believed that people were essentially fair and unselfish. In his nonfiction essay, *Two Treatises of Civil Government* (1690), Locke wrote that people were sometimes able to act for a common good. He thought that people should have great individual freedom to act. Locke also believed in a social contract between people and their government. But Locke believed that the purpose of a social contract was mostly to resolve occasional conflicts. Because people were fair, Locke thought government should be limited. He thought no one in government should have absolute power. Locke believed people could usually govern themselves.

Natural Rights

Locke thought natural law gave people natural rights. **Natural rights** are rights bestowed on people by birth. One of Locke's natural laws was that all men were equal. By equal, Locke meant that no man meeting citizenship qualifications was entitled to greater privileges than another man by birth. In England, aristocrats had hereditary privileges. Aristocrats inherited their right to serve in Parliament. For Locke, equality gave all male citizens the natural rights to life, liberty, health, and property.

Popular Sovereignty

Most important, Locke wrote that government received its sovereignty from the people. **Popular sovereignty** is the phrase for the idea that people created their government and agreed or consented to be governed by it. As part of the social contract, people expected government to protect natural rights if conflicts occurred. Locke also believed if government failed to protect natural rights, it broke the social contract. If government broke the social contract, Locke thought that people should overthrow those who governed.

Locke's ideas greatly influenced American constitutional principles. For example, when the colonists declared independence, they argued that revolution was their right because England broke its part of the social contract. England failed to preserve the colonists' natural rights.

Separation of Powers

Like Hobbes and Locke, Frenchman Baron de Montesquieu (1689–1755) also wrote about the most desirable relationship between people and their government. He expressed ideas about how to prevent government and its leaders from abusing power.

In his book *The Spirit of the Laws* (1748), Montesquieu wrote that a republic needed three separate branches of government. Otherwise, he thought power would be abused. The branches are the executive, legislative, and judicial.

The executive branch of government is the head or leader of government. The executive's job is usually to enforce laws. Examples include a monarch, a prime minister and his cabinet, or an elected president and his cabinet. The legislative branch of government is the branch that makes laws. Examples include the U.S. Congress and the two chambers of the British legislature, the House of Commons and the House of Lords. The judicial branch, or court system, interprets laws and settles disputes.

THE
Fundamental Conſtitutions
OF
CAROLINA.

◆ Initially, the *Fundamental Constitutions of Carolina* guaranteed religious freedom. However, a revision in 1670 established the Church of England as the official religion of the Carolina Colony.

FOCUS ON NORTH CAROLINA CONSTITUTION

The North Carolina Constitution, Article I, Section 2, makes it clear that the people are sovereign. It states that "All political power is vested in and derived from the people; all government of right originates from the people, [and] is founded upon their will only . . . "

FUNDAMENTAL CONSTITUTIONS OF CAROLINA

For many years John Locke served as the secretary and doctor to Sir Anthony Ashley Cooper, Earl of Shaftesbury, who was one of the aristocrats granted land from King Charles II in the Carolina Colony. Locke drafted the *Fundamental Constitutions of Carolina* (1669) as one of his secretarial duties, but he is not credited with the principles for governing established by that document. The Fundamentals gave the power to pass colony laws to the aristocracy.

✦ Known for his ideas on separation of government powers, in addition to publishing *The Spirit of the Laws* (1748), the lawyer and philosopher Montesquieu published a famous novel in 1721 called *The Persian Letters.*

Montesquieu advocated for a **separation of powers** among the three branches. By separation of powers, he meant that each branch should have different responsibilities. With different responsibilities, each branch could check the power of the others. For example, he suggested that the legislature collect and set levels of taxes. Then it could refuse to give money to the executive if it abused its power. He believed that the legislature should be divided into two bodies. More important, both bodies should approve all laws. Then one body could prevent passage of a law proposed by the other. Also, Montesquieu thought that the executive should be able to veto laws. He thought that the executive veto kept the legislature from passing a poor law. Likewise, he thought the approval of two legislative bodies kept lawmakers from creating poor laws.

Montesquieu's ideas about the separation of powers became important in the development of the American Constitution. Americans themselves can be credited with expanding and refining his ideas over time. In the colonial experience, the executive had too much influence over the business of the other branches. You will learn more in Section 3 about the rising influence of the colonial governors. When Americans first thought about applying the concept of the separation of powers to the Constitution, they particularly wanted to keep the legislature free from the power and influence of the executive.

Enlightenment Ideas for the American Government

Before they wrote the Constitution, Americans argued about the qualities of a desirable government. Some Americans believed only a strong central government could keep order and peace in the new country. Some believed the new country required a strong executive branch.

Other Americans believed that people could govern themselves. They thought that government should only step in to settle conflicts. They believed that most power should belong to individuals. Likewise, they believed that most power should be left to the states.

Eventually, when the Constitution was written, it created a mixed and balanced government. Americans embraced the constitutional principle of separation of powers. You will learn more about this in Chapter Two. Most important, they embraced the principle of shared power.

IMPORTANT TERMS

1 Match the terms in the right column with the definition in the left column.

A. The representative assembly of the English government

B. A word meaning "supreme," or the highest degree of political authority

C. Hobbes' term for pre-existing principles that arose from nature

D. Locke's term for rights bestowed on people at birth

E. Locke's term for an agreement between people and their government

Natural rights

Natural laws

Sovereignty

Social contract

Parliament

REVIEWING FACTS

2 List three responsibilities the monarchs in Europe took from the aristocrats during the Age of Absolutism.

3 The English Bill of Rights kept the monarch from doing certain things. List three.

4 Montesquieu thought a republic needed three branches of government. List the branches.

REVIEWING MAIN IDEAS

Use complete sentences to answer the following questions.

5 Define the divine right of kings.

6 Why did Hobbes believe that people formed a society and agreed to the social contract?

7 What was the purpose of the social contract for Locke?

8 What is popular sovereignty?

9 What does separation of powers mean?

UNDERSTANDING CONCEPTS

10 In our society people usually agree to behave in certain ways and expect others to behave in certain ways, often for mutual benefit. Hobbes and Locke called the agreement between people and their government a social contract. Using complete sentences, describe the social contract (agreement) in the relationships below.

• The relationship between a parent and a child

• The relationship between a school and a student

• The relationship between a hospital and a patient

Pick two of the relationships you just wrote about and describe what might happen if people broke their end of the bargain in the social contract. How are the consequences of a broken social contract in these two sets of relationships similar and/or different? How do the consequences differ from those resulting from a broken social contract between citizens and their government?

Colonial Experience and Revolution

Introduction

The knowledge colonists gained from their participation in their colonial governments influenced American thinking about constitutional principles. They also applied what they learned about the flaws of the British constitution during their struggle with the British to the American constitution. During the period immediately before the Revolutionary War, the colonists expressed many enduring principles in pre-revolutionary documents and pamphlets. These principles are found today in our Constitution.

✦ Between 1607-1733, the British established thirteen colonies in North America.

Colonial Government Experiences

The English founded the thirteen colonies in North America in three ways.

- People agreed to a compact. A compact is an agreement.

- A company or corporation received a charter of incorporation from the monarch. A charter is a type of contract.

- An aristocrat received a grant of land from the crown. The grant also gave the aristocrat power to rule the colony.

The men who founded Plymouth Colony in 1620 used a compact. They signed a document called the Mayflower Compact. This created a community of like-minded religious believers. But these believers also agreed to form a civil government. **Civil** means of the state or government. The members of Plymouth Colony agreed to follow rules of a civil government as a condition of belonging to their community. The founders of compact colonies believed that government should be based on a social compact. Another term for social compact is **social contract**.

By contrast, corporation colonies were established when the monarch granted a company a charter of incorporation. Colonists received the right to conduct colonial trade from the charter. The charter described the conditions, privileges, and rights of the company. The men who directed colony companies also received the right to establish a civil government.

Most colonies offered the colonists experience participating in government. At first, England did not have money to send governors from England as overseers. Mainly, the struggle between Parliament and the monarchy concerned the people of England. So, the colonists had great freedom in how they set up local governments. Each government was different. But by 1702, all colonial governments except Pennsylvania had

- An elected assembly
- A governor, and
- An advisory council.

Men who owned property in a colony could vote for assembly representatives. Assemblies collected taxes. They also made local laws. But the laws needed approval by the British government. Eventually, the British government started to appoint council members and the governor. The governor needed approval from the council for his actions, but the governor could also veto laws. However, the assemblies controlled the budget, including the governor's salary. Controlling the budget gave an assembly some power over the governor.

The three branches of government shared the governing. Their separate powers and functions checked and balanced the power of the others. No branch held more power than another.

FOCUS ON NORTH CAROLINA CONSTITUTION

The colonial tradition of granting elected assemblies control of the budget is found in both the U.S. Constitution and in state constitutions. Article III, Section 5, of the North Carolina Constitution gives the governor the authority to prepare a budget for the state, but Article II, section 23, requires that the General Assembly approve all spending.

Henry Bouquet served in the British Army and defended Britain's colonies during the French and Indian War. He is well known for his role in a conflict, depicted in this illustration, which occurred after the war concluded. The conflict was Pontiac's Rebellion (1764).

What is Congress?

Congress is a word that means "coming together to meet." It may also refer to the law-making or legislative body of a nation. The men who assembled at the First Continental Congress of 1774 came together to strategize ways to deal with acts or laws passed by the British Parliament. They did not intend to declare independence. Likewise, the colonists did not consider their congress to be a new national government.

Shared Sovereignty and Local Representation

After the French and Indian War (1754–1763), the British government changed its policy in the colonies. The British had four goals:

1. To establish British sovereignty, or political authority, over colonial governments

2. To manage the colonies through its central government in Great Britain

3. To collect more of the colonies' trade profits. The British government wanted colonial profits to pay for the costs of the French and Indian War

4. To make the colonial governments the same

The British Parliament passed a series of **acts**, or laws, to reach its goals. The laws changed the balance of power between the three branches of colonial government. The governor became stronger. The central government in Great Britain also became stronger. It now held more power than the local branches of government. The colonists' experiences with local governing led them to believe that the best government divided and shared power among its branches.

The colonists thought that the new laws violated the social contract between Great Britain and the colonies. At first, the colonists did not seek independence. They tried to negotiate the social contract. They believed they had certain rights. For example, they tried to keep their right to be tried in colonial courts. Parliament took away that right by passing the Coercive Acts of 1774. Under the Coercive Acts, British officials accused of a crime could be taken to England and tried.

In negotiating their rights, the colonists proposed a division of sovereignty. In other words, the colonists wanted to share power with Great Britain. They wanted to collect colonial taxes. Also, they wanted to make local laws. The colonists thought they should run the local courts, too. On the other hand, the colonists believed that the British government should make decisions about matters concerning the entire British Empire. They believed decisions about international trade, foreign affairs, and the defense of the empire belonged to government bodies in Great Britain. The colonists expressed their wish for shared sovereignty in the Declaration of Resolves of the First Continental Congress (1774). But the British Parliament rejected this proposal.

Representation in government was another area of conflict between the colonists and the British. The colonies could not elect representatives to Parliament. Most members of Parliament believed they each individually represented the interests of Great Britain as a whole. Because the colonies were part of the empire, every Parliament member represented the interests of the colonies. But the colonists believed in electing people locally to represent them in government.

Four Constitutional Principles

The colonists found it difficult to resolve their differences with the British about representation and sharing power. More and more they believed the British government had violated the terms of the social contract. During the Second Continental Congress (1775), the colonists in attendance began to act like an independent nation by officially establishing a Continental Army. This action ultimately led to a declaration of independence from Great Britain. First, however, Thomas Paine, a democratic political thinker, wrote an influential pamphlet titled *Common Sense*. In the pamphlet, published in January 1776, Paine argued that independence from Great Britain was a logical outcome of British-American history to that point. Paine offered five main arguments. First, America would be ruined by British wars for empire, which would destroy colonial international commerce. Second, it was "absurd" for a continent to be governed by an island. Third, the British system was corrupt because it gave governing powers to people through hereditary rights. Fourth, monarchy did not allow for checks and balance. The same people who made laws were appointed as ministers to serve the king. Fifth, only independence could secure peace on the continent. The pamphlet persuaded many colonists to support independence from Britain.

On August 2, 1776, every member of the Second Continental Congress signed a document called The Unanimous Declaration of the Thirteen United States of America. We know this document as The Declaration of Independence. The Declaration of Independence described four lasting American constitutional principles.

The first principle is that all men have natural rights. These rights are theirs from birth. They include the rights to life, liberty, and the pursuit of happiness. They include all other rights that support the rights to life, liberty, and the pursuit of happiness, many of which the framers of the Constitution later outlined in our Constitution.

The second principle is that government must be based on a social contract between those who agree to come together in a society to be governed by particular laws and the government that enforces those laws for the common good.

The third principle is the principle of popular sovereignty. People must consent to be governed and grant supreme political authority to government.

The fourth principle is that when government breaks the social contract, it is no longer valid. Therefore, people have the right to revolt against the government after carefully weighing all alternatives.

A fifth constitutional principle expressed in the Declaration of Independence held a different meaning in the eighteenth century from its meaning today. The principle is that all men are created equal. Equality in the eighteenth century meant that no man held greater rights by birth than any other man. The colonists believed that the British system was corrupt because it granted hereditary rights to aristocrats to sit in the House of Lords. Until 1911, the House of Lords could veto legislation. Americans did not believe that such great hereditary powers should be granted to anyone.

WHO READ COMMON SENSE?

People bought 600,000 copies of Thomas Paine's *Common Sense*. At the time, the population of the colonies was 3,000,000. Slaves made up 20 percent and indentured servants made up 50 percent of the population. Indentured servants had their passage to the colonies paid in exchange for an agreement to serve a master for 4-7 years. The servant became the property of the master for the term of the contract.

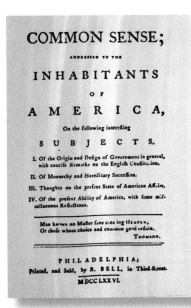

Thomas Paine's pamphlet *Common Sense* (1776) is credited with convincing many colonists to support the movement for independence from Great Britian.

The colonists did not for the most part believe that all men were truly equal. They believed that privilege and social distinctions between free men should be based on merit or achievement. In other words, the colonists believed that all free men should have the opportunity to earn social privilege. It wasn't until the Fourteenth Amendment was ratified, or approved, at the close of the American Civil War in 1865 that the Constitution finally embraced the principle that all men are truly equal under the law.

A Written Constitution

The British constitution has never existed in a single written document. It draws its principles from many sources, including acts of Parliament. Americans decided to write a constitution because of the way the British Parliament changed the British constitution and rights of the colonists through legislation after the French and Indian War. By passing legislation, the British violated the original the terms of the social contract. The colonists believed that this violation justified revolution and independence.

Americans believed that the principles of a constitution should be contained in one source separate from and above a legislature. They wanted the U.S. Constitution to outline basic principles and rights. They wanted to make sure that particular rights could not be changed or eliminated. Americans believed a written Constitution would guarantee people particular rights for all time. You will learn more about these rights in Chapter Three.

◆ The Declaration of Independence expresses defining American constitutional principles.

IMPORTANT TERMS

1 Match the terms in the right column with the definition in the left column.

A. A word meaning "coming together to meet." It may also refer to the law-making or legislative body of a nation

B. An agreement

C. A type of contract

D. Another term for social contract

E. A word for the ordinary life activities of people as opposed to religious or other type of activities

F. The constitutional principle that people must consent to be governed and grant supreme political authority to government

Compact

Civil

Congress

Popular Sovereignty

Social Compact

Charter

REVIEWING FACTS

2 List the three branches of colonial governments that existed in all colonies but Pennsylvania by 1702.

3 Name the document in which the colonists expressed their wish for shared sovereignty with Great Britain.

4 List the five constitutional principles described in the Declaration of Independence.

REVIEWING MAIN IDEAS

Use complete sentences to answer the following questions.

5 Who could vote for colonial assembly representatives?

6 How would you describe the colonists' plan for shared sovereignty with the British government?

7 How did the way the colonists view government representation differ from the view of British Parliament members?

8 What did equality mean in the eighteenth century?

9 What reason did the colonists give to justify revolution and independence from England?

10 How does the Declaration of Independence reflect the ideas of John Locke?

11 Why did Americans want a written constitution?

UNDERSTANDING CONCEPTS

12 Take a look at your state's constitution. Which of the five American constitutional principles described in the Declaration of Independence do you think it expresses? List the principles. Next, write a paragraph explaining which of the principles on your list is the most important. Provide reasons for your choice.

Going to the Source

Declaration and Resolves of the First Continental Congress

Each of the thirteen colonies sent representatives to the First Continental Congress—a meeting to strategize ways to handle the conflict with Great Britain. They met from September 5, 1774 to October 14, 1774 in Philadelphia. At their meeting, representatives wrote the *Declaration and Resolves of the First Continental Congress.* It included twelve **resolves**, or declarations, outlining the points of the British-American conflict. It also described ways to deal with the conflict. When the colonists wrote this document, they had no intention of seeking independence from Great Britain.

1. Before you read the passage below, define the following words: *immutable, cede, emigration, forfeit, provincial,* and *bona fide.* Forms of these words are used and underlined in the reading. Use a dictionary when needed.

2. Read the passage below from the Declaration and Resolves. Use complete sentences to answer the questions that follow.

That the inhabitants of the English colonies in North-America, by the <u>immutable</u> laws of nature, the principles of the English constitution, and the several charters or compacts, have the following RIGHTS:

Resolved, 1. That they are entitled to life, liberty and property: and they have never <u>ceded</u> to any foreign power whatever, a right to dispose of either without their consent.

Resolved, 2. That our ancestors, who first settled these colonies, were at the time of their <u>emigration</u> from the mother country, entitled to all the rights, liberties, and immunities of free and naturalborn subjects, within the realm of England.

Resolved, 3. That by such emigration they by no means <u>forfeited</u>, surrendered, or lost any of those rights, but that they were, and their descendants now are, entitled to the exercise and enjoyment of all such of them . . .

Resolved, 4. That the foundation of English liberty, and of all free government, is a right in the people to participate in their legislative council: and as the English colonists are not represented, and from their local and other circumstances, cannot properly be represented in the British parliament, they are entitled to a free and exclusive power of legislation in their several <u>provincial</u> legislatures, where their right of representation can alone be preserved, in all cases of taxation and internal polity, subject only to the negative of their sovereign, in such manner as has been heretofore used and accustomed . . . we cheerfully consent to the operation of such acts of the British parliament, as are <u>bona fide</u>, restrained to the regulation of our external commerce, for the purpose of securing the commercial advantages of the whole empire to the mother country, and the commercial benefits of its respective members; excluding every idea of taxation internal or external, for raising a revenue on the subjects, in America, without their consent.

Declaration and Resolves of the First Continental Congress

OCTOBER 14, 1774

CRITICAL THINKING

A. What are the four sources described in the reading that give the colonists their rights?

B. What charters and compacts do you think the colonists mean in the introduction?

C. According to resolve 1, what three rights did the colonists believe were guaranteed to them?

D. According to resolve 1, why were the colonists guaranteed their rights?

E. According to resolves 2 and 3 taken together, why else were the colonists guaranteed their rights?

F. According to resolve 4, why did the colonists think they should have the power of *provincial* legislation?

G. According to resolve 4, what did the colonists think were bona fide activities for the British Parliament in the colonies?

H. The word *polity* can mean *policy*. Reread resolve 4. What do you think the colonists wanted to control when they wrote they wanted power over "internal polity"?

I. What phrase can be used to describe the division of powers proposed by the colonists in resolve 4?

The Authority of Federal and State Governments

Many organizations, institutions, and governments share power and authority among their different parts. For example, a nonprofit organization may share power and authority among its board of directors and the executive director who is hired to run the agency. We can think about this division of power or authority as illustrating the idea of shared sovereignty. You will recall that the colonists wanted to share sovereignty with the British government before the American Revolution.

Brainstorm

In small groups, decide what kind of power you believe state governments should have and what kind of power you believe the federal government should have. What kinds of activities should each government have authority over?

In your small group, create a plan for shared sovereignty among the state governments and federal government. Provide a **rationale,** or reason, for each job or area of authority assigned to the states or federal government.

As a Class

1. Present your plans and the rationales for the different parts of the plan. Compare them. Do some aspects of some plans seem stronger than other aspects? Why?

2. After learning about the Articles of Confederation (Chapter Two), compare your class plans with the plans for shared sovereignty among the states and federal government under the Articles of Confederation. What similarities exist? What differences do you note?

3. After learning about the plan for shared sovereignty among the states and the federal government created by the U.S. Constitution (Chapter Two), including the Bill of Rights (Chapter Three), compare your class plans with the constitutional plan for shared sovereignty among the states and the federal government. What similarities exist? What differences do you note? What, if anything, surprised you about the final plan for shared sovereignty under the U.S. Constitution?

CHAPTER 7

A NEW CONSTITUTION

✦ This 19th century engraving shows George Washington presiding at the Constitutional Convention in 1787.

What You Will Learn

In this chapter, you will

★ Learn how states drafted constitutions after America broke ties with England in the Declaration of Independence.

★ Learn about the first national government in the United States, and the strengths and weaknesses of the Articles of Confederation.

★ Discover how an armed rebellion in Massachusetts led states to agree to attend a convention to revise the Articles of Confederation.

★ Learn more about the debates and disagreements that shaped the Constitution of the United States.

★ Explore all seven articles of the Constitution, learn about the debates played out in the Federalist Papers and the Anti-Federalist Papers, and learn about subsequent ratification.

A Fragile Union

Introduction

In 1776 the Declaration of Independence formally broke America's ties with England. In the years that followed, the states wrote constitutions and created new, independent governments. The states also ratified the first national constitution, the Articles of Confederation. This document created a confederation of states called the United States of America. The lessons the founders learned in these early years of independence later helped them craft the United States Constitution.

✦ This map shows the original thirteen colonies.

New Hampshire
Massachusetts
New York
Rhode Island
Connecticut
Pennsylvania
New Jersey
Maryland
Delaware
Virginia
North Carolina
South Carolina
Georgia

State Constitutions

In the years after the Declaration of Independence, all of the states created republican governments. A **republic** is a political system in which supreme power is held by the people, who elect representatives to make decisions on their behalf. These new state governments drafted new state constitutions.

Most state constitutions clearly set out the rights of the people, such as freedoms of religion, speech, and the press. These state constitutions also reflected the revolutionary ideal of popular sovereignty. Each state constitution provided for the people to elect their representatives in government. Each state created a legislature. A **legislature** is the branch of government that makes laws. The legislature is composed of members who are elected by the people. These state legislatures could appoint a governor to carry out the laws and a court to resolve disputes.

The legislature had great power. But there were several ways in which its power was limited. Most states created a **bicameral legislature**, which is a legislature composed of two separate chambers. In those states, laws had to be passed by both legislative chambers, so each chamber kept an eye on the other.

In addition, all of the states' constitutions provided for elections every year. If the people weren't happy with what the legislature had (or hadn't) done, the people could vote representatives out of office. However, frequent elections meant that the representatives often focused on improving things in the short term. Little thought was given to the long term. And some state governments focused on the wishes of the majority of voters, which meant that they passed laws that were unfair to minorities. Laws changed quickly; no one could be sure what the law was from one year to the next. Over time, state legislatures started to take over the powers of the state governor and the state courts.

Articles of Confederation

Most colonists were strongly attached to their state and their local community. Many colonists were suspicious of powerful government, and every colony had its own government. The thirteen colonies were like thirteen different countries.

However, the colonists did have some things in common. They spoke the same language and shared a resentment of Britain. When war broke out, they needed to fight together to defeat a common enemy.

After the Declaration of Independence was signed in 1776, representatives from the colonies discussed the need to create a national government to coordinate the fight against the British. These representatives had two main goals: They wanted to create a government with enough power to make important decisions for the nation, but they also wanted to leave much of the power to govern in the hands of the states. With both of these concerns in mind, a committee of colonial representatives drafted a document called the **Articles of Confederation**.

Did You KNOW?

Article 11 of the Articles of Confederation invited Canada to join the United States!

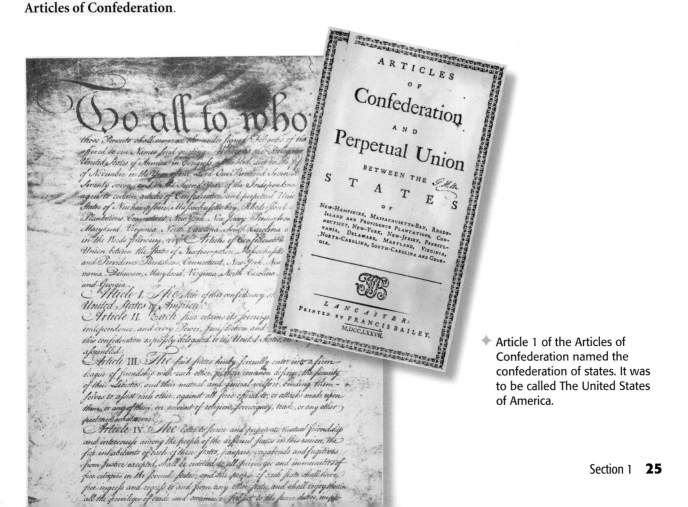

◆ Article 1 of the Articles of Confederation named the confederation of states. It was to be called The United States of America.

Creating a Confederation

The Articles of Confederation created a confederation of states. A **confederation** is a loose union of independent states. A confederation seemed to address both concerns that the representatives had. For example, Article 2 of the Articles of Confederation stated that each state retained its "sovereignty, freedom, and independence." A confederation allowed each state to retain the right to govern within its own borders. But the confederation also gave states the power to join together to deal with some issues, such as fighting the war against Britain and conducting foreign relations with other countries.

The Articles of Confederation created a national Congress to make decisions. The members of this Congress represented the interests of the states. They did not directly represent the people. Under Article 5 of the Articles of Confederation, each state could nominate between two and seven delegates to represent it in Congress. However, each state was entitled to only one vote, no matter how many delegates it had.

Problems Emerge

This first Congress had some important powers, such as the powers to declare war, sign treaties, and appoint ambassadors. But soon after the Articles of Confederation were ratified, states realized that the Articles had some serious problems. It was difficult for Congress to make a decision, because 9 states out of 13 had to agree to important measures. When the Congress did make a decision, it had to depend on the individual states to enforce it—the national Congress had no enforcement power.

Congress also had no power to collect taxes. It had to rely on the states to contribute money to pay for such things as a national army. By the end of the Revolutionary War in 1783, Congress had huge debts to pay to soldiers who had fought in the army. Congress also owed money to citizens who had lent supplies or money to the government during the war. But the national government was broke, and the individual states wouldn't give it any money.

✦ After the Revolutionary War, each state issued its own currency. States often did not accept currency from other states.

Another problem with the Articles was that Congress could not regulate commerce among the states. This weakness led to bitter fighting among states as they squabbled over boundaries, currency, and trade.

Meanwhile, overseas, the reputation of the new United States of America was suffering. European nations knew that the national government had little control over the states and treated the United States with contempt. For example, Britain refused to move soldiers stationed in forts on American territory.

Some states wanted to change, or **amend**, parts of the Articles of Confederation. But Congress could only amend the Articles if all 13 states agreed. The states could never unanimously agree to an amendment.

Shays's Rebellion

Daniel Shays was a farmer who left his land in Massachusetts to fight against the British in the Revolutionary War. When he returned home after the war, times were hard. Farmers could no longer sell their goods to the British, so they didn't have much money coming in. The state government of Massachusetts owed large debts, and in order to pay them, Massachusetts raised taxes. Raising taxes on the poor farmers was hard enough, but if a farmer couldn't afford to pay the taxes, his land was seized and he was imprisoned.

In August 1786, Daniel Shays organized an armed rebellion of farmers to protest these economic problems. The group barred access to court buildings, which prevented the trial and imprisonment of debtors. In January of 1787, Shays led 1200 rebels to capture a federal store of weapons. State armed forces quickly suppressed the uprising and most of the rebels surrendered. But this rebellion didn't go unnoticed.

During the chaos of the rebellion, more states realized how important it was to have a strong national government. The uprising highlighted the fact that the debt-ridden states were unstable. Some landowners feared that dissatisfied citizens would rebel against other state governments. In February, 1787, Congress authorized a meeting of the states in Philadelphia "for the sole and express purpose of revising the Articles of Confederation." Representatives from 12 states agreed to attend.

◆ A portrait of Daniel Shays, leader of Shays's Rebellion. This woodcut was probably made after his death in 1825.

IMPORTANT TERMS

1 Match the terms in the right column with the definition in the left column.

A.	A union of independent states	**Amend**
B.	A word describing a legislature with two chambers	**States**
C.	A system in which the people elect a government to represent them and make decisions on their behalf	**Confederation**
D.	A word you can use to mean *change*, if you are talking about political documents	**Republic**
E.	The word used to describe the colonies in the Articles of Confederation	**Bicameral**

REVIEWING FACTS

2 Why did the states decide to create a national government?

3 List three powers that the Articles of Confederation gave to the national Congress.

4 List three problems that emerged with the Articles of Confederation.

REVIEWING MAIN IDEAS

Use complete sentences to answer the following questions.

5 What are the advantages of having a written constitution, instead of legal protections that are generally accepted but not written down? Why did the American colonists, in particular, think it was important to have a written constitution?

6 The popularly elected legislatures of the state governments had most of the power. What are the disadvantages of concentrating power in the hands of the legislature?

7 List at least two ways in which the power of the legislature could be limited. Which option is more effective? Can you think of any other ways the power of one part of government could be limited?

UNDERSTANDING CONCEPTS

8 Imagine you are asked to help draft a new constitution in 1787. Think carefully about the strengths and weaknesses of the Articles of Confederation and the state constitutions. In complete sentences, suggest the things you would change about the Articles of Confederation.

The Constitutional Convention

Introduction

In May 1787, 55 delegates from the states met in Philadelphia. A **delegate** was a person sent to a conference or a meeting to represent his state. At first, many delegates in Philadelphia simply planned to change the Articles of Confederation. Instead, they created the Constitution of the United States.

Who Was There?

Some of the best and brightest minds in the United States attended the Convention, including George Washington, Benjamin Franklin, Alexander Hamilton, and James Madison. Many delegates were highly educated. Most of them also had practical experience in leadership. Some men had helped draft state constitutions and had been active in state politics. About three-fourths of them had served in the national Congress.

There were also some notable absences. Rhode Island refused to send any delegates. It was afraid that a strong national government would injure its trade. Rhode Island wanted to keep the Articles of Confederation. Also, some of the most important men in politics were absent. For example, Thomas Jefferson and John Adams were both working as ambassadors in Europe.

LESSONS LEARNED

The delegates learned valuable lessons from the weaknesses of the Articles of Confederation. For one, the national government needed more power to be effective. It had to be able to raise taxes and regulate commerce among the states.

The delegates also learned from their observations of state government. Some delegates believed that the elected representatives in state governments were, by simple majority votes, passing unfair laws. These delegates wanted to ensure that the Constitution limited the power of popularly elected representatives.

✦ This sketch shows Independence Hall in Philadelphia, where delegates met to create and sign the Constitution.

✦ In a democracy, the ultimate power to govern rests with the people of the country. That's why the Constitution begins "We the People of the United States . . ."

FOCUS ON NORTH CAROLINA CONSTITUTION

In 1967, then-Governor Dan K. Moore recognized that North Carolina needed constitutional reform. The constitutional changes suggested by the North Carolina State Constitution Study Commission in 1970 were approved by the General Assembly, then approved by the voters. These proposals became the 1971 North Carolina Constitution.

THE DELEGATES

The delegates were from all over the United States and had many different perspectives. But they had a few things in common. Every single delegate was male. Almost every delegate was a landowner. And every delegate was white. Remember that in the 1700s, women, slaves, and Native Americans did not have the right to vote. They had no political power. The founding fathers probably couldn't imagine seeking the input of these groups.

The Virginia Plan

James Madison drafted a plan for the new government before the Convention started. This **Virginia Plan** proposed the creation of a strong national government with separate legislative, executive, and judicial branches. Does this sound familiar? In fact, the Virginia Plan included some features that made it into the Constitution we have today. But the delegates debated other parts of the Virginia Plan, and it changed dramatically over the course of the Convention.

The Great Compromise

The first issue with the Virginia Plan was the representation of the states in Congress. Under the Articles of Confederation, each state was entitled to one vote in Congress. The large states thought this system was unfair. The Virginia Plan proposed that each state should have a number of representatives proportionate to its population. The larger the state, the more representatives it would have. But the small states opposed this plan: They thought such a system would reduce their power and influence.

It looked for a while like the Convention might collapse. Then Roger Sherman, a well-respected delegate from Connecticut, proposed a solution. The people would elect the lower house of Congress, called the House of Representatives, and each state would have a number of representatives proportional to its population. The lower house would then select the upper house, called the Senate, in which every state would have two representatives.

After another two weeks of debate, Sherman's solution was accepted. This solution became known as the **Connecticut Compromise**, or the **Great Compromise**. The Compromise created a federal system that represents both the people and the states.

Congressional Power

Most of the delegates at the Convention agreed that the national government needed to be more powerful. But they disagreed over how power should be divided between the national government and the states.

The Virginia Plan suggested that the national government should have broad powers to legislate in all the areas where states were "incompetent." Some delegates feared that this would give the national government power to legislate on just about anything. An alternative proposal was to limit Congress to specific powers. But James Madison thought that this would limit Congress too much. Eventually, the issue was resolved when a committee wrote the first draft of the Constitution. This draft listed the specific powers of Congress. It did, however, include one potentially broad power, the "necessary and proper" clause. This will be discussed in the next section.

Slavery

Many of the delegates were antislavery. Benjamin Franklin, for example, thought that slavery was "an atrocious debasement of human nature" and "a source of serious evils." However, other delegates supported slavery. Many delegates owned slaves. In order to get unified support for the Constitution, delegates who were pro-slavery and delegates who were antislavery had to make some compromises.

Some of the southern states had large populations of slaves. Delegates from those states wanted to count slaves in the population of their states, which would entitle them to more representatives in the lower house. The northern states pointed out that slaves were not free, and so slaves should not be counted. Antislavery delegate James Wilson of Pennsylvania proposed a compromise. For the purposes of representation and taxation, each slave would be counted as three-fifths of a person. The delegates agreed.

The pro-slavery delegates also insisted that Congress protect the slave trade. As the result of another compromise, the Constitution stated that Congress could not abolish the slave trade for 20 years—until 1808. This did not prevent states from restricting or outlawing the slave trade, which many had already done. Congress passed a national prohibition on trade in slaves at the first moment it was able to do so—effective January 1, 1808.

Signing the Constitution

After months of debate and compromise, only three of the delegates at the Convention refused to sign the new Constitution of the United States; 38 delegates signed. The next step was ratification by the states.

◆ Delegates to the Constitutional Convention used a quill and inkwell, such as the ones shown here, to write and sign the Constitution.

IMPORTANT TERMS

1 **Match the terms in the right column with the definition in the left column.**

A.	The word used to refer to the people who attended the Constitutional Convention	**Two**
B.	The man who drafted the Virginia Plan	**Proportional**
C.	The number of senators in each state	**Delegates**
D.	The type of representation in the House of Representatives	**House of Representatives**
E.	The name of the part of Congress that was originally designed to represent the people	**James Madison**

REVIEWING FACTS

Are the following statements true or false?

2 In the Great Compromise, the delegates agreed that the states would have equal representation in the House of Representatives.

3 The delegates agreed that Congress should have power to legislate in all areas in which the states were incompetent.

4 The delegates decided that each woman in a state should count as three-fifths of a person for the purposes of representation.

REVIEWING MAIN IDEAS

Use complete sentences to answer the following questions.

5 The Constitutional Convention was not open to the public. Why do you think the delegates chose to meet privately? What do you think the advantages of secrecy might be? What might be the disadvantages?

6 Why did the founding fathers believe that they had to place limits on the power of the popularly elected part of Congress?

7 State two ways in which the Constitution was different from the Articles of Confederation.

UNDERSTANDING CONCEPTS

8 The Constitutional Convention brought together 55 men from all over the country to represent their states. The youngest delegate was Jonathan Dayton (who was 26 in 1787); the oldest delegate was Benjamin Franklin, at 81. Most of the delegates were well-educated landowners, who had worked in national or state politics in the 1770s and 1780s.

If you were holding a convention to revise the constitution or charter of your school, who would you invite? Make a list of all the groups you would like to see represented at such a Convention. What other characteristics would you take into account when choosing delegates?

The Structure of Government

Introduction

The Constitution is divided into seven parts called articles. An **article** is a clause or a portion of a document. The first three articles establish the three branches of government: the legislative, the executive, and the judicial. The Constitution creates a **separation of powers**, which gives each branch its own specific functions and duties. This separation of powers means that no one branch can control the other branches. The Constitution also creates a **balance of powers**, which keeps any branch from becoming too powerful. For example, the president is commander in chief of the armed forces, but Congress must appropriate funds for the military and must vote to declare war. This divided system prevents any branch from having complete power and prevents the president from becoming a dictator.

A SEPARATION OF POWERS
James Madison wrote in Federalist Paper No. 47: *The accumulation of all powers, legislative, executive, and judiciary, in the same hands, whether of one, a few, or many, and whether hereditary, self appointed, or elective, may justly be pronounced the very definition of tyranny.*

Article I: The Legislative Powers

Article I of the Constitution establishes the legislature. The Legislature is the part of government that makes laws.

A Bicameral Legislature

The Constitution created a **bicameral legislature**. A bicameral legislature is composed of two houses. The United States has a **House of Representatives** (also called the **lower house**) and a **Senate** (also called the **upper house**). The number of representatives for each state is proportional to its population. This means that a state with a large population has more representatives than a small one does. For example, California has 53 Representatives. Wyoming has only one. Every state, regardless of its population, has two senators.

◆ The number of members of the House of Representatives, shown above, is fixed by law at 435.

FOCUS ON NORTH CAROLINA CONSTITUTION

The North Carolina Constitution parallels the U.S. Constitution in several ways. For example, it establishes each branch of state government separately: Article II establishes the legislative branch, Article III the state executive branch, and Article IV the judicial branch. Article XIII provides the mechanism for amending the North Carolina Constitution.

✦ Both the House and the Senate meet in the Capitol building in Washington, D.C.

Electing the Legislature

The Constitution originally provided that the people would elect the lower house, and then the lower house would select the upper house. Eventually, people realized that this system didn't work. House members chose senators on the basis of their connections rather than on the basis of merit. The Seventeenth Amendment, which was ratified in 1913, changed this system. This amendment provided that senators were also to be elected directly by the citizens of each state. Representatives serve for two years, and every House member runs for election every two years. Senators serve for six years, and one-third of the Senate is up for election every two years.

Why does Congress need to be divided into two houses? The most important reason is that this system allows the federal legislature to represent both the people and the states. Each house also has a role in making sure that the other does not pass unreasonable laws.

Powers of Congress

Article I, Section 8 is one of the most important sections in the Constitution. It contains a long list of the powers of Congress. It gives Congress many more powers than it had under the Articles of Confederation. Among other things, Congress is given the power to:

- collect taxes
- spend for the general welfare
- borrow money
- regulate commerce among the states and between countries
- regulate immigration
- regulate the mail
- declare war
- raise and support military forces, and
- establish federal courts

Congress also has power "To make all Laws which shall be necessary and proper for carrying into Execution the foregoing Powers." The "necessary and proper" clause—sometimes called the elastic clause—is important because it enables Congress to make laws in circumstances that the founders could not imagine. For example, Congress is able to pass laws under the commerce clause to regulate railways; telephones, radio, television, and the Internet; and airlines—none of which existed when the Constitution was written.

Powers of the States

The Constitution does not list the powers of the states. It does not need to. The states retain every power that the federal government is not given. The Tenth Amendment of the Constitution makes this explicit. It says, "The powers not delegated to the United States by the Constitution, nor prohibited by it to the States, are reserved to the States respectively, or to the people."

The national government cannot take away the powers of state governments, but state governments cannot pass laws that are inconsistent with federal laws. It is this division and separation of lawmaking power between the national government and state governments that makes the United States a **federal** nation.

Limits on Congress

There are two important limits on the power of Congress built into the Constitution.

1. The executive acts as a check on the legislative branch. The president has the ability to block legislation that has been passed by both houses. This is called the **veto** power.

2. The Constitution also creates an independent judicial branch with the power to hear all cases arising under the Constitution. The Court has used this power to declare laws unconstitutional (see discussion on Article III below).

DEATHS AND ASSASSINATIONS

Only four U.S. Presidents have been assassinated while in office: Abraham Lincoln in 1865, James Garfield in 1881, William McKinley in 1901, and John F. Kennedy in 1963. Four other presidents have died in office of natural causes: William Henry Harrison in 1841, Zachary Taylor in 1850, Warren G. Harding in 1923, and Franklin Delano Roosevelt in 1945.

Article II: The Executive Powers

Article II of the Constitution establishes the **executive** branch of government. The executive is the body of government that carries out the laws. The President of the United States of America is the head of the executive branch.

The President

Article 2 sets the qualifications to be president: the president must have been born in the United States, be at least 35 years of age, and have lived in the United States for at least 14 years. The Twenty-second Amendment, ratified in 1951, limits the president to two elected terms. The Twenty-fifth Amendment states that if the president dies or is disabled, he is succeeded by the vice-president.

Article 2 also states that the President must swear an oath or affirmation before taking office. The President takes this oath before the Chief Justice of the Supreme Court at the inauguration ceremony. The President must say, "I do solemnly swear (or affirm) that I will faithfully execute the Office of President of the United States, and will to the best of my Ability, preserve, protect and defend the Constitution of the United States."

✦ The inauguration of President Washington, shown in this painting, took place at Federal Hall in New York City, on 30 April 1789.

WASHINGTON, D.C.

Washington, D.C., has a larger population than 13 of the states. But because it is not a state, it is not entitled to any representatives or senators. However, the Twenty-third Amendment does entitle residents of Washington to vote in presidential elections. The district is not allowed to have any more electors than the least populous state. At the moment, D.C. has three electors.

The Electoral System

The Constitution sets out a complex system for electing the president. People do not elect the president directly. Each state nominates a number of **electors** equal to the state's total number of senators and representatives. These electors then vote for a presidential candidate.

The Constitution originally provided that each elector had to cast two votes for president. At least one vote had to be for a candidate from another state. The person with the most votes became the president, and the person who came in second became the vice-president. In the election of 1800, this system led to a strange result. Thomas Jefferson and Aaron Burr received the same number of votes from electors. The Constitution provided that the House of Representatives would vote to decide the winner. The House had to vote 36 times before Jefferson was finally declared the winner. This fiasco led to the passage of the Twelfth Amendment in 1804. This amendment limited each elector to only one vote for president and a separate vote for vice president.

The Constitution gives states the power to decide how to choose electors. Today, the selection system in most states works like this:

- Each political party creates a list of electors and gives it to the state. The electors on each list are individuals who are loyal to their presidential candidate.
- Voters select their choice for president on the ballot. The names of the electors are not even listed on the ballot.
- The candidate that wins the most votes in the state gets the votes of all of their chosen electors.

✦ This map shows the total number of electors (members of the House of Representatives and Senate) for each state.

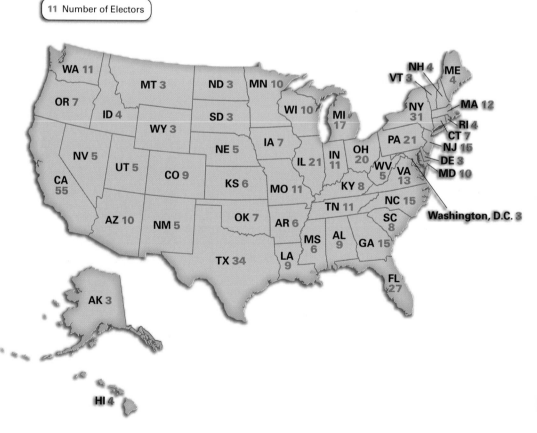

11 Number of Electors

WA 11, OR 7, ID 4, MT 3, ND 3, MN 10, WI 10, NH 4, VT 3, ME 4, NY 31, MA 12, NV 5, UT 5, WY 3, SD 3, IA 7, MI 17, PA 21, RI 4, CT 7, NJ 15, CA 55, CO 9, NE 5, IL 21, IN 11, OH 20, WV 5, VA 13, DE 3, MD 10, AZ 10, NM 5, KS 6, MO 11, KY 8, NC 15, Washington, D.C. 3, OK 7, AR 6, TN 11, SC 8, TX 34, MS 6, AL 9, GA 15, LA 9, FL 27, AK 3, HI 4

Powers of the Executive

Article II of the Constitution says that the president "shall take Care that the Laws be faithfully executed." To carry out this responsibility, the president oversees most of the federal government, which includes more than 4 million employees. As part of this role, the president can issue executive orders. These are rules, like laws, that employees of the executive branch must obey.

The President also has some specific powers, listed in section 2. He has the power to:

- nominate judges to the Supreme Court and the lower federal courts, subject to approval by the Senate
- pardon criminals who have broken a federal law, and
- make treaties with other countries, subject to approval by the Senate

Today, the President has a cabinet of 15 members. Each cabinet member is the head of a government agency.

The president is also the commander in chief of the armed forces. This means that the president can direct the movements of the armed forces. During times of war, Congress may give the president even broader powers.

Article II also gives the president the right to create a cabinet to give advice and make policies. George Washington's cabinet consisted of a secretary of state, a secretary of war, a secretary of the treasury, and an attorney general. Today the presidential cabinet consists of 15 people.

The Constitution envisions the president working closely with Congress. It states that the president shall "from time to time give to the Congress Information of the State of the Union." The president traditionally gives his State of the Union address in January. In practice, the executive branch of government proposes much of the legislation discussed by Congress.

Limits on the Executive

The president can veto legislation that has been passed by both houses. In this way, the executive acts as a check on the legislature. But the legislature can override the president's veto if it has a two-thirds majority in both houses. Section 4 of Article II of the Constitution gives the legislature another important check on the power of the president. Congress can impeach the president. **Impeachment** is a process authorized by the Constitution to bring charges against the president and certain other officials of the federal government for misconduct while in office. The House of Representatives has the sole power to impeach. After impeachment, the Senate may hold a trial on the accusations. If the Senate convicts the president, it may remove him from office for "Treason, Bribery, or other high Crimes and Misdemeanors."

Did You KNOW?

- Only two presidents have been impeached: Andrew Johnson in 1868 and Bill Clinton in 1998. Neither of them was convicted or dismissed from office.
- In 2004, the president earned a salary of $400,000 a year.
- The Secret Service uses an acronym to refer to the president of the United States: POTUS. The First Lady is referred to as FLOTUS.

Article III: The Judiciary

Article III of the Constitution establishes the judicial branch of government. The Supreme Court is the only court required by the Constitution. Congress creates all the other federal courts.

Powers of the Judiciary

The Constitution gives the Supreme Court the authority to hear cases that arise under the Constitution, federal laws, and treaties. The Supreme Court also hears appeals from all the state courts and the lower federal courts, but only if an issue of federal law needs to be decided. The Court can also hear cases in which there is a dispute among the states.

Chief Justice John Marshall's decision in *Marbury* v. *Madison* (1803) dramatically shaped the powers of the Supreme Court. Marshall stated that the Court had the power of **judicial review**. This is the power to declare that laws passed by Congress are inconsistent with the Constitution. The Court can declare such laws unconstitutional. If a law is unconstitutional, that law cannot be enforced.

The power of judicial review is not mentioned explicitly in the Constitution. But judicial review is absolutely necessary for our democratic government. Congress is given the power to make laws; Congress should not also decide whether the laws it makes are constitutional. Judicial review means that the judiciary, which has no power to make laws, has the final word on whether a law is consistent with the Constitution.

Limits on the Judiciary

Obviously, the ability to strike down laws as being contrary to the Constitution gives the Court enormous power. But several things keep the judicial branch in check. For one thing, courts can only decide the cases that come before them. Judges have no power to act on their own.

Also, the Constitution states that judges "shall hold their Offices during good Behaviour." This means that, in effect, judges are appointed for life. But if a judge behaves badly, the Senate can impeach him or her and remove the judge from office. Only 13 federal judges have been impeached since 1789.

Another check on the judiciary is Congress's power to amend the Constitution. (See discussion of Article V.) Congress has amended the Constitution to overturn a Supreme Court decision several times. For example, the Court's opinion in the 1857 case of *Dred Scott* v. *Sandford* stated that slaves were property and were not citizens of the United States. The Fourteenth Amendment, passed in 1868, overruled that decision.

A Limited Judiciary

Alexander Hamilton wrote about the limits on the judiciary in Federalist Paper No. 78:

The judiciary . . . has no influence over either the sword or the purse; no direction either of the strength or of the wealth of society; and can take no active resolution whatever. It may truly be said to have neither force nor will but merely judgment.

✦ The Supreme Court meets in the Supreme Court building, which was built in 1935. Before that, the Court met in a few rooms in the Capitol.

Article IV: The States

Article IV describes

- the relationship between the federal government and the states
- the relationship among the states

Section 1 contains the "full faith and credit" clause. This is the clause that requires that every state recognize the laws and court decisions of every other state. For example, New York courts must recognize the decisions of courts in Texas or Iowa.

Section 2 contains the "privileges and immunities" clause. This clause means that a state may not discriminate against citizens of other states in favor of its own citizens. For example, imagine that two people commit a crime in Utah. One person is from Utah, and the other person is from California. The privileges and immunities clause means that the law and courts in Utah must treat the two people equally. Utah cannot treat the person from California more harshly than its own citizen just because that person is not from Utah.

Section 3 says that Congress can admit new states to the Union. Today this power may seem unimportant. But it was this clause that allowed the United States to grow from the 13 original states to today's 50 states.

✦ This painting shows Betsy Ross sewing the first US flag. The original flag had only 13 stars, representing the 13 states. The modern flag has 50 stars to represent the 50 states.

Article V: Amendments

One of the problems that emerged with the Articles of Confederation was the fact that all 13 states needed to agree to an amendment. This system made it very difficult to amend the Articles. The Constitution's method makes amending it a little easier. Amendments must be proposed by two-thirds of both houses. If an amendment is successfully proposed, then it must be approved by the legislatures of three-quarters of the states or by conventions in three-quarters of the states. Article V also states that the Constitution can be amended if a Convention is called by two-thirds of the state legislatures, and proposed amendments are later ratified by three-fourths of the state legislatures. This method of amendment has never been used.

Thousands of amendments have been suggested. Congress has only proposed 33 amendments. Only 27 amendments have been ratified by the states.

FOCUS ON NORTH CAROLINA CONSTITUTION

The North Carolina Constitution may be amended in two ways. First, Article XIII allows a proposed amendment to be submitted to voters if a three-fifths vote of each house of the General Assembly approves. If a majority of the voters approve the amendment, it becomes part of the state constitution. Second, Art. XIII allows the legislature, by a two-thirds vote of each house, to call a Convention of the People, which may then submit proposed amendments to voters for approval.

In the North Carolina Constitution, Article I, Sections 3, 4, and 5, expressly state that the constitution and government of North Carolina are subordinate to the Constitution and government of the United States. Similarly, the North Carolina Constitution gives the North Carolina General Assembly the power to create county, city, and other local governments, including special districts. This power makes all local governments subordinate to the state government.

Article VI: Supremacy

Article VI provides that the Constitution, and the laws and treaties made under it, is the "supreme Law of the Land." This means that if there is a conflict between a federal law and a state law, only the federal law is valid. Even state constitutions are subordinate to federal law.

Article VII: Ratification

After months of debate and compromise at the Constitutional Convention, 38 of the delegates signed the new Constitution of the United States. But the Constitution was not in force until it was **ratified**. This means that the states had to agree to accept the Constitution. Article VII required that 9 states out of the existing 13 states had to ratify the Constitution before it could be adopted.

A convention was held in each state, at which delegates debated the Constitution and voted on ratification. Some people welcomed the new Constitution. They were known as **Federalists**. But many people were opposed to the Constitution because it gave such strong powers to the national government. They also feared that the proposed Constitution did not adequately safeguard their rights. People opposed to the Constitution were called **Antifederalists**.

The Antifederalist Papers

In New York, several essays were published attacking the new Constitution. These antifederalist essays were written by a number of different people. Often the authors wrote under false names, or **pseudonyms**. One author used the name Cato, another took the name Brutus, and another called himself the Federalist Farmer. Some of these essays were re-published in newspapers across the country.

The essays criticized the broad powers of the proposed government and the removal of power from the states. They criticized the lack of a Bill of Rights guaranteeing individual freedoms. The authors of these essays hoped to sway public opinion, and the opinion of the delegates to the state conventions, against the Constitution.

◆ A portrait of Alexander Hamilton, one of the strongest supporters of the new Constitution. Hamilton wrote about two-thirds of the essays in the *Federalist Papers.*

The Federalist Papers

John Jay, James Madison, and Alexander Hamilton decided to mount a counterattack. They used the pseudonym Publius. This pseudonym referred to Publius Valerius Publicola, a great defender of the ancient Roman Republic. In late 1787, Hamilton wrote the first of a series of essays defending the Constitution in New York newspapers. The authors made sure the essays were distributed in every state. Hamilton wrote the majority of the 85 Federalist essays over the next crucial months. These essays became known as the *Federalist Papers*. The essays pointed out the weaknesses of the Articles of Confederation, and made a case for a strong national government. Thomas Jefferson later called the *Federalist Papers* the "best commentary on the principles of government ever written." In the two centuries since they were published, the *Federalist Papers* have become valuable tools for judges in interpreting the Constitution.

Ratification

Delaware was the first state to ratify the new Constitution in December 1787. Pennsylvania and New Jersey also ratified the Constitution that month. Connecticut and Georgia ratified it in early 1788. But some powerful states, including Massachusetts, New York, and Virginia, withheld their support.

To win ratification in these states, the Federalists had to compromise. The Constitution did not contain any guarantees of individual rights, like the right to worship freely or the right to freedom of speech. The Federalists thought that such explicit protections were unnecessary.

But many citizens worried that their rights would not be protected unless the protections were in writing. The *Antifederalist Papers* played up their concerns. Eventually, some conventions ratified the Constitution on the condition that it be amended as soon as possible by a Bill of Rights. The Federalists agreed.

Massachusetts ratified the Constitution in a close vote in February 1788, Maryland ratified in April, and South Carolina ratified in May. On June 21, 1788, New Hampshire became the ninth state to ratify the document, and the Constitution was finally in force.

The two largest states, Virginia and New York, ratified the Constitution by close margins in June and July. North Carolina, which had initially voted against ratification, ratified the Constitution in November 1789. Rhode Island was the hold out state: it finally ratified the Constitution almost three years after it had been signed, in May of 1790.

✦ This cartoon, from the mid-20th century, shows Uncle Sam climbing a ladder that leads from the Articles of Confederation to the U.S. Constitution.

STEPS IN THE ESTABLISHMENT OF A MORE STABLE GOVERNMENT

The FEDERAL CONSTITUTION

PHILADELPHIA CONVENTION 1787

ANNAPOLIS CONVENTION 1786

MT. VERNON CONVENTION 1785

ARTICLES OF CONFEDERATION

IMPORTANT TERMS

1 Match the terms in the right column with the definition in the left column.

A.	The body of government that makes laws	**Judiciary**
B.	The body of government that carries out the laws	**House of Representatives**
C.	The body of government that interprets the laws to resolve disputes	**Antifederalists**
D.	Another name for the lower house	**Legislature**
E.	Another name for the upper house	**Executive**
F.	The name given to people in favor of the Constitution	**Federalists**
G.	The name given to people who were not in favor of the Constitution	**Senate**

REVIEWING FACTS

Use complete sentences to answer the following questions.

2 List three powers of Congress and three checks on the power of Congress.

3 List three powers of the executive and two checks on the power of the executive.

4 Explain the role of the federal judiciary, and list three checks on the power of the judiciary.

REVIEWING MAIN IDEAS

Use complete sentences to answer the following questions.

5 What compromise did the Federalists make in order to ensure that the Constitution was ratified in all the states? What made them take this step?

6 Do you think there are disadvantages to the electoral system? Explain your answer.

UNDERSTANDING CONCEPTS

7 The Constitution was created by the founding fathers. They were white men, and most of them were landowners who were active in politics. These citizens had a good idea of what their position under the Constitution would be.

The twentieth century philosopher John Rawls imagined a clever way to design a fair society. He suggested that people should design a society before they know what their position in it will be. The designers would work under a "veil of ignorance." That way, the designers would try to make the system fair for everyone.

Now, try a thought experiment. Imagine the founding fathers wrote the Constitution under a "veil of ignorance"—not knowing what their own position would be in the new system. In the new system, they could be rich or poor, black or white, male or female. In what ways, if any, do you think the Constitution might have been different?

Island Society Constitution

You are shipwrecked on a deserted island in the South Pacific with about 100 other students from your school. There are no teachers or other adults. You need to create a stable society on the island. You want to make sure that everyone has enough food, that there are no fights over resources, and that everyone works together for your long-term goal—rescue. You decide to draft an island society constitution.

Brainstorm

On a piece of paper, write down some ideas for your constitution. You might want to consider some of the following questions:

★ How will the group make decisions about important issues on the island?

★ Will there be a single leader or a committee to make sure that decisions are carried out? What are the advantages of each option? What are the disadvantages?

★ What will happen if someone is unfairly treated in some way?

★ What if someone is accused of breaking the island's rules?

★ What steps could you take to make sure that the people who have power on the island do not abuse it?

★ Are there some rights that are so important to you that they should be guaranteed in the constitution? If so, what are they?

★ If it became necessary, how would you amend the constitution?

In groups of 4–6 people, discuss your ideas about the planned constitution. Work together to come up with a one-page list of proposed articles. This is your draft of a new constitution.

As a Class

Present your proposed constitution to the class. You may need to explain or defend some articles. Use your skills in debate to persuade other students in your class that your ideas for the constitution are important. You may need to make some compromises.

Your teacher will write up a list of the articles that everyone can agree on. When it is complete, read it carefully to see if you have created a system that will work. Then take a class vote on the constitution. If a majority agrees that the constitution is a good one, then it is complete. Your constitutional convention has been a success.

Going to the Source

An Enduring Constitution

When the Constitution was drafted, some framers believed it would only be in force for a few years. More than two hundred years on, the Constitution is the oldest written constitution in the world that is still in force. Why do you think the Constitution has endured? Read the extracts below and answer the questions that follow.

Benjamin Franklin wrote the following words, which were read on his behalf at the Constitutional Convention in 1787:

> I agree to this Constitution with all its faults, if they are such: because I think a General Government necessary for us, and there is no Form of Government but what may be a Blessing to the People if well-administered; and I believe farther that this is likely to be well administered for a Course of Years and can only end in Despotism as other Forms have done before it, when the People shall become so corrupted as to need a Despotic Government, being incapable of any other.

In a letter to James Madison written on September 6, 1789, Thomas Jefferson suggested that a new Constitution should be drafted every twenty years or so. He wrote,

> ...it may be proved that no society can make a perpetual constitution, or even a perpetual law. The earth belongs always to the living generation... They are masters too of their own persons, and consequently may govern them as they please.

James Madison, as painted by popular portrait artist Gilbert Stuart.

Benjamin Franklin drew this cartoon in 1754, during the French and Indian Wars. It was the first political cartoon published in an American newspaper, and it was widely published again during the 1770s. What do you think Franklin was trying to say with this image? What do you think the rattlesnake represents?

JOIN, or DIE.

In the 1819 case of *McCulloch v. Maryland,* the Supreme Court was asked to interpret the "necessary and proper" clause of the Constitution to decide whether Congress had power to create a national bank. Chief Justice John Marshall wrote,

This provision is made in a constitution intended to endure for ages to come, and, consequently, to be adapted to the various crises of human affairs.

In 2003, Supreme Court Justice Antonin Scalia gave a speech to students at the University of Mississippi. He said,

If you have a living Constitution, the only kind of Constitution that you'll have is the kind of Constitution the society of that time wants.

CRITICAL THINKING

1. Explain Benjamin Franklin's quote from 1787 in your own words. What other forms of government might Franklin have personally experienced? Why might he be negative about the future of the government established by the Constitution?

2. Why does Thomas Jefferson think that a society cannot write a constitution that will last indefinitely? List some advantages and disadvantages of having the same constitution for more than two hundred years.

3. Consider the quotes of the two Supreme Court Justices—Chief Justice John Marshall and Justice Scalia—and answer the following questions:

   - What arm of government has the power to interpret the Constitution?

   - Do you think the Constitution should be interpreted and adapted to apply to modern dilemmas? Are there dangers in interpreting the Constitution broadly?

   - The Constitution could be amended if Congress disagreed with a Supreme Court interpretation of the Constitution. With this in mind, does it matter if the Supreme Court interprets the Constitution broadly to adapt it to the issues of modern society? Why or why not?

THE BILL OF RIGHTS

What You Will Learn

In this chapter you will

★ Learn about the origin of individual rights in English history.

★ Find out how the American colonists defined their rights as English subjects.

★ Discover why the states objected to the absence of a bill of rights in the U.S. Constitution.

★ Explore the first 10 amendments to the U.S. Constitution, which form the Bill of Rights.

★ Compare the U.S. Bill of Rights to the French Declaration of the Rights of Man and of the Citizen.

◆ John Peter Zenger's papers are burned in colonial New York on November 6, 1734.

The History of Individual Rights

Introduction

The U.S. Constitution's Bill of Rights protects such liberties as freedom of speech, freedom of religion, and the right to jury trial. The idea that citizens were entitled to these **individual rights** developed over hundreds of years. English history was the source of many of these rights. American citizens claimed these rights as their own and gave them new protections in the Bill of Rights.

The English Experience

Magna Carta

Magna Carta (the Great Charter) is one of the earliest sources of individual rights. In 1215, a group of **barons** rebelled against King John of England. The barons were powerful noblemen who supported the king in exchange for large estates of land. In the Magna Carta, they demanded that the king recognize their rights in writing.

The barons did not care very much about the rights of common people. But one part of the Magna Carta provided that no "free man" could be imprisoned or lose his rights "except by the lawful judgment of his equals or by the law of the land." From this grew the concept of **due process of law**. Due process means that people must have their rights determined fairly, according to established laws. In England, this body of established law is known as the **common law**. English common law was defined by custom, acts of Parliament and the monarch, and judicial decisions. It was used throughout the American colonies until the Revolutionary War. The common law's emphasis on due process of law became an important principle in the legal system of the new United States.

◆ King John signs the Magna Carta, which recognized and protected the rights of the English barons.

A portrait of Sir Edward Coke, the English lawyer who argued that even the king is subject to the law.

The Petition of Right

In the seventeenth century, English lawyer **Sir Edward Coke** used Magna Carta to argue that England's king was not above the law. King Charles I claimed that he was answerable only to God. But Coke was convinced that Magna Carta had made the common law England's supreme authority. Even the monarch was subject to it.

In 1628, Coke and other members of Parliament presented the **Petition of Right** to King Charles. The Petition of Right accused the king of:

- Taxing people without Parliament's consent.
- Imprisoning, trying, and executing people without due process of law.
- Forcing people to provide lodging for the king's soldiers in their private homes.

The Petition of Right was a major event in the seventeenth-century struggle between Parliament and the king. This struggle resulted in the English Civil Wars and Parliament's beheading of King Charles I in 1649. In 1660, Parliament asked Charles II (Charles I's son) to return to England to serve as king. This event is known as the **Restoration**. But the Restoration was soon followed by another struggle between the monarchy and Parliament.

English Bill of Rights

Charles II died in 1685. His brother, **James II**, took over the throne. James was a practicing Catholic in a mostly Protestant England. Parliament feared that James would try to make England a Catholic nation. It invited James's daughter, **Mary**, and her husband, the Protestant Dutch prince **William of Orange**, to take over the English throne.

In 1689, Parliament presented William and Mary with the **English Bill of Rights**. The English Bill of Rights established Parliament's **supremacy**—or control—over the monarch. It also provided for:

- The right to petition the king and his government.
- Freedom of speech and debate in Parliament.
- The right of Protestants to keep arms for their defense.
- The right to trial by jury.
- Prohibitions on excessive bail, excessive fines, and cruel and unusual punishment.

This map, made in 1688, shows the arrival of William of Orange and his fleet at Torbay, England, to claim the English throne.

English Writers

English writers also called for stronger protection of individual rights. Their defenses of free speech and religious freedom helped define the rights protected in the First Amendment to the U.S. Constitution. Two of the most important works were John Milton's ***Areopagitica*** and John Locke's ***Letter Concerning Toleration***.

Areopagitica

John Milton published ***Areopagitica*** in 1644. It asked Parliament to reconsider a **licensing law** it had passed in 1643. The law required a government **license**, or approval, before printed material could be published. Such a law is known as a **prior restraint** on speech. Milton argued that in passing this law Parliament was weakening the liberties it claimed to protect. By the end of the seventeenth century, licensing laws had ended in England. A free press had been established.

Letter Concerning Toleration

In 1689, **John Locke** published his Letter Concerning Toleration. The letter called for a firm **separation between church and state**. This meant that the state had no place making laws that tried to control individuals' religious beliefs. It also meant that religious groups should have no power to limit the **civil rights** of someone who violated the religion's rules or practiced a different religion. For Locke, civil rights included life, liberty, health, and property ownership.

THE LIMITS OF TOLERATION

John Locke felt that most religious groups should be tolerated. He did not think toleration should extend to **atheists**. Atheists are people who do not believe in God. In Locke's day, promises and oaths were sworn to God. Locke defined these promises and oaths as "the bonds of human society." Because atheists deny the existence of God, Locke felt that these social bonds had no meaning to them. Because atheists had no religion, they had no religious beliefs for which they could claim toleration.

Colonial American Experiences

The English history of rights had a strong impact on the American colonists. Many American colonists were English and claimed the rights of English people. Three good examples of how colonists asserted these rights are

- Maryland's Act Concerning Religion (1649)
- The trial of John Peter Zenger (1735)
- The Virginia Declaration of Rights (1776)

Act Concerning Religion

Even before John Locke wrote on religious toleration, Maryland's colonial government had passed a religious tolerance act. The 1649 **Act Concerning Religion** provided that all Christians would enjoy free exercise of religion. The act's tolerance did not extend beyond Christianity. Many conflicts existed between different Christian faiths at that time, however, and the Maryland act tried to promote toleration among them.

◆ John Milton's *Areopagitica* helped to establish a free press in England.

Trial of John Peter Zenger

In 1735, an important trial helped define **free speech rights** in the American colonies. **John Peter Zenger** was a printer in New York. Beginning in 1733, Zenger published several newspaper articles criticizing William Cosby, who was New York's colonial governor.

Cosby had Zenger put on trial for **seditious libel**. Seditious libel laws punished people who criticized the government or public officials. If a statement was found to damage the public's respect for the government, the truth of the statement could not be a defense.

Almost 50 years before the Constitution, the trial of John Peter Zenger showed how highly the American colonists valued freedom of speech.

The judges at Zenger's trial told the jury that truth was not a defense, but the jury acquitted Zenger. The verdict demonstrated the New York colonists' commitment to a free press. It also showed how trial by jury could protect individual rights from government interference.

Virginia Declaration of Rights

On June 12, 1776, the Virginia Constitutional Convention adopted the **Virginia Declaration of Rights**. Virginia and the other former colonies used these conventions to draft new state constitutions after the Revolutionary War began (see Chapter 2, Section 1). The Virginia Declaration of Rights became a model for both the Declaration of Independence and the Bill of Rights.

Some of the rights in the Virginia Declaration are taken directly from Magna Carta and the English Bill of Rights. These include

- guarantees of due process
- the right to trial by jury
- prohibitions on excessive bail, excessive fines, and cruel or unusual punishments
- the right of the people to form militia in defense of the state

The Virginia Declaration also names freedom of speech and religious belief as fundamental individual rights. For example, the Declaration guarantees free exercise of religion without force or violence. It calls freedom of the press one of the greatest protectors of liberty.

By 1776, centuries of conflict in England and America had created a strong commitment to individual rights. But the new U.S. Constitution, adopted in 1787, mentioned few of these rights by name. Under pressure from the states, Congress quickly proposed a set of constitutional amendments that would become the Bill of Rights.

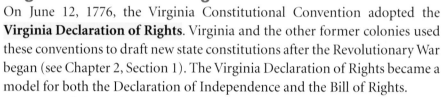

★ ★ ★ ★ ★ ★ ★

HOW FREE IS A FREE PRESS?

The removal of **prior restraints** on publishing does not mean that people can publish whatever they want without punishment. In both England and the United States, publishers can be sued for **libel** if they intentionally publish false statements about a person or organization. A publisher who is found guilty of libel will usually have to pay a certain sum of money, called **damages**, to the person whose reputation has been harmed by the false statement.

IMPORTANT TERMS

1 Match the terms in the right column with the definitions in the left column.

A. The body of established law in England

B. A law that punishes people who criticize the government or public officials

C. Laws requiring government approval before printed material can be published

D. The term John Locke uses to describe such things as life, liberty, health, and property ownership

Prior restraints

Civil rights

Seditious libel

Common law

REVIEWING FACTS

2 Name three objections members of the British Parliament made in the Petition of Right.

3 What relationship between the British Parliament and the monarchy did the English Bill of Rights establish?

4 Who was protected by Maryland's 1649 Act Concerning Religion?

REVIEWING MAIN IDEAS

Use complete sentences to answer the following questions.

5 What is meant by the concept of due process of law?

6 What limits does separation of church and state place on the government? What limits does it place on religious groups?

7 How do prior restraints on speech affect the development of a free press? Does a free press mean that people can publish whatever they want without fear of punishment?

UNDERSTANDING CONCEPTS

8 John Locke called for a firm separation between church and state. He thought that religious belief should be freely chosen. He said it was wrong for government to try to force people to believe in a religion.

The First Amendment to the U.S. Constitution supports Locke's ideas in two ways. First, it says that government cannot choose to support one religion over another. Second, it says that all people are free to practice their own religion.

Consider the following examples. Do any of them violate Locke's idea of separation between church and state? Why or why not?

A. Your city puts up a Christmas tree in a city park.

B. A religious leader says a prayer at a school event.

C. The U.S. currency says "In God We Trust."

Going to the Source

Freedom of Speech and Religion

England's turbulent seventeenth century resulted in a new emphasis on individual rights to free expression, such as speech and religion. Read the following excerpts and then read the First Amendment to the U.S. Constitution. Answer the questions that follow.

From John Milton, *Areopagitica* (1644)

✷ Where there is much desire to learn, there of necessity will be much arguing, much writing, many opinions; for opinion in good men is but knowledge in the making.

✷ When God shakes a kingdom with strong and healthful commotions to a general reforming, 'tis not untrue that many sectaries* and false teachers are then busiest in seducing; but yet more true it is, that God then raises to his own work men of rare abilities, and more than common industry, not only to look back and revise what hath been taught heretofore, but to gain further and go on some new enlightened steps in the discovery of truth. For such is the order of God's enlightening his Church, to dispense and deal out by degrees his beam, so as our earthly eyes may best sustain it.

*A sectary is someone who separates from an established religion or belief.

John Locke's ideas about religious freedom strongly influenced people in the American colonies. (19th century engraving by Freeman, from a painting by Sir Godfrey Kueller, 1697.)

From John Locke, *Letter Concerning Toleration* (1689)

✷ The business of laws is not to provide for the truth of opinions, but for the safety and security of the commonwealth and of every particular man's goods and person. And so it ought to be. For the truth certainly would do well enough if she were once left to shift for herself. She seldom has received and, I fear, never will receive much assistance from the power of great men, to whom she is but rarely known and more rarely welcome. She is not taught by laws, nor has she any need of force to procure her entrance into the minds of men.

✷ It is not the diversity of opinions (which cannot be avoided), but the refusal of toleration to those who are of different opinions (which might have been granted), that has produced all the bustles and wars that have been in the Christian world upon account of religion.

The First Amendment to the U.S. Constitution (1789)

✳ Congress shall make no law respecting an establishment of religion, or prohibiting the free exercise thereof; or abridging the freedom of speech, or of the press, or the right of the people peaceably to assemble, and to petition the Government for a redress of grievances.

CRITICAL THINKING

1. **Both Milton and Locke emphasize the importance of discovering truth in their arguments.**

   - If truth is important, why shouldn't the government be able to forbid speech or religious belief that it believes is wrong?

   - Do either Milton or Locke suggest how differences of religious belief or opinion could help discover the truth? Do you agree? Explain your answer.

2. **Milton describes a nation shaken by "strong and healthful commotions," while Locke describes the "bustles and wars" that religion has caused in the world.**

   - Do you think disagreement can be a good thing, as Milton suggests? What does Locke think of disagreement?

   - How does Locke think disagreements can be kept from turning into "bustles and wars"? Do you agree with him?

3. **The First Amendment forms part of the U.S. Constitution's Bill of Rights. The Bill of Rights protects the individual freedoms of U.S. citizens.**

   - How fully do you think the First Amendment protects freedoms of speech and religious belief?

   - Do the freedoms of speech and religious belief protected in the First Amendment make the United States a stronger and healthier nation? Why or why not?

The Bill of Rights

Introduction

Thomas Jefferson said, "A bill of rights is what the people are entitled to against every government on earth, general or particular, and what no just government should refuse, or rest on inference." The Bill of Rights is the name given to the first 10 amendments to the U.S. Constitution. Many of the states that ratified the Constitution also demanded that it be amended to include a Bill of Rights. The Bill of Rights guarantees the protection of key individual rights. It also recognizes that the American people have rights beyond those explicitly described in the Bill of Rights.

Demand for an Amended Constitution

The Constitution produced at the Philadelphia convention in 1787 did not please all the delegates. Several delegates refused to sign the Constitution because it failed to include a bill of rights. Their objections were debated when the states decided whether to ratify the Constitution.

Federalist supporters of the Constitution had resisted including a bill of rights. They argued that a bill of rights was unnecessary for several reasons:

- Under the new form of government in the United States, the people held the power. They did not have to protect rights from a power that they themselves held.
- A bill of rights could be dangerous. Listing certain rights in the Constitution might suggest that other rights did not deserve the same degree of protection.
- Bills of rights did not offer much protection. James Madison described bills of rights in state constitutions as "parchment barriers" that were often ignored.

Despite Federalist objections to a bill of rights, more than half of the states that ratified the Constitution recommended that it be amended to include one. Shortly after Congress assembled in 1789, work began on the list of amendments that would become the Bill of Rights.

Did You KNOW?

Congress originally submitted twelve amendments to the states for ratification. The states ratified ten of these twelve, which became the Bill of Rights. One of the two amendments that were not ratified, dealing with the pay of representatives and senators, was eventually ratified in 1992 and became the Twenty-seventh Amendment!

The Bill of Rights

James Madison had at first opposed adding a bill of rights to the Constitution. But he wrote the 12 amendments that Congress submitted to the states for ratification. The states ratified only 10 of the 12 amendments. These 10 amendments became known as the Bill of Rights.

The Bill of Rights protects six categories of rights:

- Rights of religion and expression (First Amendment)
- Right to bear arms (Second Amendment)
- Right to be secure in one's person and home (Third and Fourth Amendments)
- Right to private property (Fifth Amendment)
- Rights to a fair trial (Fifth, Sixth, Seventh, and Eighth Amendments)
- Additional rights held by the people and the states (Ninth and Tenth Amendments)

✦ James Madison drafted the amendments that became the Bill of Rights, although he was initially opposed to the idea of adding them to the Constitution.

Rights of Religion and Expression— The First Amendment

The first two clauses of the First Amendment protect religious freedoms. The **establishment clause** provides that "Congress shall make no law respecting an establishment of religion." This means that Congress is not able to name a national religion.

The second clause protecting religious freedom is the **free exercise clause**. This clause prohibits Congress from making any law interfering with an individual's free exercise of his or her religious beliefs. This means that every individual is free to hold and practice religious beliefs as he or she sees fit.

✦ The First Amendment protects religious freedom. It prohibits Congress from both choosing a national religion and telling a person what religious beliefs he or she must hold.

An Established Religion

The Church of England is the national religion of England. Earlier in English history, members of **nonconforming religions** were punished for their beliefs. Nonconforming religions were those that differed from the beliefs of the Church of England. Many American colonists were members of nonconforming religions. The First Amendment's establishment clause ensured that no religious belief would prevail over others through government support.

The next cluster of rights in the First Amendment address freedom of expression. Two of these, defined in the **freedom of speech** and **freedom of the press** clauses, protect the rights of individuals and the media to express their beliefs free of government restraints. The Supreme Court has interpreted these clauses very broadly but has allowed some restrictions. For example, government can restrict:

- The **time, place, and manner** of certain forms of speech. For example, a city could decide that a sound truck blasting political messages at high volumes could not drive through a residential neighborhood late at night.
- Speech that is **harmful to children**. For example, the government can require that television programs with mature content be broadcast only after a certain time.
- Speech that presents a **clear and present danger** of immediate harm to others. No one, for example, has a right to scream "Fire!" in a crowded theater when there is no fire.
- **Obscene speech**. Obscene speech is vulgar or sexually explicit speech that deeply offends the standards of a community and has no political or artistic value.

The remaining rights protected by the First Amendment are those of **assembly** and **petition**. The right to assembly means that people can peacefully come together in protest of a government policy. It also means that people have a right to form associations based on common interests or beliefs, such as political parties, labor unions, or community service organizations. The right to petition the government means that individuals can seek change by going directly to the government. Filing a lawsuit to protest a government action is a good example of the right to petition.

✦ This civil rights march in 1963 was part of the movement that sought to guarantee that every person's Constitutional rights were guaranteed and protected by the government.

Right to Bear Arms—The Second Amendment

The Second Amendment provides that "a well regulated militia, being necessary to the security of a free State, the right of the people to keep and bear Arms, shall not be infringed." The idea of citizens bearing arms to protect their freedoms stretched back into English history. Moreover, the United States had won the Revolutionary War with the help of **militia** made up of armed citizens. Militia are "citizen-soldiers" who can be called upon for military service in times of emergency.

Today there is disagreement over the Second Amendment right to bear arms. Some say that the right is limited to citizens who bear arms to serve in a state-organized militia. Others argue that it is an individual right to bear arms that the government cannot restrict. The Supreme Court has not made a clear ruling on the Second Amendment's meaning. However, the government has placed some restrictions on gun ownership. For example, federal law requires background checks of people who purchase firearms to make sure they do not have a previous criminal record.

Right to Be Secure in One's Person and Home—The Third and Fourth Amendments

The Third and Fourth Amendments protect our rights to be secure in our persons and homes. The Third Amendment, prohibiting the **quartering of troops**, may seem irrelevant to us today. But it was a major concern for people in the eighteenth century. Quartering of troops is the requirement that private individuals give soldiers lodging at the individuals' own expense.

The Fourth Amendment also provides that no person, residence, private papers, or other private property (called "effects" in the amendment) can be searched without a proper warrant. A **search warrant** is an order, usually issued by a judge, which allows government authorities to search for and seize certain items. These can include

- Items that might be evidence in a criminal case, such as a murder weapon.
- Goods that have been criminally obtained, such as stolen property.
- Items that it is against the law to possess, such as illegal drugs.

The government might also seek a search warrant if it believes a criminal suspect is hiding in a particular place.

The Fourth Amendment requires that the government demonstrate **probable cause** in order to get a search warrant. This means that the government must show it has good reason to believe that a search will uncover evidence of a crime. The Fourth Amendment also requires that the warrant be backed by an **oath or affirmation**. Someone must swear that the government is acting in good faith in requesting the warrant. Finally, the warrant must specify the place where the search is to be conducted and the person or items that the government intends to seize.

◆ The Second Amendment protects a person's right "to keep and bear arms." The limits of that right are not clearly defined.

FOCUS ON NORTH CAROLINA CONSTITUTION

In the U.S. Constitution, the Bill of Rights consists of the first ten amendments. In the North Carolina Constitution, a separate article, Article I, Declaration of Rights, defines and affirms the rights and protections of the people of North Carolina. Article I includes 37 sections. In some ways it is similar to the U.S. Bill of Rights—both guarantee freedom of speech and religion, for example. However, North Carolina lists additional items, such as the right to an education and the rights of crime victims.

◆ The Fourth Amendment's protection against random government searches depends in part on your expectation of privacy. This expectation is less at school than at home.

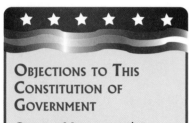

OBJECTIONS TO THIS CONSTITUTION OF GOVERNMENT

George Mason, author of the Virginia Declaration of Rights, was one of the delegates who refused to sign the Constitution. He wrote a pamphlet called "Objections to This Constitution of Government" that began, "There is no Declaration of Rights." This pamphlet circulated throughout the states as they debated ratifying the Constitution.

The Fourth Amendment clearly protects us against random government searches of our persons and homes. But how far do its protections go? Can a school official, for example, search your locker without a search warrant? Often, the answer is yes. The first question a court would ask is whether you have an **expectation of privacy** in using the school locker. Your school probably has a policy that states that lockers are school property over which the school has control. In this case, your expectation of privacy would be very low.

Right to Private Property—The Fifth Amendment

The Fifth Amendment's **takings clause** provides that private property shall not "be taken for public use without just compensation." Imagine, for example, that the government decides to build a new highway that will run right through your home. The government does have the power, called **eminent domain**, to take private property for public use. It cannot do so, however, without paying the property owner **just compensation**. If, for example, your family's home would have been worth $150,000 before the government announced its highway plans, you should be entitled to this amount as just compensation from the government.

More difficult questions arise when the government does not so clearly take private property. Imagine that the government decides to build a new airport a few miles from your house. You can now hear the noise of aircraft taking off and landing over your neighborhood. Your property has remained intact and you have not been forced to leave it. But because of the increased noise in your neighborhood, people might be willing to pay less to buy homes in the area. Your property has probably lost some value because of the new airport. But is this a loss that should be compensated if you are able to use the property in much the same way as you did before the airport was built? How exactly should that loss be valued? Such questions have made the takings clause a subject of lively debate in the courts.

Rights to a Fair Trial—
The Fifth, Sixth, Seventh, and Eighth Amendments

Four of the 10 amendments in the Bill of Rights address the individual's right to a fair trial. These amendments give special attention to the rights of individuals accused in a criminal case. The government has great power in a criminal trial. If the accused is found guilty, the government can make him or her pay a fine or serve a prison sentence. In the most serious cases, it can even sentence a convicted criminal to death. The Bill of Rights tries to balance this power by making sure that the accused is guaranteed a fair trial.

Rights Before Trial   Before a suspect can be brought to trial, the suspect must be **indicted**. An indictment is a formal written accusation of a suspect.

The Fifth Amendment requires that "for a capital, or otherwise infamous crime," the suspect must be indicted by a **grand jury**. Grand juries are panels of citizens who hear charges against a suspect. Unlike a trial jury, a grand jury does not decide on a suspect's guilt or innocence. It simply decides whether there is enough evidence to justify putting a suspect on trial. Grand juries are larger than trial juries, which traditionally have 12 members. Federal law requires at least 16 members on a grand jury. Grand juries also have powers to investigate crimes and can request to examine physical evidence or hear witnesses testify.

The Fifth Amendment's provision for grand jury indictment has been interpreted to mean that suspects are entitled to a grand jury indictment in all federal **felony** cases. Felonies are the most serious crimes and are typically punished by a prison sentence exceeding one year or, in capital cases, by death.

Unlike a trial jury, a grand jury does not decide on a suspect's guilt or innocence. It simply decides whether there is enough evidence to justify putting a suspect on trial. The grand jury's written indictment satisfies the Sixth Amendment's requirement that the suspect "be informed of the nature and cause of the accusation."

Our justice system presumes a criminal suspect is innocent until proven guilty. One way to preserve the suspect's liberty before trial is to allow the suspect to post **bail**. Bail is a sum of money that the suspect deposits with the court as a promise to appear at trial. If the suspect doesn't appear, the bail money is forfeited to the government.

The Eighth Amendment prohibits excessive bail. This means that bail cannot exceed what is necessary to protect the state's legitimate interests in trying the suspect and protecting the community. A suspect can be kept in jail before trial without bail if the court believes releasing the suspect would pose a danger to the community. This might be the case if a suspect is charged with a violent crime.

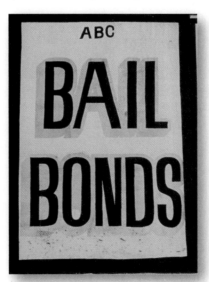

✦ By posting bail, a suspect may remain free until trial.

Rights at Trial   The Sixth Amendment gives a suspect the right to a **speedy and public trial**. Someone who is in fact innocent will want to clear his or her name as soon as possible. A speedy trial also helps guarantee that facts and events will be fresh in the mind of potential witnesses. Members of the public, including the press, must be able to observe trials. This ensures that the government respects the rights of suspects.

The Sixth Amendment gives suspects the right to **trial by jury**. It requires that the jury be from the state and district in which the crime was committed. This reflects the idea that the jury should speak for the community affected by the crime. The Sixth Amendment also requires that jurors be **impartial**. They must, in other words, be willing to consider evidence for and against the suspect with an open mind.

Additional Sixth Amendment rights include:

- The right to be represented by a lawyer. The Supreme Court has held that this right also applies to suspects who cannot afford a lawyer. These individuals are provided with a lawyer at government expense.
- The right to confront **adverse witnesses**. Adverse witnesses are witnesses who testify against the suspect. This right gives the suspect a chance to hear what the adverse witnesses say and to ask questions of the witnesses.
- The right to **compulsory process** for making a witness appear at court. Compulsory process means that the suspect can ask the court to order a witness to appear at trial. This order is called a **subpoena**. If the witness refuses to appear, the court can punish him or her for disobeying the subpoena with a fine or imprisonment.

Finally, the Fifth Amendment provides that no one "shall be compelled in any criminal case to be a witness against himself." This is called the right against **self-incrimination**. It means that the suspect cannot be forced to testify about his or her alleged involvement in the crime.

◆ The right to a trial by an impartial jury in a criminal case is protected by the Sixth Amendment.

Rights after Trial   At the end of a criminal trial, the jury delivers its verdict of guilty or innocent. If the jury decides the suspect is innocent, the suspect can never again be tried for the same offense. This is because the Fifth Amendment guarantees the right against **double jeopardy**. Double jeopardy means being put on trial more than once for the same crime. The right is based on the idea that the government, with all of its powers, should only be given one chance to try an individual for a criminal offense.

If, on the other hand, the jury finds the suspect guilty of the crime, the Eighth Amendment provides that the suspect cannot suffer **cruel and unusual punishments**. The meaning of cruel and unusual punishment has changed over time. Today some argue that the death penalty is a cruel and unusual punishment. The Supreme Court has not accepted this argument. It has, however, decided that arbitrary or racially biased uses of the death penalty can violate the Eighth Amendment.

Unenumerated Rights and Reserved Powers— The Ninth and Tenth Amendments

The last two amendments in the Bill of Rights name no specific rights. The rights and powers referred to in these amendments are unenumerated because they are not explicitly named.

The Ninth Amendment provides that "the enumeration in the Constitution of certain rights shall not be construed to deny or disparage others retained by the people." Remember the fear that the Federalists had expressed about the idea of a Bill of Rights? If certain specific rights were granted, did that mean that other rights that were not listed were no longer protected? This amendment speaks to that fear by stating that the people have other rights than those listed in the Bill of Rights. In the last fifty years, the Supreme Court has based several decisions on a **right to privacy** that it has found is implied, but not expressly described, in the Constitution.

The Tenth Amendment makes clear that any powers not delegated to the federal government are reserved to the states and, ultimately, to the people.

The Tenth Amendment restates the principle of federalism that governs the relationship between the federal and state governments. It provides that "the powers not delegated to the United States by the Constitution, nor prohibited by it to the States, are reserved to the States respectively, or to the people." In other words, the Constitution grants specific and limited powers to the federal government. Additional powers of government not granted to the federal government are reserved to state governments or to the people, who are the ultimate source of government in the United States.

The Bill of Rights and the Fourteenth Amendment

The rights protected in the Bill of Rights initially protected individuals against the actions of the federal government only. The Fourteenth Amendment, which was ratified in 1868, provides that "no state shall make or enforce any law which shall abridge the privileges and immunities of citizens of the United States." It also provides that no state shall "deprive any person of life, liberty, or property, without due process of law." These provisions of the Fourteenth Amendment, called the **privileges and immunities clause** and the **due process clause**, became the basis for a series of Supreme Court decisions over the twentieth century that gradually extended the Bill of Rights to protect individuals against improper actions by state governments as well as the federal government.

Most, but not all, of the rights protected by the Bill of Rights have been extended to the states. For example, the Fifth Amendment right to indictment by a grand jury has not been extended. You will learn more about this process of extending the Bill of Rights to the states, called **incorporation**, in Chapter Four.

IMPORTANT TERMS

1 Match the terms in the right column with the definitions in the left column.

A. First Amendment provision that prohibits the government from naming a national religion

B. Being put on trial more than once for the same crime

C. The government's power to take private property for public use

D. A court order used to make a witness appear at a trial

E. Citizen soldiers who can be called on in times of emergency

Militia

Eminent domain

Subpoena

Establishment clause

Double jeopardy

REVIEWING FACTS

Are the following statements true or false?

2 Congress submitted 10 amendments to the states for ratification as the Bill of Rights.

3 Fourth Amendment protections against search and seizure depend in part on one's expectation of privacy.

4 The Supreme Court has ruled that juveniles are entitled to trial by jury.

REVIEWING MAIN IDEAS

Use complete sentences to answer the following questions.

5 Why do you think the Supreme Court has allowed some restrictions on free speech? What do you think is the purpose of the restrictions it has allowed?

6 Why does your expectation of privacy affect whether the government can conduct a search without a search warrant?

7 Why is it important that criminal trials be open to the public?

UNDERSTANDING CONCEPTS

8 The government usually needs a search warrant before it can search you, your house, your personal property, or your private correspondence. In cases where you have a low expectation of privacy, however, the government may not need a search warrant if it suspects illegal activity is going on.

Consider the following examples. Do you think you would have a high or low expectation of privacy in these situations?

A. You are sitting in a car parked in a public parking lot.

B. You are inside a tree house in your backyard.

C. You are sending an e-mail from a computer at your school.

Comparing the Bill of Rights and the French Declaration of Rights

✦ This coin, minted in 1792, show Louis XVI as "King of the French" three years after the French Revolution began in 1789. Louis' reign ended with his execution in 1793.

Introduction

In 1789, the same year that the U.S. Bill of Rights was written, a revolution began in France. The French Revolution would come to rival the impact of the American Revolution. It also produced a document that would stand with the Bill of Rights as a model for individual liberty. This document is the Declaration of the Rights of Man and of the Citizen. Comparing the U.S. Bill of Rights to the French Declaration of the Rights of Man helps us better understand the rights we enjoy. It also helps us understand different interpretations of these rights.

The French Revolution

France, like England, was a monarchy. Expensive wars and the extravagance of life at the royal court had made the monarchy virtually bankrupt. Facing a financial crisis, the French King Louis XVI called for the assembly of the **Estates-General** of France to approve needed financial reforms.

The Estates-General was made up of people representing the traditional **three estates**, or social classes, of French society. The **first estate** was the Roman Catholic clergy (Catholicism was France's official religion). The **second estate** was the aristocracy, individuals who had inherited titles and special social standing by virtue of their birth. The **third estate** represented everyone else, including peasants, artisans, merchants, lawyers, and doctors. The first and second estates had special privileges, including the ability to avoid paying many of the taxes that supported the kingdom. The third estate bore the burden of financing the king and his administration.

Jacques-Louis David, an artist who sympathized with the French Revolution, produced this famous image of the Tennis Court Oath, taken by members of the newly formed National Assembly on June 20, 1789.

The Estates-General met at the palace of Versailles, just outside Paris, in May 1789. It soon became clear that the third estate's representatives were concerned about issues beyond the king's finances. They demanded greater representation of the third estate in the Estates-General. When these demands were not met, the third estate declared itself a **National Assembly** and took over an indoor tennis court at the Versailles palace. The third estate established the National Assembly as an alternative to the Estates-General that would better represent the French people.

The third-estate representatives, joined by some sympathetic members of the nobility and clergy, took what is known as the **Tennis Court Oath**. The Tennis Court Oath was a pledge that the representatives would stay assembled until a constitution had been written. The Tennis Court Oath is often called the beginning of the **French Revolution**, as it asserted the people's political will against the monarch's wishes. Louis eventually agreed to meet the third estate's demands. The first and second estates were joined into the new National Assembly, and the Estates-General ceased to exist.

On August 4, 1789, the National Assembly declared an end to the special privileges of the aristocracy and the clergy. These privileges had supported what we now call the *ancien régime*. Ancien régime is a French term that means "old government." It describes the political and social order based on a monarchy that existed before the French Revolution. The National Assembly also declared that anyone was now eligible to hold office in France, regardless of social class.

On August 26, 1789, the National Assembly formally adopted a document known as the **Declaration of the Rights of Man and of the Citizen**. This document would become the foundation for a new French political system.

THE FIFTH REPUBLIC

Unlike the United States, France has rewritten its constitution several times since 1789. The most recent constitution was written in 1958, which began the period in French political history called the Fifth Republic. The preamble to the 1958 constitution proclaims France's continuing commitment to the Declaration of the Rights of Man.

◆ King Louis XVI of France is executed at the guillotine on January 21, 1793.

The immediate impact of the Declaration of the Rights of Man was affected by the course of the French Revolution. In the early years of the Revolution, it looked as if France would adopt a system of **limited monarchy** similar to Britain. In a limited monarchy, as you learned in Chapter One, the monarch is subject to a constitution and the laws enacted under it. But in 1793, both Louis XVI and his queen, Marie-Antoinette, were executed.

The French Revolution now entered a more radical phase known as the **Reign of Terror**. Thousands of people were declared enemies of the revolution and beheaded at the guillotine. The excesses of this period turned many foreign observers, including many American political leaders, against the French Revolution.

In subsequent years, France went through many forms of government before its identity as a republic was firmly established. Throughout these changes in government, the Declaration of the Rights of Man has been a cornerstone of the French constitution.

THE GUILLOTINE AND THE REIGN OF TERROR

The guillotine was a device intended to efficiently and quickly behead someone who was sentenced to death for a crime. It was intended to be a humane alternative to more painful punishments, including beheading with an axe. Its efficiency in delivering death made it a gruesome symbol of the Reign of Terror in France.

Comparing the Bill of Rights and the Declaration of the Rights of Man

Similarities

The leaders of the French and American revolutions were inspired by the writings of the same Enlightenment philosophers whom you read about in Chapter One. The drafters of the Declaration of the Rights of Man were also familiar with the American Declaration of Independence and the Virginia Declaration of Rights. These documents had a strong influence on the French Declaration of the Rights of Man.

Among the rights guaranteed by both the Declaration of the Rights of Man and the Bill of Rights are

- Freedoms of conscience, speech, and religious belief.
- Private property rights, including the right to compensation if the government takes private property for public use.
- Rights of the accused in criminal trials.

The Declaration of the Rights of Man also shares principles found elsewhere in the U.S. Constitution. These include:

- The need for separation of powers within the government.
- The need for the government to have the power to tax citizens and to provide for the common defense through support of public military forces.
- The prohibition of **ex post facto laws**. Ex post facto laws are laws that punish someone "after the fact." For example, if your state legislature decided to pass a law that made it illegal to chew gum in public, it could not punish you if you had publicly chewed gum before the law was passed.

Finally, the Declaration of the Rights of Man shares many of the principles asserted in the American Declaration of Independence. These include the belief that all men possess certain natural and unalienable rights. The Declaration of Independence describes the rights of life, liberty, and the pursuit of happiness, while the Declaration of the Rights of Man describes the rights of liberty, property, security, and resistance to oppression.

Both documents assert the equality of all men. This is the idea, discussed in Chapter One, that no one is entitled to greater privileges by virtue of birth. Both documents also share similar assumptions about the proper source of government power. The Declaration of Independence defines that source as the consent of the governed, while the Declaration of the Rights of Man defines it as the expression of the general will of the people.

This subway station in Paris, France, gives French citizens a public space for freedom of expression.

Differences

Despite its many similarities to the founding documents of the United States, the Declaration of the Rights of Man also defines a society that differs in several important respects from the American model.

You have learned that the Bill of Rights and the Declaration of the Rights of Man both protect freedoms of religion and expression. Now look at how the Declaration of the Rights of Man defines these freedoms:

- "No one shall be disquieted on account of his opinions, including his religious views, provided their manifestation does not disturb the public order established by law" (Article 10).
- "Every citizen may . . . speak, write, and print with freedom, but shall be responsible for such abuses of this freedom as shall be defined by law" (Article 11).

Like the U.S. Constitution, the North Carolina Constitution protects freedom of speech and the press, and says that these freedoms "shall never be restrained." (Article I, Sec. 14) However, unlike the U.S. Constitution, the North Carolina Constitution explicitly says that "every person shall be held responsible for their abuse." This language is an example of the principle that every right carries a responsibility.

Compare this to the language of the First Amendment. What differences do you notice? Look carefully at the first five words of the First Amendment: "Congress shall make no law. . . ." Is there a similar ban on laws that might restrict the rights of religion and expression in the Declaration of the Rights of Man?

To the contrary, the Declaration of the Rights of Man allows the making of laws that define, and potentially limit, freedoms of religion and expression. Article 10 provides that **manifestations** of religious beliefs—religious practices, in other words—can be limited if they "disturb the public order established by law." Similarly, Article 11 provides that the law can hold people responsible if they abuse their freedom of expression.

The different approaches to freedoms of religion and expression in the Bill of Rights and the Declaration of the Rights of Man illustrate a basic difference between the documents. In neither the United States nor France are individual freedoms absolute. But in the Bill of Rights, individual freedoms tend to act as a limit on government actions. In the Declaration of the Rights of Man, the interests of the nation as a whole tend to act as a limit on individual freedoms.

Let's look at an example that illustrates the different approaches of the American and French models. In both the U.S. and France, **hate speech** has been a subject of concern in recent years. Hate speech is speech that is meant to offend someone based, for example, on the person's race, gender, or religion.

In the United States, courts have often struck down laws that try to restrict hate speech. Their reasoning is that the First Amendment protects an individual's free speech, no matter how offensive it is. French law, on the other hand, bans hate speech.

U.S. citizens might argue that it is better for hate speech to be out in the open, where it can be debated and discredited by others. French citizens might argue that restrictions on hate speech support a national interest in civility and tolerance and takes little away from the right to engage in legitimate debate.

✦ The United States and France take different approaches to hate speech. Here, an American neo-Nazi Party leader comments in 1978 on the U.S. Supreme Court's decision to allow neo-Nazi party members to march in Chicago's Marquette Park.

Both decisions demonstrate that the freedoms fundamental to democracy can and do take different forms.

Today the Declaration of the Rights of Man and the U.S. Bill of Rights stand together as perhaps the two most important sources of modern democratic ideals. They have had a deep influence on national constitutions around the world. As you will read in Chapter Five, they have also affected how the world thinks of human rights. They continue to support two of the world's most vigorous and prosperous democracies.

IMPORTANT TERMS

1 Match the terms in the right column with the definitions in the left column.

A. A law that punishes someone "after the fact"

B. A radical phase of the French Revolution that saw thousands beheaded at the guillotine

C. The pledge by representatives of France's third estate to stay assembled until a constitution was written

D. The French term for "old government"

Ancien régime

Tennis Court Oath

Ex post facto

Reign of Terror

REVIEWING FACTS

2 What social classes did the three estates in France represent?

First Estate:

Second Estate:

Third Estate:

3 Name three of the rights guaranteed by both the U.S. Bill of Rights and the French Declaration of the Rights of Man.

4 What form of government did France have before the French Revolution?

REVIEWING MAIN IDEAS

Use complete sentences to answer the following questions.

5 Why did the third estate break away from the Estates-General to form the National Assembly?

6 How did the special privileges given to the first and second estates in France affect the third estate?

UNDERSTANDING CONCEPTS

7 Article 2 of the 1958 French Constitution states that the French government avoids open support of any religion and that the nation of France respects all beliefs.

In 2003, the French government passed a law that says students cannot wear "conspicuous" religious symbols at public schools. This means that while they are at school, Muslim girls cannot wear headscarves and Christian students cannot wear large crosses.

Do you think that the language of the 1958 French Constitution and the 2003 law banning religious symbols at French public schools fit within the Declaration of the Rights of Man's definition of religious freedom? Do you think the 2003 French law would violate the First Amendment to the U.S. Constitution?

A New Bill of Rights?

The U.S. Bill of Rights is now over 200 years old. The U.S. government has asked you and your classmates to review the Bill of Rights. The government wants to know if you think the Bill of Rights needs any changes to better protect the rights of Americans in the twenty-first century.

Organize Your Thoughts

First, read through the 10 amendments in the Bill of Rights. Then take out a sheet of paper and answer the following questions:

1. Are there any rights described in the Bill of Rights that you think no longer need constitutional protection?

2. Are there any rights that you think should stay, but should be defined differently? You might think that some rights need to be strengthened. Or perhaps you think some rights need to be limited.

3. Are there any rights not currently described in the Bill of Rights that you think should be added?

Teamwork

Get into groups of 4 to 6 students. First, compare your answers to the above questions. Are there areas you all agree on? What are your areas of disagreement? Working together, come up with a list of recommendations that everyone in your group can agree upon. Your recommendations should include rights that you think should be removed, added, or defined differently.

As a Class

Have each group report their recommendations to the class as a whole. Your teacher will make a list of

- Any rights you think should be removed from the Bill of Rights,
- Any rights currently described in the Bill of Rights that you think should be defined differently, and
- Any rights you think should be added to the Bill of Rights.

After all the groups have reported, discuss the lists of recommendations. Focus on how these recommendations might affect your lives as U.S. citizens. At the end of your discussion, have the class vote on a final list of recommendations.

THE LIFE OF THE CONSTITUTION:
Historical Milestones

✦ This illustration depicts Abraham Lincoln reading the Emancipation Proclamation to the members of his Cabinet.

What You Will Learn

In this chapter you will

★ Learn about the end of slavery and how the Thirteenth Amendment abolished slavery in all the states.

★ Explore how the Fourteenth Amendment sought to protect the civil rights of former slaves and end discrimination against them.

★ Discover how the right to vote has been expanded over time by the Fifteenth, Nineteenth, and Twenty-sixth Amendments.

An End to Slavery

Introduction

The word *slavery* does not appear in the Constitution. But there are several sections in the Constitution that deal specifically with the issue of slavery. Article I includes the Three-Fifths Compromise and prevents Congress from ending the slave trade, as discussed in Chapter Two. Article IV says that a slave who has escaped into another state has to be returned to his or her slaveholder.

These provisions appear in the Constitution as a result of compromises made at the Constitutional Convention in 1787. Many delegates from the northern states opposed slavery, but they made these compromises in order to get delegates from the southern states to agree to the Constitution.

The Thirteenth Amendment ended slavery.

✦ Farmers in the South depended on slaves to pick cotton by hand. This photo, taken after the Civil War in 1870, shows a woman balancing a basket of cotton on her head at a farm in Augusta, Georgia.

Abolition in the Northern States

After the Constitution was ratified, the states' differences of opinion on slavery increased. By the 1830s slavery had been abolished in the northern states. People who campaigned to end slavery were called **abolitionists**.

Meanwhile, in the South, the economy was increasingly dependent on enslaved Africans. Farmers needed slaves to harvest labor-intensive crops like cotton and tobacco. They wanted to continue to exploit slave labor.

It was a generally accepted constitutional principle that slavery was an area over which the states had control.

This map shows in red the states in which slavery was legal after the Missouri Compromise of 1820

Slavery in the Territories and New States

The United States grew quickly in the first decades of the 1800s. The territories began petitioning for statehood. The North and South disagreed about whether the territories should enter the Union as free states or slave states.

In 1819 Missouri tried to enter the Union as a slave state. The southern states supported it. The northern states opposed it, fearing that slavery would spread. After two years of controversy, a compromise was struck. Missouri was admitted as a slave state, while Maine was admitted as a free state. This maintained a balance between 12 slave states and 12 free states. Congress also agreed to prohibit slavery forever in the territories of the Louisiana Purchase that were north of Missouri's southern border.

The tension over slavery continued between the North and South over the years. Then in 1854, Congress passed the Kansas-Nebraska Act. This overruled the Missouri Compromise. The act said that all the territories had the right to decide issues of slavery. This act made it possible for slavery to spread into the North.

The Civil War Begins

In 1858 Abraham Lincoln was the leader of the Republican Party in Illinois. Lincoln was opposed to slavery. He said slavery was "a moral, a social, and a political wrong." He argued that the federal government had a duty to prevent the spread of slavery into the territories.

This photograph shows Abraham Lincoln in 1863.

In the 1860 election, Lincoln was elected president of the United States. The southern states seceded a short time later. **Secession** is the act of withdrawing from a country or union. When the southern states seceded, they were no longer a part of the United States. They formed a confederation of independent states called the Confederate States of America, or the Confederacy. The Civil War began a few months later in April 1861.

Emancipation

During the Civil War, public opinion in the North increasingly turned against slavery. Many slaves escaped from the South to fight in the Union army alongside white soldiers. The president wanted to free slaves in order to deprive the South of its labor supply. The North also wanted to recruit more black soldiers to help win the war. In 1862 Congress passed an act stating that the slaves in the rebellious South who were captured or crossed Union lines were free and would never be slaves again.

On New Year's Day, 1863, Lincoln read the Emancipation Proclamation. **Emancipation** means freeing a person from the social or legal control of another. When slaves were freed they were said to be emancipated. The Emancipation Proclamation read:

> As a fit and necessary war measure for suppressing the rebellion ... slaves within any State, or designated part of a State ... then ... in rebellion, ... shall be then, thenceforward, and forever free.

This Proclamation freed all slaves in Confederate states that were still in rebellion against the Union—more than 3 million slaves in total. However, the Proclamation did not free slaves in the loyal border states of Maryland, Delaware, Kentucky, and Missouri, and in southern areas controlled by the Union military.

After the Emancipation Proclamation, there was widespread public acceptance that a Union victory would lead to general emancipation. There was one small problem. Lincoln issued the Proclamation under the broad war powers of the president. But by tradition and law, the states had power over slavery. Some people raised questions about whether Lincoln's Proclamation was legally valid.

The Civil War ended four years after it had begun, in April 1865.

FOCUS ON NORTH CAROLINA CONSTITUTION

The North Carolina Constitution, in Article I, Section 17, forever prohibits slavery. It also forever prohibits involuntary servitude, "except as a punishment for crime whereof the parties have been adjudged guilty."

Did You KNOW?

In 1861, a month before the start of the Civil War, both Houses passed an amendment that prohibited any further amendments allowing Congress to interfere with slavery. The amendment was only ratified by two states.

The Thirteenth Amendment

In the closing days of the war, Congress drafted the Thirteenth Amendment. This amendment removed any doubt about the legality of the Emancipation Proclamation and freed slaves in all states. The amendment declared that slavery would no longer exist in the United States. Any remaining slaves were free. Remember, before the war, the states had power over slavery. The Thirteenth Amendment gave power over slavery to the federal government.

President Andrew Johnson encouraged the southern states to ratify the amendment. Eight southern states ratified it, and the Thirteenth Amendment was passed by three-quarters of the states in December 1865.

IMPORTANT TERMS

1 Match the terms in the right column with the definitions in the left column.

A. People who campaigned to end slavery

B. The word used to describe the action of the southern states in withdrawing from the Union

C. The organization of states that withdrew from the Union

D. The word used to describe a slave who was freed

Secession

Emancipated

Confederacy

Abolitionists

REVIEWING FACTS

Are the following statements true or false?

2 The U.S. Constitution explicitly states that slavery is legal.

3 The Missouri Compromise meant that each state had the right to decide whether to legalize slavery.

4 The Emancipation Proclamation did not free all slaves in all states.

REVIEWING MAIN IDEAS

Answer the following questions using complete sentences.

5 Give two reasons why President Lincoln made the Emancipation Proclamation during the Civil War.

6 Why did Congress pass the Thirteenth Amendment?

UNDERSTANDING CONCEPTS

7 Look at the illustration below.

◆ This wood engraving appeared in the "Anti-Slavery Almanac" in 1839. Its original caption was 'A Northern Freeman Enslaved by Northern Hands'."

Do you think this illustration would persuade people that slavery should be abolished? Explain why you think it would or would not be effective.

Design a poster to persuade people to pass the Thirteenth Amendment. Explain why you think your poster would convince people to vote in favor of the Thirteenth Amendment.

Emancipation

Read the excerpt from the Emancipation Proclamation and Dr. John Fields's description of slavery during the Civil War. Then answer the questions below.

Abraham Lincoln issued the Emancipation Proclamation on January 1, 1863. The opening sentence read:

> [A]ll persons held as slaves within any State or designated part of a State, the people whereof shall then be in rebellion against the United States, shall be then, thenceforth, and forever free...

Dr. John W. Fields was born in Owensville, Louisiana. He was a slave. He was separated from his mother and family when he was 6 years old and was sent to work in Kentucky. At the time of the Emancipation Proclamation he was 15 years old and still living in Kentucky.

King & Baird, Printers, 607 Sansom Street, Philadelphia.

Entered according to Act of Congress, in the year 1863, by J. W. UMPEHENT, in the Clerk's Office of the District Court of the United States, for the Eastern District of Pennsylvania.

Published by S. BOTT. No. 43 South Third Street, Philadelphia, Penna.

◆ This is a version of an illustration by Thomas Nast that appeared in Harper's Weekly on January 24, 1863. The original caption read, "The Emancipation of the Negroes . . . The Past and the Future." What do you think of the artist's representation of the past and the future?

In 1937 Dr. Fields was interviewed about his life as a part of the Federal Writers' Project. This project recorded more than 2,000 interviews with ex-slaves. Dr. Fields's description of his memories of slavery and the Civil War is recorded in his own words.

At the beginning of the Civil War I was still at this place as a slave. It looked at the first of the war as if the South would win, as the South won most of the big battles. This was because we slaves stayed at home and tended the farm and kept their families.

To eliminate this solid support of the South, the Emancipation Act was passed, freeing all slaves. Most of the slaves were so ignorant they did not realize they were free. The planters knew this and as Kentucky never seceded from the Union, they would send slaves into Kentucky from other states in the South and hire them out to plantations.

✦ This photograph of John W. Fields was taken in Indiana between 1936 and 1938, when Dr. Fields was 89 years old.

CRITICAL THINKING

1. Does the Emancipation Proclamation apply to all the slave states?

2. Why is Dr. Fields's narrative a valuable primary resource? What can it teach us about the past? What are the limitations of this kind of resource?

3. In your own words, explain why Dr. Fields thinks the Emancipation Proclamation was issued. In full sentences, describe any other reasons you think President Lincoln might have had for issuing the Emancipation Proclamation.

4. Dr. Fields describes one consequence of the Emancipation Proclamation in Kentucky. In your own words, explain what happened. What effect did the Thirteenth Amendment have on Kentucky and other slave states in the Union?

The Fourteenth Amendment and the Dawn of Civil Rights

Introduction

The Thirteenth Amendment may have abolished slavery, but former slaves found they were openly discriminated against, particularly in the South. Some of the newly elected southern legislatures passed laws called **Black Codes**, which deprived African Americans of many basic rights. These laws acknowledged that former slaves were free, but

- limited their job opportunities,
- controlled their movements,
- restricted the places where they could live, and
- excluded them from jury duty, public office, and voting.

The Fourteenth Amendment, ratified in 1868, was intended to extend the Bill of Rights to the states and compel the states to respect the fundamental rights of all people.

> **RECONSTRUCTION**
>
> Reconstruction is the period after the Civil War when the southern states were rebuilt and readmitted to the Union.

President vs. Congress: The Battle for Control Over Reconstruction

The Fourteenth Amendment was ratified in the context of a struggle between Congress and President Johnson. Andrew Johnson, a Democrat from Tennessee, was Abraham Lincoln's vice-president. Johnson had been a supporter of slavery in the late 1850s. However, he was also the only southern Democrat who stayed in the federal Senate during the Civil War. Lincoln chose him in an attempt to appeal to Democrats and build "national unity."

Just over a month after President Lincoln's second inauguration in March 1865, Lincoln was assassinated by John Wilkes Booth. Vice president Johnson became president. He pursued a plan for reconstructing the Confederate southern states. His plan involved pardoning Confederates and restoring southern governments. As a result of his policies, many Confederates entered state politics again and had a role in passing the Black Codes.

◆ This engraving shows President Andrew Johnson, the seventeenth President of the United States.

The Freedmen's Bureau was established by the federal government in 1865 to provide former slaves with food, clothing and other assistance. In 1866, Congress passed a Bill to extend the life and expand the powers of the Bureau. This illustration, which appeared in *Harpers Weekly* on April 14, 1866, shows President Johnson kicking the Freedmen's Bureau. Can you guess what happened to the Bill?

Republicans dominated Congress. They thought that President Johnson was being too easy on the Confederate states and were angered by the discriminatory laws passed by governments in the South. In December 1865, Congress refused to seat congress members from the former Confederate states.

Congress started to take control of the reconstruction process from President Johnson. Congress proposed several acts to try to protect the rights of former slaves. One of its most important pieces of legislation was the 1866 Civil Rights Act, which made it a federal crime to deprive a person of his or her civil rights. President Johnson vetoed this bill, saying it gave too much power to the states. A couple of weeks later, Republicans in Congress banded together to override the president's veto. The Constitution requires a two-thirds majority vote in both the House of Representatives and the Senate to override the president's veto. This was the first time in American history that a bill became law by a congressional override of a presidential veto.

In the election in 1866, Republicans gained seats in both houses of Congress, ensuring that Congress would easily be able to override any more vetoes by President Johnson. Congress took charge of the reconstruction process.

★ ★ ★ ★ ★ ★

THE IMPEACHMENT OF ANDREW JOHNSON

After Republicans won seats in the 1866 elections, Congress passed the Tenure of Office Act. This act prevented the president from firing one of his officers without the approval of the Senate.

Soon after, President Johnson fired his secretary of war. The Senate reinstated the secretary. President Johnson fired him again. Congress voted to impeach the president.

The president was put on trial in the Senate. The majority was one vote short of a two-thirds majority, and Andrew Johnson was not convicted.

The Fourteenth Amendment

Congress drafted the Fourteenth Amendment during the first six months of 1866, while the South was not represented in Congress. The amendment was passed in June 1866 and then submitted to the states for ratification.

By the end of that year 14 northern states and two border states—Missouri and West Virginia—had ratified the amendment. But only one former Confederate state, Tennessee, had ratified it. In response, the Republican Congress passed three Reconstruction Acts (over President Johnson's veto) during 1867.

These acts declared that there were no legal state governments in the former Confederate states. States had to hold constitutional conventions to create new state constitutions. Only black men and loyal white men were allowed to participate. All state constitutions had to grant voting rights to African American men. As a result of these acts, elections in the states created Republican-dominated, biracial legislatures.

The acts also stated that the former Confederate states would not be re-admitted to the Union until they ratified the Fourteenth Amendment and it became part of the U.S. Constitution. New legislatures in the South quickly ratified the Fourteenth Amendment, and it became part of the Constitution on July 9, 1868.

✦ This portrait of Dred Scott was painted from a photograph in 1882.

There are five sections of the Fourteenth Amendment. Section 2 removed the Three-Fifths Compromise by stating that all people, black and white, would be counted to determine how many representatives a state could have in Congress. Section 3 prevented former Confederates from holding office in state or federal government. Section 4 dealt with some issues relating to debt after the Civil War. Section 5 gave Congress the power to pass legislation to enforce the Fourteenth Amendment.

Section 1 is the most significant section of the Fourteenth Amendment. It states that every person born or naturalized in the United States is a citizen of both the nation and their state. This clause overturned the Supreme Court's decision in the *Dred Scott* case and made all former slaves citizens of the United States. Section 1 also sought to extend the Bill of Rights to the states to protect the human rights of former slaves, as explained in the discussion of the privileges and immunities clause and the equal protection clause below.

Privileges and Immunities, Due Process, and the Bill of Rights

The first 10 amendments to the Constitution, also known as the Bill of Rights, guarantee individual rights and restrict the actions of government (the Bill of Rights is discussed in Chapter Three). But the Supreme Court said in an 1833 case that the Bill of Rights only applied to the federal government and did not apply to state governments. This meant, for example, that states could pass laws limiting free speech and could perform unreasonable searches.

Section 1 of the Fourteenth Amendment contains one guarantee of rights: It says that states cannot deprive any person of life, liberty or property without "due process of law." Due process means that laws must be clear and fair. It also means that people have a right to a fair trial. Section 1 also prohibits states from making or enforcing any law that abridges the "privileges and immunities" of citizens.

When Senator Jacob Howard of Michigan introduced the Fourteenth Amendment, he said that the privileges and immunities clause in Section 1 would extend the other protections of the Bill of Rights to state governments. Senator Howard thought that the Fourteenth Amendment would make the Bill of Rights apply to the states as well as the nation.

However, the Supreme Court did not interpret the privileges and immunities clause in this way. In the *Slaughterhouse Cases* in 1873, the Court held that the Fourteenth Amendment did not make the Bill of Rights apply to the states. The Court said that states had control over laws about the basic civil rights and liberties of citizens. As a result of this decision, states were able to continue to pass laws that abridged the human rights of citizens.

This narrow interpretation of the Fourteenth Amendment started to change in the twentieth century. The Supreme Court made a series of decisions in which it interpreted the privileges and immunities clause and the due process clause to mean that parts of the Bill of Rights should apply to the states. The process of extending the Bill of Rights to the states was called **incorporation**. Almost all the rights in the Bill of Rights had been incorporated by the 1960s.

✦ This 1890 etching shows Justice John Marshall Harlan, who wrote the only dissent in the case of *Plessy v. Ferguson*.

★ CASE ★

THE CASE OF *PLESSY V. FERGUSON*

In 1892 a man named Homer Plessy sat down in a train car that was reserved for whites in accordance with state segregation laws. The train conductor asked him to move to a train car reserved for African Americans. Plessy refused and was arrested. At his trial, Plessy argued that the law prohibiting African Americans from sitting in train cars reserved for whites was unconstitutional under the Fourteenth Amendment.

In the case of *Plessy v. Ferguson,* the Supreme Court upheld the constitutionality of segregation laws. The Court interpreted the equal protection clause narrowly. It said that segregation was acceptable if the facilities provided for blacks and whites were equal. This decision led to more than 50 years of legal segregation between blacks and whites.

Justice Harlan wrote the only dissenting judgment in the case of *Plessy v. Ferguson.* He said that the purpose of state segregation laws was to discriminate against African Americans. He said:

In view of the constitution, in the eye of the law, there is in this country no superior, dominant, ruling class of citizens...
Our Constitution is color-blind, and neither knows nor tolerates classes among citizens.

◆ The 1954 photograph shows Linda Brown (left) with her parents and sister in front of their house in Topeka, Kansas.

Discrimination, Segregation, and the Equal Protection Clause

The equal protection clause says that states cannot deny people in the state "equal protection of the laws." It was intended to ensure that former slaves were treated equally with other citizens.

At the time that the Fourteenth Amendment was passed, former slaves did not just face discriminatory laws such as the Black Codes. They also faced racism and prejudice in their private dealings with individuals. In 1875 Congress passed the Civil Rights Act on the basis of the equal protection clause to try to prevent private discrimination. The act said that all people, black and white, should be entitled to use inns, public transportation, theaters, and other public places.

★ CASE ★

THE CASE OF BROWN V. BOARD OF EDUCATION

Until the 1950s, some state laws provided for segregation of elementary schools. Linda Brown was a third-grade student. She had to walk several miles to school every morning to attend a school for African American students. When her parents tried to enroll her at an all-white school closer to their home, their application was rejected because Linda was black.

Linda's parents and the parents of African American children from four other states brought a case to the Supreme Court. The lawyers for the children argued that even if equal schools were provided for black and white students, segregation meant that African American students felt they were inferior. Segregation itself produced inequality. In 1954 the Supreme Court issued its decision in the case of Brown v. Board of Education. The Court decided that segregation was unconstitutional under the equal protection clause of the Fourteenth Amendment.

In 1883 the constitutionality of this act was challenged in the Supreme Court in the Civil Rights Cases. The Supreme Court decided that the 1875 Civil Rights Act was unconstitutional. It said the Fourteenth Amendment did not prevent discrimination by individuals, such as a refusal to serve food or give lodging in a hotel to an African American.

The decision in the Civil Rights Cases paved the way for state segregation laws. **Segregation laws** separated blacks and whites in transport, hotels, restaurants, theaters, parks, schools, and even elevators in public buildings. These laws were also known as Jim Crow laws. Segregation continued in many states across the nation until the Supreme Court decided that such laws were unconstitutional in the 1954 case of *Brown* v. *Board of Education* (see explanation on previous page).

After the Supreme Court's decision in *Brown*, segregation laws could no longer be enforced. However, this did not stop people in some parts of the country from resisting desegregation. For example, in 1957, nine African-American students in Arkansas attempted to attend Little Rock Central High School, which had previously been an all-white school. The state governor ordered the state's National Guard to surround the school to prevent any African-American students from entering. President Eisenhower intervened by sending 1,000 United States Army troops to protect the African-American students as they entered the school.

In 1964, Congress passed the Civil Rights Act. The Act made discrimination and segregation illegal in all public places, in government and in employment. The Jim Crow laws of the South were finally swept away.

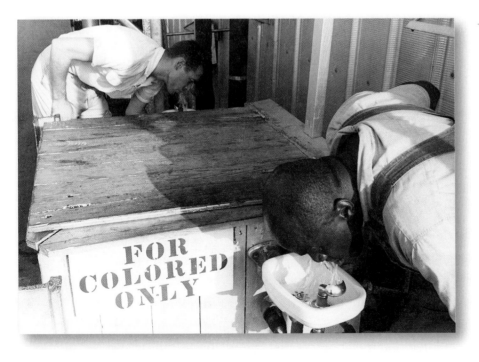

✦ This photograph shows two people using separate drinking fountains in the segregated south.

IMPORTANT TERMS

1 **Match the terms in the right column with the definitions in the left column.**

A. Laws passed by former confederate states after the Civil War that discriminated against African Americans

Segregation

B. The period during which the former confederate states were reorganized and admitted to the Union

Incorporation

C. The process of extending the Bill of Rights to the states

Reconstruction

D. The separation of races in public places

Black Codes

REVIEWING FACTS

2 What was the first act passed by Congress over a presidential veto?

3 What 1857 Supreme Court case did the Fourteenth Amendment overrule?

4 The Supreme Court said in the case of *Plessy* v. *Ferguson* that segregation was legal. What did the Court say about the facilities that had to be provided?

REVIEWING MAIN IDEAS

Answer the following questions using complete sentences.

5 The drafters of the privileges and immunities clause of the Fourteenth Amendment intended it to enable the federal government to extend the Bill of Rights to the states. Which Supreme Court decision interpreted the clause narrowly? What was the effect of this decision?

6 Which Supreme Court decision ended segregation? What argument did the lawyers in the case make?

UNDERSTANDING CONCEPTS

7 The Fourteenth Amendment sought to protect the civil rights of former slaves. Write a definition for the term *civil rights,* and list five rights that you think of as important civil rights. Then look at a copy of the Constitution and answer the following questions.

- Does the Constitution directly protect any of the rights on your list? If so, write the article and section number next to the civil right you have listed.

- Are there any rights you have listed that might be protected by interpreting the Constitution broadly? Explain your answer.

- Are there any rights you have listed that are not protected by the Constitution? Do you think there are some kinds of rights that cannot or should not be protected by the Constitution? Explain your answer.

Expanding the Right to Vote

Introduction

One of the most important civil rights is the right to vote. The Fifteenth Amendment granted the right to vote to African American men in 1870. It was seen as the peak achievement of the Reconstruction Congress. Despite this, it was not properly enforced until almost 100 years later, when the Twenty-fourth Amendment was passed. The Nineteenth Amendment granted the vote to women in 1920. The right to vote was extended to all people over 18 in 1971.

Did You KNOW?

In colonial America, some women had the right to vote. For example, in Massachusetts, women who owned property had voting privileges between 1691 and 1780.

The Fifteenth Amendment and the Twenty-fourth Amendment

The Fourteenth Amendment stated that all persons were citizens, but it did not directly give African American men the right to vote. In 1867, Congress passed the Reconstruction Acts, which allowed southern states to re-enter the Union if they adopted new constitutions that allowed black men to vote. But voting was seen as a matter for the states, and African Americans were still not entitled to vote in most of the northern states.

The black vote became a big issue after the elections in 1868, in which presidential candidate Ulysses S. Grant won only 52 percent of the popular vote. Other Republican candidates won by small margins. In the South, white Democrats used violence and intimidation to prevent blacks from voting. The Republican Congress came to believe that all African Americans needed to have the vote in order to balance the strengthening Democratic Party. The only way to guarantee blacks the vote in every state was to pass a constitutional amendment.

◆ This cartoon, from 1876, was published six years after the Fifteenth Amendment was ratified. The original caption was "Cartoon showing the freedom of the Negro voter in the South." What point do you think the cartoonist is trying to make?

The Fifteenth Amendment, ratified on February 3, 1870, stated that the right of citizens of the United States to vote should not be denied or abridged by the United States or by a state on account of "race, color, or previous condition of servitude." This section entitled African American men to vote. Federal troops were stationed in the states to ensure that the amendment was honored. Thousands of black men enrolled to vote. Former slaves were elected to public office, in positions from local official to U.S. senator.

During the 1890s and early 1900s, however, some states introduced laws and practices that discouraged blacks from voting:

• **Poll Tax**

Many states charged voters a poll tax. A **poll tax** is a tax that voters must pay if they want to vote. This was usually only a small amount per year, but it was a cumulative tax. This meant that the unpaid poll tax added up year after year. If a person wanted to vote they had to pay everything they owed for past years. The poll tax reduced the voting privileges of the poorer citizens in the states, many of whom were minorities.

• **Literacy Tests**

Some states required voters to pass literacy tests or to explain a clause of the Constitution before they could vote. The Supreme Court said these requirements were not inconsistent with the Fifteenth Amendment because they appeared to apply to all men, black and white.

However, in some states, grandfather clauses said that the literacy requirements did not apply if a voter's father or grandfather had been able to vote before the Civil War. Obviously, such clauses only benefited white men.

• **White Primaries**

In some states the Democratic Party prohibited blacks from voting in their primaries. In states where the Democratic Party was very strong, this effectively excluded blacks from political participation.

✦ This 1966 photograph shows African-American men voting in Alabama after the passage of the 1966 Voting Rights Act.

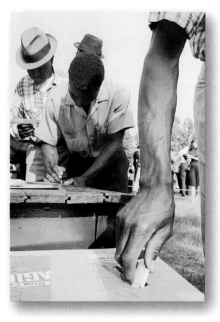

• **Discrimination**

Voting officials in many states discriminated against African American men by administering literacy tests and Constitution tests unfairly. Organizations like the Ku Klux Klan used violence and intimidation to try to prevent blacks from voting.

African Americans made some advances in voting in the first half of the twentieth century. In 1915, the Supreme Court ruled that grandfather clauses were unconstitutional. It decided that white primaries were unconstitutional in 1932.

In 1949 it ruled that literacy requirements were unconstitutional where they were drafted with the intent of preventing African-Americans from voting. However, such an intent was difficult to prove. The poll tax survived several challenges to its constitutionality. Almost 100 years after the Fifteenth Amendment, five states still required voters to pay a poll tax.

As the civil rights movement gathered speed in the 1950s and 1960s, Congress decided that a constitutional amendment was necessary to remove the poll tax in the states that still had it. The Twenty-fourth Amendment stated that the right of citizens to vote should not "be denied or abridged by the United States or any State by reason of failure to pay poll tax or any other tax." The Amendment was ratified on January 23, 1964.

Nineteenth Amendment

African American men were not the only people deprived of the vote. Women also faced a struggle for the right to vote.

When the founding fathers drafted the Constitution after the American Revolution, they gave states the power to determine who could vote. At first states only gave the vote to men who owned property or paid taxes. By the early nineteenth century most states had extended voting rights to all adult men. After the Fifteenth Amendment was passed, white and black men were entitled to vote (in theory if not in practice). But all women, even women who owned property and paid taxes, were excluded from voting.

Women started campaigning for the right to vote in the 1840s and 1850s. They worked with abolitionist leaders, seeking the vote for former slaves and for women. But the leaders of the women's movement felt betrayed when the Fifteenth Amendment was passed without any reference to a vote for women.

Women formed two groups to fight for their right to vote. The **National Woman Suffrage Association** sought to enact a federal law guaranteeing women the vote. The **National American Woman Suffrage Association** worked to secure the vote for women gradually, state by state. The two groups merged in 1890.

ATTEMPTS TO VOTE

Some women were determined to interpret the Fifteenth Amendment to mean that it gave women the vote. Susan B. Anthony went to the polls in Rochester, New York, in 1872. She persuaded the election inspectors to let her and 15 other women register to vote. Two weeks later all the women, and the voting officials, were arrested. Anthony appeared before a judge who repeatedly made anti-feminist remarks and fined Anthony $100. She refused to pay, and the judge, fearing that she might appeal to higher courts, let her go free.

FOCUS ON NORTH CAROLINA CONSTITUTION

Article VI of the North Carolina Constitution deals with suffrage and eligibility for office. Section 1 states that "Every person born in the United States and every person who has been naturalized, 18 years of age, and possessing the qualifications set out in this Article, shall be entitled to vote at any election by the people of the State . . ." Section 2 denies convicted felons the right to vote unless their rights have been restored in the manner prescribed by law.

✦ This photo shows women in Manhattan marching to campaign for the right to vote.

Women in England also campaigned for the right to vote. In this 1914 photograph, three policemen arrest a woman campaigning for the right to vote outside Buckingham Palace in London.

Wyoming, a territory at the time, gave women the right to vote in 1869. By 1919, about 30 states had granted women voting rights of some kind. Some states allowed women to vote in municipal (city) elections and for presidential electors, but did not allow women to vote in elections for state or federal government. Others gave women the right to vote in all elections.

On August 18, 1920, the Nineteenth Amendment to the Constitution ensured women the right to vote in all elections. It stated, in the same language as the Fifteenth Amendment, "the right of citizens of the United States to vote shall not be denied or abridged by the United States on account of sex."

Twenty-sixth Amendment

Throughout the Vietnam War, any male over 18 years of age could be conscripted. **Conscription** is compulsory service in the military. In most states, people had to be 21 or older before they were allowed to vote. It seemed unfair that people who could be sent to die for their country were not allowed to vote in its elections. Similar arguments had been made after the Civil War and during World War II.

According to polls, the majority of the public supported voting rights for those over 18, because:

- They were treated as adults in most respects—18-year-olds could get married, buy property, and pay taxes;

- 18-year-olds were considered to be physically and emotionally mature enough to vote; and

- People thought that extending the right to vote to young people would bring idealism and commitment into American democracy.

Theodore Sorenson former special counsel to President John F. Kennedy, said, "If taxation without representation was tyranny, then conscription without representation is slavery."

Voters in Miami-Dade County stand in line to vote in the Presidential elections on November 2, 2004.

Congress proposed the Twenty-sixth Amendment on March 21, 1971. It swept through the states faster than any previous constitutional amendment and was ratified on July 1, 1971. It took the same form as the Fifteenth Amendment and stated, "the right of citizens of the United States, who are eighteen years of age or older, to vote shall not be denied or abridged by the United States or by any state on account of age." The amendment meant that all citizens who were 18 years or older had the right to vote in federal, state, and local elections.

IMPORTANT TERMS

1 Look up these words in the dictionary:

suffrage
franchise

2 Apply what you've learned to write definitions for these three words:

suffragette
enfranchised
disenfranchised

Check your work in the dictionary. Are your definitions correct?

REVIEWING FACTS

Are the following statements true or false?

3 African American men were not allowed to vote in any state until the Fifteenth Amendment was passed.

4 The Fifteenth Amendment gave Native Americans the right to vote.

5 Women had the right to vote in some elections in the majority of states before the Nineteenth Amendment was passed.

6 The Twenty-sixth Amendment was passed during World War II.

REVIEWING MAIN IDEAS

Answer the following questions in complete sentences.

7 List three tactics that states used to try to prevent African American men from voting.

8 Explain how court decisions, laws, or amendments overcame each of those tactics.

9 Look at Article V of the Constitution. It outlines two ways in which amendments may be proposed and ratified. What are they? Which method of amendment is usually used?

UNDERSTANDING CONCEPTS

10 Would you agree with a constitutional amendment that stated, "The right of citizens of the United States, who are **ten years of age or older,** to vote shall not be denied or abridged by the United States or by any state on account of age?" Give reasons for your answer.

Would you agree with a constitutional amendment that stated, "The right of **non-citizens,** who are legal residents in the United States, to vote shall not be denied or abridged by the United States or by any state on account of citizenship status?" Give reasons for your answer.

Amending the Constitution

Hundreds of amendments have been proposed in Congress in the last decade, including:

★ An amendment to allow any person who has been a citizen of the United States for 20 years or more to be eligible for the presidency. (This would limit the Constitution's current ban on foreign-born presidents.)

★ An amendment to permit laws preventing desecration of the U.S. flag. (This would overrule the Supreme Court's decision that flag burning is a form of speech protected by the First Amendment.)

★ An amendment to guarantee the right of people to pray on public property, including schools. (This would overrule Supreme Court decisions that organized prayer sessions in schools are contrary to the establishment clause of the First Amendment.)

None of these proposed amendments have received the two-thirds vote in Congress necessary to send them to the states for ratification.

Organize Your Thoughts

Review the amendments covered in this chapter, and write short answers to the following questions:

★ In what circumstances is a constitutional amendment necessary?

★ What kinds of issues are important enough to require a constitutional amendment?

Brainstorm

Divide into groups of 4 to 6 people. Each group should consider one of the amendments listed above. Write out a list of arguments in favor of the amendment and a list of arguments against the amendment.

As a Class

Each group should present their arguments for and against the amendment to the rest of the class. Your teacher will hold a Class Congress vote on each amendment. The teacher will write on the board any amendments passed by two-thirds of the class.

Did any of the amendments pass? Remember, real amendments that are passed by two-thirds of Congress must also be ratified by the legislatures of three-quarters of the states. Do you think that the Constitution is difficult to amend? Do you think the amendment process is a good one? Explain your answer. Can you think of a different or better way to amend the Constitution?

CHAPTER 5

CONSTITUTIONS AROUND THE WORLD

◆ A demonstrator hammers away at the Berlin Wall upon the fall of East Germany's communist government in 1989.

What You Will Learn

In this chapter you will

★ Learn how constitutionalism has supported the growth of democracy around the world.

★ Read about the struggle between democracy and totalitarianism in the twentieth century.

★ Find out why human rights have become an issue of international concern.

★ Discover how international human rights have affected the U.S. Constitution.

★ Explore the fundamental requirements for a successful democracy.

A Movement Spreads around the World

Introduction

The U.S. Constitution has had an impact on many nations. The United States was the first nation to adopt a written constitution. It has provided a model for **constitutionalism** in other countries. Constitutionalism is the idea that law should limit the power of government.

During the twentieth century, constitutionalism encouraged the growth of democracy around the world.

✦ Norwegian citizens celebrate their constitution, which dates back to 1814.

Early Constitutions

The influence of the U.S. Constitution on other nations began almost immediately after it was ratified. As you learned in Chapter Three, France began to develop a new constitutional government only two years after the U.S. Constitution was ratified. Soon, other countries began to follow the American and French examples.

In Europe, the constitution of modern Norway dates back to 1814. Belgium's constitution dates back to 1831. Switzerland and Luxembourg both have constitutions written before 1880. As in the United States, constitutions have helped these countries establish long-lasting governments.

In Central and South America, many colonies of Spain and Portugal became independent nations in the nineteenth century. The U.S. and French constitutions provided models for constitutions in countries including Venezuela, Argentina, Chile, and Brazil. In Africa, freed American slaves established the nation of Liberia. Liberia based its 1847 constitution on the U.S. Constitution.

This postcard from 1919 reflects Britain's colonial presence around the world in the early twentieth century.

Constitutionalism in the Twentieth Century

The development of constitutional governments grew quickly in the twentieth century. There are several reasons for this growth.

Factors in the Growth of Constitutionalism

- World War II. **Totalitarian governments** in Germany and Japan were primarily responsible for starting World War II. A totalitarian government claims total authority over its subjects in their public and private lives. When World War II ended in 1945, the United States led the effort to build new democratic governments in Germany and Japan.

- The end of the colonial era. Many parts of Asia and Africa were colonies of European nations well into the twentieth century. Following World War II, independence movements in Asia and Africa produced many new nations. Most of these nations adopted constitutional governments.

- The collapse of the Soviet Union. In 1991, the Soviet Union broke up into 15 separate nations. Around the same time, **communist governments** in East European nations that had been allies of the Soviet Union also collapsed. These communist governments were controlled by a single political party. Only members of the ruling party could select the political leaders. After the collapse of these governments, many nations in eastern Europe and the former Soviet Union sought to establish constitutional democracies.

CONSTITUTIONS OLD AND NEW

Older constitutions, including the U.S. Constitution, tend to focus on **negative freedoms**. Negative freedoms are individual rights that limit what the government can do. More modern constitutions, especially those written in the twentieth century, often include positive freedoms as well. These are individual rights that require the government to act. An example is the right to free public education protected in many national constitutions.

To get an idea of how many new nations have been formed in the twentieth century, consider the membership of the United Nations. The United Nations is an international organization of nations. It was formed at the end of World War II to promote world peace and security. Nations that join the United Nations are called **member states**. The United Nations began in 1945 with 51 original member states. Today, 191 nations are member states of the United Nations.

Democracy's Century

The twentieth century has been called Democracy's Century because of the increase in the number of democratic nations. One element of a democracy is the way in which people choose their political leaders. In a democracy:

- Political leaders are chosen in **multiparty elections**. This means that citizens have the right to choose among candidates from more than one political party. **Opposition candidates** are members of political parties that oppose the policies of the party that holds power.
- Political leaders are chosen in **competitive elections**. This means that opposition candidates have a real chance at winning the election. The rules for holding elections cannot be stacked against opposition candidates.
- Political leaders are chosen by **universal suffrage**. Universal suffrage means that all adults have the right to vote regardless of their race, gender, or beliefs.

In 1900, no country met this definition of democracy. Even in the United States, women and African Americans were denied voting rights by law or by practice at the beginning of the twentieth century. As you learned in Chapter Four, the U.S. Constitution was amended several times in the twentieth century to give all adult Americans the right to vote. Today, well over 100 countries meet this definition of democracy. These countries represent almost 60 percent of the world's population.

A country that has a constitution does not necessarily have a democracy. However, constitutions can protect the political rights that define a democracy. The U.S. Constitution, for example, sets out the basic rules for national elections. As amended, it also guarantees the voting rights of adult American citizens.

◆ At left, women in Afghanistan participate in the 2004 election, the first popular election of Afghanistan's head of state. At right, a South African man votes in the 1994 election, South Africa's first democratic election.

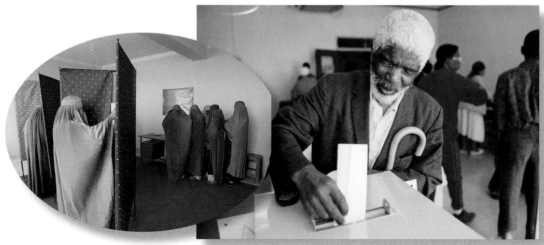

IMPORTANT TERMS

1 Match the terms in the right column with the definitions in the left column.

A. The right of all adults to vote regardless of race, gender, or beliefs

B. The idea that law should limit the power of government

C. A government that claims total authority over its subjects

D. The nations that belong to United Nations

Totalitarian government

Universal suffrage

Constitutionalism

Member states

REVIEWING FACTS

2 Name three reasons for the growth of constitutional governments during the twentieth century.

3 In 1900, how many nations could say that their political leaders were democratically elected through universal suffrage?

4 Which two nations had primary responsibility for starting World War II?

REVIEWING MAIN IDEAS

Use complete sentences to answer the following questions.

5 How do people choose their political leaders in a democracy?

6 How can a constitution help support a democracy?

7 Why might you question a communist government's claim that it represents the people?

UNDERSTANDING CONCEPTS

8 In this section, you learned how people in democratic nations select their political leaders. In some democracies today, including the nations of Australia and Belgium, the right to vote is also a legal obligation. Citizens who fail to vote in national elections can be punished with a fine. This is described as **compulsory voting**.

Supporters of compulsory voting say that the decisions of political leaders in a democracy are more legitimate if the highest possible number of citizens have elected those leaders. Those who oppose compulsory voting say that it is inconsistent with democratic freedom. If voters do not think any candidates would represent their interests, they should be free to refuse to vote.

Do you think compulsory voting is a good idea? Explain your answer.

Constitutions and Human Rights

Introduction

In Chapter Three, you learned how individual liberties were protected in the constitutions of the United States and France. These individual liberties formed the basis for what we call **human rights** today. Human rights are those rights that people around the world recognize as essential to human dignity and freedom. Human rights suffered greatly under totalitarian governments early in the twentieth century. After World War II, most nations of the world agreed on the Universal Declaration of Human Rights. The Declaration has influenced constitutions and laws in many nations. It has also affected how Americans understand the rights guaranteed by our own Constitution.

World War II: A Crisis for Democracy and Human Rights

✦ Millions of people throughout Europe were murdered by Nazi forces during the Holocaust. This picture shows survivors at a Nazi concentration camp in Sandbostel, Germany, which was liberated by Allied forces in 1945.

The Rise of Totalitarianism

The twentieth century is sometimes called Democracy's Century. But early in the twentieth century, democracy was in real danger. Totalitarian governments in Germany and Japan developed powerful military forces. Beginning in the 1930s, they started to invade neighboring countries in Europe and Asia. They were joined by Italy, where a totalitarian government had also taken power. These three nations formed a coalition called **the Axis**.

Human rights were suppressed in the Axis nations. Individuals were forced to follow what the government defined as the nation's interests. In Germany, the **Nazis** were the ruling government party. The Nazis launched an effort to create a "racially pure" Germany. This effort led to **the Holocaust**. The Holocaust is the name given to the Nazis' mass murder of millions of Jews throughout Europe. Others were murdered for their political beliefs, nationality, or social status. In Asia, human rights abuses were also severe. In the Chinese city of Nanking, for example, invading Japanese soldiers killed an estimated 300,000 civilians.

The Four Freedoms

On January 6, 1941, U.S. President Franklin D. Roosevelt gave his State of the Union address to Congress. President Roosevelt described the looming crisis of World War II. He urged Congress to prepare for a defense of freedom. "Freedom," President Roosevelt declared, "means the supremacy of human rights everywhere."

President Roosevelt's speech outlined "four essential human freedoms" necessary to create a secure world. These **Four Freedoms** are:

- Freedom of speech and expression.
- Freedom of every person to worship in his or her own way.
- Freedom from want.
- Freedom from fear of armed aggression.

In August 1941, President Roosevelt met Winston Churchill, prime minister of the United Kingdom, on a ship off the coast of Canada. The two leaders agreed on a document called the **Atlantic Charter**. The Atlantic Charter sets forth shared goals of the United States and the United Kingdom in promoting a better future for the world.

The influence of the Four Freedoms is clearly visible in the Atlantic Charter. The charter calls for governments to act according to the "freely expressed wishes of the peoples concerned." It calls for "the right of all peoples to choose the form of government under which they will live." It calls for the right of all people in all lands to "live out their lives in freedom from want and fear." The Atlantic Charter helped guide the efforts of the United States and the United Kingdom against the Axis nations during World War II.

THE FOUR FREEDOMS AT HOME IN WORLD WAR II

The Four Freedoms were an important part of the United States' war effort. The American artist Norman Rockwell painted four images showing how the Four Freedoms affected the lives of ordinary Americans (see Going to the Source for this chapter). The U.S. government used these images to help explain why we were fighting World War II.

The Universal Declaration of Human Rights

World War II ended in 1945. Millions of innocent people in Europe and Asia had been killed. Human rights were now an issue of international concern. On April 25, 1945, delegates from nations around the world met in San Francisco to form the United Nations. The assembled nations agreed that the new United Nations would have to protect individual human rights.

✦ Members of the United Nations General Assembly listen to a speech by U.S. President Jimmy Carter in 1977.

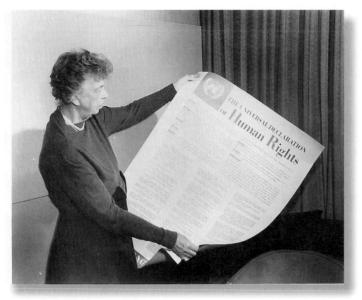

The United Nations appointed a Commission on Human Rights to identify fundamental human rights shared by all people in all nations. The Commission elected Eleanor Roosevelt as their chairperson. Eleanor Roosevelt had been the First Lady of the United States. As chairperson of the Commission on Human Rights, she led a three-year effort to write the Universal Declaration of Human Rights. The Declaration was approved by almost all of the United Nations' member states on December 10, 1948.

Roosevelt described the Universal Declaration of Human Rights as an "international Magna Carta." She also compared it to the U.S. Bill of Rights and the French Declaration of the Rights of Man. Many of the rights described in the Universal Declaration show the influence of these earlier documents. For example, the Universal Declaration calls for

✦ Eleanor Roosevelt reviews a copy of the Universal Declaration of Human Rights, which was approved by United Nations member states in 1948.

- Freedom of opinion and expression.
- Freedom of thought, conscience, and religion.
- Freedom of assembly and association.
- Right to due process of law.
- Right to a fair trial.
- Right to be secure in one's person and home.
- Protection of private property rights.

The Universal Declaration also includes rights that reflect more modern concerns. Examples include

- Right to rest and leisure.
- Right to education.
- Right to social security.

With the Universal Declaration of Rights, the international community agreed for the first time on a list of rights and freedoms for people around the world. The Universal Declaration has shaped the protection of human rights in the constitutions and laws of many nations. It has formed the basis for international agreements protecting human rights. It has also strengthened the efforts of individuals and organizations working to improve human rights worldwide.

FOCUS ON NORTH CAROLINA CONSTITUTION

The North Carolina Constitution, in Article XIV, Section 5, makes it a policy and a function of the state to acquire property to protect and conserve its land and waters for the benefit of its citizens, and for the purpose of controlling and limiting pollution and excessive noise.

Did You KNOW?

When Eleanor Roosevelt died in 1962, former U.S. presidential candidate and friend Adlai Stevenson said, "She would rather light candles than curse the darkness, and her glow has warmed the world."

Human Rights and the U.S. Constitution

The United States was a leader in the effort to promote human rights worldwide after World War II. But the U.S. support of human rights abroad also made it look at its situation at home. The United States needed to ensure that all Americans enjoyed the protections guaranteed in our Constitution.

When World War II ended, much of the United States was still divided by race. In Chapter Four, you learned about the U.S. Supreme Court's decision in *Plessy* v. *Ferguson*. That decision said that the Fourteenth Amendment's promise of equal protection of the laws allowed segregation of Americans by race. It said that laws could require black Americans to use separate facilities from those provided to whites as long as the separate facilities were equal.

Even as the United States was fighting for democracy in World War II, Americans at home were fighting against segregation. Their biggest victory came in 1954, when the U.S. Supreme Court decided the case of *Brown* v. *Board of Education*. In *Brown*, the Court decided that laws separating schools by race were unconstitutional.

The U.S. government joined the parents of black students in calling for the Supreme Court to end school segregation in *Brown*. In its arguments to the Court, the government said:

> *The United States is trying to prove to the people of the world, of every nationality, race, and color, that a free democracy is the most civilized and most secure form of government yet devised by man. We must set an example for others by showing firm determination to remove existing flaws in our democracy.*

Brown gave momentum to the civil rights movement that continued through the 1960s and 1970s. The civil rights movement fought to secure full rights for all Americans—in school, in the workplace, and in the voting booth.

The United States could not promote human rights abroad if it could not provide them at home. Our support of international human rights, in other words, did more than influence the constitutions of other nations. It encouraged us to close the gap between what our own Constitution said and how we treated one another as citizens.

Did You KNOW?

No member state voted against the Universal Declaration of Human Rights, but eight nations abstained from voting. These included the Soviet Union and five other allied communist governments, South Africa, and Saudi Arabia.

✦ The African American students who integrated Central High School in Little Rock, Arkansas, in 1957 encountered hostility from residents opposed to desegregation.

IMPORTANT TERMS

1 Match the terms in the right column with the definitions in the left column.

    A. The coalition of totalitarian nations during World War II

    B. An agreement between the United States and the United Kingdom on the goals necessary to promote a better future

    C. The document that represents the first time the international community agreed on a list of freedoms for people around the world

    D. The name given to the Nazis' mass murder of millions of Jews in Europe

Holocaust

Atlantic Charter

Universal Declaration of Human Rights

Axis

REVIEWING FACTS

2 Name the Four Freedoms President Roosevelt described in his 1941 State of the Union address.

3 How many nations abstained from voting to approve the Universal Declaration of Human Rights in 1948?

4 What is the name of the U.S. Supreme Court decision that said it was unconstitutional to separate schools by race?

REVIEWING MAIN IDEAS

Use complete sentences to answer the following questions.

5 What was the impact of totalitarian governments on human rights early in the twentieth century?

6 What are some differences between the rights protected in the Universal Declaration of Human Rights and those in the U.S. Bill of Rights?

7 What effect have international human rights had on the U.S. Constitution?

UNDERSTANDING CONCEPTS

8 Can you think of a situation where the rights of one individual might conflict with those of another? Consider the following example.

Article 26 of the Universal Declaration of Human Rights provides that "everyone shall have a right to education." It also states that "parents have a prior right to choose the kind of education that shall be given to their children."

Your community's public school offers an excellent education in most areas, but it has no courses in religious studies. The parents of a 10-year-old girl are disputing where she will attend school. The girl's mother wants her to continue to attend the public school. The girl's father wants her to attend a private school that has a strong religious education program. The girl has said that she would prefer to stay with her friends at the public school.

Whose rights are at stake here? Should anyone's rights be given preference? How would you resolve this disagreement?

Making Constitutions Work

Introduction

A constitution begins as words on paper. These words mean nothing if they are not given meaning by the government they create and the people whose rights they are supposed to protect. A constitution must be lived, not just read. A constitution does not guarantee a democracy, but the constitutions of successful democracies share some important features.

Constitutional Features of Successful Democracies

Limited Powers

A successful democracy has a constitution that limits government power. The United States has chosen to separate the powers of government among the executive, legislative, and judicial branches. Each branch has its own unique powers, but each is limited in what it can do. Each branch has the power to check and balance the power of the other branches. Regular elections give people the opportunity to vote for or against their elected officials.

◆ The British Parliament. Like most of its European neighbors, Britain uses a parliamentary system of government.

Other democracies use a **parliamentary system**. A parliamentary system combines the powers of the executive and the legislature. The judiciary remains separate. Most nations in Europe have a parliamentary system.

In a parliamentary system, the people elect their representatives to the parliament. The political party that gets a majority of its members elected to parliament chooses the person who will serve as prime minister. If no party gets a majority, two or more parties will form a majority coalition to choose the prime minister. The prime minister is head of the executive branch but must answer to the parliament.

Constitutions in parliamentary nations limit the powers of parliament and the prime minister, just as the U.S. Constitution limits the powers of the executive and legislative branches. They also require that elections be held at regular intervals. If the people disagree with the policies of the majority party in parliament and the prime minister, they can vote for representatives of other parties.

Judicial Independence

A nation might select a government with power separated among the three branches or a parliamentary system. In either case, if the power of the legislative and executive branches is to be checked, the constitution must give the judiciary the power to tell these branches when their actions violate the constitution. Because the judiciary has this power, it must also be independent of both the executive and legislative branches.

To help protect judicial independence, a constitution should have several features. The salary of judges should be guaranteed so that angry legislators cannot punish judges with a salary reduction if they make an unpopular decision. Judges should also have a protected **tenure**. Tenure is the term of years that a judge serves in office. A judge's tenure should be interrupted only if the judge engages in serious wrongdoing.

Transparent Government

A constitution must make sure that the workings of government are **transparent** to the people. This means that the people must be able to find out whether the government is doing its job. The U.S. Constitution's guarantees of public trials and a free press are examples of provisions that support transparent government. People should also have easy and inexpensive access to government records. Public access should be restricted only in limited circumstances—to protect, for example, personal privacy or national security interests.

Respect for Human Rights

A democracy is sure to fail if the human rights of all citizens are not respected. Most nations of the world have now agreed on the rights described in the Universal Declaration of Human Rights. A constitution must protect these fundamental human rights.

Creating a Culture of Democracy

Many nations adopted constitutions in the twentieth century. Most of these nations have tried to establish democratic societies. Their constitutions have the essential features for democracy described above. But a constitution also needs a culture of democracy in which it can take root and grow.

The Example of the Czech Republic

The Czech Republic used to be part of the communist nation of Czechoslovakia. In 1989, massive popular demonstrations against the communist government convinced the government to step down. Elections were held and the people chose a new parliamentary system of government. It ratified a new constitution.

In 1997, the Czech Republic faced an economic and political crisis. The prime minister and his government resigned in 1997. President Václav Havel gave a speech to the parliament. He said he did not think that the Czech Republic's culture was supporting the nation's goal of becoming a democracy.

One problem was disrespect for human rights. The Roma (or Gypsies) are an ethnic minority in the Czech Republic. They faced discrimination, and at times physical violence, from other Czech citizens. Havel condemned "the dreadful behavior of some of our own people toward their fellow humans simply because of the different color of their skin."

Another problem was the lack of **civil society** in the Czech Republic. Civil society means the many organizations, associations, and groups that people join voluntarily to pursue shared interests, goals, or values.

Under most communist governments, civil society is suppressed. If the ruling party wants to protect itself and avoid change, it tries to make people so dependent on the government that they believe they cannot live without it. Civil society encourages independence from the power of the state. The Czech Republic had not yet built the civil society it lacked under a communist government.

The Czech Republic recovered from its 1997 crisis. But the challenges that Havel highlighted in his 1997 speech are challenges that every democracy must face. How does a nation support a culture of tolerance and respect among citizens of different races, traditions, and beliefs? How does it encourage its citizens to actively and responsibly exercise the power that a democracy gives them?

Foundations of a Democratic Culture

A constitution and a popularly elected government are only starting points for a truly democratic nation. The constitution and the government it forms must be supported by a democratic culture. Important foundations of a democratic culture include a free press, an educational system that encourages independent thought, and a thriving civil society.

Did You KNOW?

The fall of Czechoslovakia's communist government in 1989 is called the Velvet Revolution. This is because the government was transformed without bloodshed.

✦ Massive demonstrations preceded the fall of Czechoslovakia's communist government in 1989.

Education is important to the people of North Carolina. Unlike the U.S. Constitution, which makes no mention of education, the North Carolina Constitution includes Article I, Section 15, which makes education a right guaranteed by the state. Article IX of the North Carolina Constitution covers educational issues, such as providing for a general and uniform system of free public schools. Article IX also requires that the benefits of higher education "as far as practicable, be extended to the people of the State free of expense."

A Free Press

Democratic citizens need to know what the government is doing in order to be able to exercise their power over the government intelligently. We know that a constitution must provide for a transparent government. But how can any one citizen sift through all the information that the government produces?

The democratic role of a free press is to act as a watchdog for citizens. When a nation has a free press, journalists are free to investigate the actions of government officials and report their findings to the public. In nations without a free press, the government controls what journalists can report to the public.

Journalists cannot do all the work. A democratic citizen takes advantage of a free press by reading newspapers, watching news programs, and seeking out the different perspectives that a free press offers. With this information, the democratic citizen can make intelligent decisions about how the government is working and whether the government needs to change.

Civil Society

You participate in civil society when you join a religious group, volunteer to help an organization that feeds the hungry, or give money to a cause that you believe in. You are recognizing that government does not and should not provide everything a citizen needs to live a full and engaged life. Your participation in civil society is a commitment to the ideal of the active citizen on which a democracy depends. A thriving civil society is a mark of a thriving democracy.

Education

Almost every nation today provides some level of education to its people. But education in a democratic society must accomplish specific tasks. Democratic societies are **open societies**. This means that they encourage the free and open exchange of ideas and information.

Schools and universities in a democratic society must encourage students to question ideas and form reasoned opinions. They must give students the tools they need to express themselves effectively. And they must encourage students to accept that commitment to their own beliefs must be accompanied by tolerance of those who believe differently.

The political elements of a democracy are its constitution and a popularly elected government. When these political elements are combined with a culture of democracy—one that produces citizens who are informed, inquisitive, tolerant, and engaged—a nation is likely to flourish.

◆ A volunteer helps feed homeless men and women Thanksgiving dinner. Civil society depends upon the voluntary efforts of engaged citizens.

IMPORTANT TERMS

1 Match the terms in the right column with the definitions in the left column.

A. A political system that combines the powers of the legislative and executive branches

B. The term of years that a judge serves in office

C. The ability of people to find out whether the government is doing its job

D. The organizations, associations, and groups people join voluntarily to pursue shared interests, goals, or values

Parliament

Civil society

Tenure

Transparency

REVIEWING FACTS

2 List three features that a constitution should include to support a democracy.

3 Name two things that help protect judicial independence.

4 Give one reason why Václav Havel thought the Czech Republic's culture was not supporting the nation's goal of becoming a democracy in 1997.

REVIEWING MAIN IDEAS

Use complete sentences to answer the following questions.

5 How does a parliamentary government differ from the government we have in the United States?

6 How can disrespect for human rights harm a democracy?

7 Why do most communist governments try to suppress civil society?

UNDERSTANDING CONCEPTS

8 Consider civil society in your local community. Begin by listing the names of voluntary organizations in your community. Then make a list of the activities they offer and the services they provide to the members of your community.

What needs do these organizations fill in your community? Why do you think people volunteer to join these organizations? What would life be like in your community if these organizations ceased to exist?

Going to the Source

The Four Freedoms

On January 6, 1941, President Franklin D. Roosevelt gave his State of the Union Address that defined the Four Freedoms. President Roosevelt's speech inspired the American artist Norman Rockwell to create four images showing how the Four Freedoms affected the daily lives of people in the United States. Look carefully at these images.

OURS...to fight for

FREEDOM FROM FEAR

SAVE FREEDOM OF WORSHIP
EACH ACCORDING TO THE DICTATES OF HIS OWN CONSCIENCE

BUY WAR BONDS

SAVE FREEDOM OF SPEECH

BUY WAR BONDS

OURS...to fight for

FREEDOM FROM WANT

Eleanor Roosevelt on Human Rights

On March 27, 1958, Eleanor Roosevelt gave a speech at the United Nations commemorating the tenth anniversary of the Universal Declaration of Human Rights. Read the following excerpt from that speech.

✳ Where, after all, do universal human rights begin? In small places, close to home—so close and so small that they cannot be seen on any map of the world. Yet they are the world of the individual person: the neighborhood he lives in; the school or college he attends; the factory, farm or office where he works. Such are the places where every man, woman, and child seeks equal justice, equal opportunity, equal dignity without discrimination. Unless these rights have meaning there, they have little meaning anywhere. Without concerted citizen action to uphold them close to home, we shall look in vain for progress in the larger world.

CRITICAL THINKING

1. Norman Rockwell's images show how he envisioned the Four Freedoms in the daily lives of Americans in the 1940s. If you were asked to illustrate how the Four Freedoms affect the daily lives of Americans today, what images would you use?

2. Both Norman Rockwell's images and Eleanor Roosevelt's speech emphasize the meaning of human rights close to home. When you look around your community, what meaning do you see being given to human rights? Can you think of any examples where the human rights described by the Four Freedoms have been given value in your community? Can you think of any examples where more attention should be given to these rights?

3. Eleanor Roosevelt speaks of the need for "concerted citizen action" to uphold human rights close to home. What do you think she means by this? What can citizens do to help ensure that the rights of others are upheld?

Defining Democracy

You and your classmates have been asked to prepare for a meeting with delegates from the nation of Civitas. For many years, a totalitarian government controlled Civitas. That government has recently stepped down in the face of popular protests. The delegates you will be meeting with will be working on a new constitution for Civitas. They want Civitas to become a democracy.

Many people in Civitas are unfamiliar with the concept of democracy. At your first meeting with the delegates, you have been asked to offer a definition of democracy. The delegates will use your definition to help explain democracy to the people of Civitas.

The delegates have requested a short definition – no more than 3 or 4 sentences – that you think highlights the most important elements of democracy.

Working Individually

Write your own personal definition of democracy. Remember that this definition should be no more than 3 or 4 sentences long. When you have written your definition, circle the one word or concept that you think is the most important part of your definition.

Teamwork

Get into small groups of 4 to 6 students. Begin by asking the group members to read their own definitions of democracy and the one word or concept they selected. Then work together to produce a group definition of democracy that is acceptable to all the small group members. Again, your small group definition should be no more than 3 or 4 sentences long.

As a Class

Have each small group report their definition of democracy to the class as a whole. Your teacher will write the small group definitions on the board.

Consider the group definitions. What similarities do you see among them? What are the differences? Have your discussions with your small group and your class changed your personal definition of democracy? Is there a definition of democracy that everyone in the class can agree upon?

THE U.S. CONSTITUTION
ANNOTATED VERSION

What You Need to Know

★ The following document is an Annotated Constitution. This means it is a copy of the entire text of the Constitution with additional explanatory notes and definitions.

★ If a part of the Constitution is crossed out, it means one of two things. The part may no longer be in force because it was drafted to expire at a certain time. Alternatively, the part may no longer apply because of an amendment to the Constitution.

★ All of the amendments to the Constitution are listed after the Constitution itself.

The Constitution of the United States

Preamble
The short and dignified preamble explains the goals of the new government under the Constitution.

We the People of the United States, in Order to form a more perfect Union, establish Justice, insure domestic Tranquility, provide for the common defense, promote the general Welfare, and secure the Blessings of Liberty to ourselves and our Posterity, do ordain and establish this Constitution for the United States of America.

Note: The parts of the Constitution that have been lined through are no longer in force or no longer apply because of later amendments. The titles of the sections and articles are added for easier reference. For example, in Article I, section 2, the portion known as the "three-fifths compromise" is crossed out. This language was replaced by the 14th amendment.

Article I   The Legislature

Section 1.   Congress

All legislative Powers herein granted shall be vested in a Congress of the United States, which shall consist of a Senate and House of Representatives.

Section 2.   The House of Representatives

1. Elections The House of Representatives shall be composed of Members chosen every second Year by the People of the several States, and the Electors in each State shall have the Qualifications requisite for Electors of the most numerous Branch of the State Legislature.

2. Qualifications No Person shall be a Representative who shall not have attained to the Age of twenty five Years, and been seven Years a Citizen of the United States, and who shall not, when elected, be an Inhabitant of that State in which he shall be chosen.

3. Number of Representatives Representatives and direct Taxes shall be apportioned among the several States which may be included within this Union, according to their respective Numbers, which shall be determined by adding to the whole Number of free Persons, including **those bound to Service**[1] for a Term of Years, and excluding Indians not taxed, three fifths of **all other Persons**.[2] The actual **Enumeration**[3] shall be made within three Years after the first Meeting of the Congress of the United States, and within every subsequent Term of ten Years, in such Manner as they shall by Law direct. The Number of Representatives shall not exceed one for every thirty Thousand, but each State shall have at Least one Representative; and until such enumeration shall be made, the State of New Hampshire shall be entitled to choose three, Massachoosetts eight, Rhode-Island and Providence Plantations one, Connecticut five, New-York six, New Jersey four, Pennsylvania eight, Delaware one, Maryland six, Virginia ten, North Carolina five, South Carolina five, and Georgia three.

4. Vacancies When vacancies happen in the Representation from any State, the Executive Authority thereof shall issue Writs of Election to fill such Vacancies.

5. Officers and Impeachment The House of Representatives shall choose their Speaker and other Officers; and shall have the sole **Power of impeachment.**[4]

Legislative Branch

Article I explains how the legislative branch, called Congress, is organized. The chief purpose of the legislative branch is to make laws. Congress is made up of the Senate and the House of Representatives.

The House of Representatives

The number of members each state has in the House is based on the population of the individual state. In 1929 Congress permanently fixed the size of the House at 435

Vocabulary

[1] **those bound to Service** indentured servants

[2] **all other Persons** slaves

[3] **Enumeration** census or official population count

[4] **Power of impeachment** the right to charge a government official with wrongdoing

Section 3. The Senate

1. Number of Senators The Senate of the United States shall be composed of two Senators from each State, ~~chosen by the Legislature thereof,~~ for six Years; and each Senator shall have one Vote.

2. Classifying Terms Immediately after they shall be assembled in Consequence of the first Election, they shall be divided as equally as may be into three Classes. The Seats of the Senators of the first Class shall be vacated at the Expiration of the second Year, of the second Class at the Expiration of the fourth Year, and of the third Class at the Expiration of the sixth Year, so that one third may be chosen every second Year; ~~and if Vacancies happen by Resignation, or otherwise, during the Recess of the Legislature of any State, the Executive thereof may make temporary Appointments until the next Meeting of the Legislature, which shall then fill such Vacancies.~~

3. Qualifications No Person shall be a Senator who shall not have attained to the Age of thirty Years, and been nine Years a Citizen of the United States, and who shall not, when elected, be an Inhabitant of that State for which he shall be chosen.

4. Role of Vice-President The Vice President of the United States shall be President of the Senate, but shall have no Vote, unless they be equally divided.

5. Officers The Senate shall choose their other Officers, and also a President **pro tempore**,[5] in the Absence of the Vice President, or when he shall exercise the Office of President of the United States.

6. Impeachment Trials The Senate shall have the sole Power to try all **Impeachments**.[6] When sitting for that Purpose, they shall be on Oath or Affirmation. When the President of the United States is tried, the Chief Justice shall preside: And no Person shall be convicted without the Concurrence of two thirds of the Members present.

7. Punishment for Impeachment Judgment in Cases of Impeachment shall not extend further than to removal from Office, and disqualification to hold and enjoy any Office of honor, Trust or Profit under the United States: but the Party convicted shall nevertheless be liable and subject to Indictment, Trial, Judgment and Punishment, according to Law.

The Vice President

The only duty that the Constitution assigns to the vice president is to preside over meetings of the Senate. Modern presidents have usually given their vice presidents more responsibilities.

The Senate

The Senate was originally chosen by the state legislatures. Now, like the House, the Senate is chosen by the people of each state.

EXPLORING THE DOCUMENT If the House of Representatives charges a government official with wrongdoing, the Senate acts as a court to decide if the official is guilty. **How does the power of impeachment represent part of the system of checks and balances?**

Vocabulary

[5] **pro tempore**
temporarily

[6] **Impeachments**
official accusations of federal wrongdoing

Federal Office Terms and Requirements QUICK FACTS

Position	Term	Minimum Age	Residency	Citizenship
President	4 years	35	14 years in the U.S.	natural-born
Vice President	4 years	35	14 years in the U.S.	natural-born
Supreme Court Justice	unlimited	none	none	none
Senator	6 years	30	state in which elected	9 years
Representative	2 years	25	state in which elected	7 years

Section 4. Congressional Elections

1. Regulations The Times, Places and Manner of holding Elections for Senators and Representatives, shall be prescribed in each State by the Legislature thereof; but the Congress may at any time by Law make or alter such Regulations, except as to the Places of choosing Senators.

2. Sessions ~~The Congress shall assemble at least once in every Year, and such Meeting shall be on the first Monday in December, unless they shall by Law appoint a different Day.~~

Section 5. Rules/Procedures

1. Quorum Each House shall be the Judge of the Elections, Returns and Qualifications of its own Members, and a Majority of each shall constitute a **Quorum**[7] to do Business; but a smaller Number may **adjourn**[8] from day to day, and may be authorized to compel the Attendance of absent Members, in such Manner, and under such Penalties as each House may provide.

2. Rules and Conduct Each House may determine the Rules of its Proceedings, punish its Members for disorderly Behaviour, and, with the Concurrence of two thirds, expel a Member.

3. Records Each House shall keep a Journal of its Proceedings, and from time to time publish the same, excepting such Parts as may in their Judgment require Secrecy; and the Yeas and Nays of the Members of either House on any question shall, at the Desire of one fifth of those Present, be entered on the Journal.

4. Adjournment Neither House, during the Session of Congress, shall, without the Consent of the other, adjourn for more than three days, nor to any other Place than that in which the two Houses shall be sitting.

Section 6. Payment

1. Salary The Senators and Representatives shall receive a Compensation for their Services, to be ascertained by Law, and paid out of the Treasury of the United States. They shall in all Cases, except Treason, Felony and Breach of the Peace, be privileged from Arrest during their Attendance at the Session of their respective Houses, and in going to and returning from the same; and for any Speech or Debate in either House, they shall not be questioned in any other Place.

2. Restrictions No Senator or Representative shall, during the Time for which he was elected, be appointed to any civil Office under the Authority of the United States, which shall have been created, or the **Emoluments**[9] whereof shall have been increased during such time; and no Person holding any Office under the United States, shall be a Member of either House during his **Continuance**[10] in Office.

Vocabulary

[7] **Quorum** the minimum number of people needed to conduct business

[8] **adjourn** to stop indefinitely

[9] **Emoluments** salary

[10] **Continuance** term

EXPLORING THE DOCUMENT The framers felt that because members of the House are elected every two years, representatives would listen to the public and seek its approval before passing taxes. **How does Section 7 address the colonial demand of "no taxation without representation"?**

EXPLORING THE DOCUMENT The veto power of the president is one of the important checks and balances in the Constitution. **Why do you think the framers included the ability of Congress to override a veto?**

Section 7. [How a Bill Becomes a Law]

1. Tax Bills All **Bills**¹¹ for raising Revenue shall originate in the House of Representatives; but the Senate may propose or concur with Amendments as on other Bills.

2. Lawmaking Every Bill which shall have passed the House of Representatives and the Senate, shall, before it become a Law, be presented to the President of the United States: If he approve he shall sign it, but if not he shall return it, with his Objections to that House in which it shall have originated, who shall enter the Objections at large on their Journal, and proceed to reconsider it. If after such Reconsideration two thirds of that House shall agree to pass the Bill, it shall be sent, together with the Objections, to the other House, by which it shall likewise be reconsidered, and if approved by two thirds of that House, it shall become a Law. But in all such Cases the Votes of both Houses shall be determined by yeas and Nays, and the Names of the Persons voting for and against the Bill shall be entered on the Journal of each House respectively. If any Bill shall not be returned by the President within ten Days (Sundays excepted) after it shall have been presented to him, the Same shall be a Law, in like Manner as if he had signed it, unless the Congress by their Adjournment prevent its Return, in which Case it shall not be a Law.

3. Role of the President Every Order, Resolution, or Vote to which the Concurrence of the Senate and House of Representatives may be necessary (except on a question of Adjournment) shall be presented to the President of the United States; and before the Same shall take Effect, shall be approved by him, or being disapproved by him, shall be repassed by two thirds of the Senate and House of Representatives, according to the Rules and Limitations prescribed in the Case of a Bill.

How a Bill Becomes a Law

❶ A member of the House or the Senate introduces a bill and refers it to a committee.

❷ The House or Senate Committee may approve, rewrite, or kill the bill.

❸ The House or the Senate debates and votes on its version of the bill.

❹ If the bill is passed, then it is sent to the other house for a debate and a vote.

❺ If the bill is amended, then it is sent back to the house that originated it for another debate and vote.

❻ If the the bill is passed without amendment, then it is sent to the President.

Section 8.

Powers Granted to Congress

1. Taxation The Congress shall have Power To lay and collect Taxes, **Duties**,[12] **Imposts**[13] and **Excises**,[14] to pay the Debts and provide for the common Defense and general Welfare of the United States; but all Duties, Imposts and Excises shall be uniform throughout the United States;

2. Credit To borrow Money on the credit of the United States;

3. Commerce To regulate Commerce with foreign Nations, and among the several States, and with the Indian Tribes;

4. Naturalization and Bankruptcy To establish an uniform **Rule of Naturalization**,[15] and uniform Laws on the subject of Bankruptcies throughout the United States;

5. Money To coin Money, regulate the Value thereof, and of foreign Coin, and fix the Standard of Weights and Measures;

6. Counterfeiting To provide for the Punishment of counterfeiting the **Securities**[16] and current Coin of the United States;

7. Post Office To establish Post Offices and post Roads;

8. Patents and Copyrights To promote the Progress of Science and useful Arts, by securing for limited Times to Authors and Inventors the exclusive Right to their respective Writings and Discoveries;

9. Courts To constitute Tribunals inferior to the supreme Court;

10. International Law To define and punish Piracies and Felonies committed on the high Seas, and Offences against the Law of Nations;

LINKING TO TODAY

Native Americans and the Commerce Clause

The commerce clause gives Congress the power to "regulate Commerce with . . . the Indian Tribes." The clause has been interpreted to mean that the states cannot tax or interfere with businesses on Indian reservations, but that the federal government can. It also allows American Indian nations to develop their own governments and laws. These laws, however, can be challenged in federal court. Although reservation land usually belongs to the government of the Indian group, it is administered by the U.S. government.

Drawing Conclusions How would you describe the status of American Indian nations under the commerce clause?

Vocabulary

[12] **Duties** taxes on the import or export of goods

[13] **Imposts** taxes

[14] **Excises** internal taxes on the manufacture, sale, or consumption of goods

[15] **Rule of Naturalization** a law by which a foreign-born person becomes a citizen

[16] **Securities** a general name for stocks, bonds, and other investments

7 The president signs or vetoes the bill.

8 Two-thirds majority vote of Congress is needed to approve a vetoed bill. Bill becomes a law.

ANALYSIS SKILL **ANALYZING INFORMATION**

Why do you think the framers created this complex system for adopting laws?

Vocabulary

[17] Letters of Marque and Reprisal documents issued by governments allowing merchant ships to arm themselves and attack ships of an enemy nation

11. War To declare War, grant **Letters of Marque and Reprisal**,[17] and make Rules concerning Captures on Land and Water;

12. Army To raise and support Armies, but no Appropriation of Money to that Use shall be for a longer Term than two Years;

13. Navy To provide and maintain a Navy;

14. Regulation of the Military To make Rules for the Government and Regulation of the land and naval Forces;

15. Militia To provide for calling forth the Militia to execute the Laws of the Union, suppress Insurrections and repel Invasions;

16. Regulation of the Militia To provide for organizing, arming, and disciplining, the Militia, and for governing such Part of them as may be employed in the Service of the United States, reserving to the States respectively, the Appointment of the Officers, and the Authority of training the Militia according to the discipline prescribed by Congress;

17. District of Columbia To exercise exclusive Legislation in all Cases whatsoever, over such District (not exceeding ten Miles square) as may, by Cession of particular States, and the Acceptance of Congress, become the Seat of the Government of the United States, and to exercise like Authority over all Places purchased by the Consent of the Legislature of the State in which the Same shall be, for the Erection of Forts, Magazines, Arsenals, dock-Yards, and other needful Buildings;—And

18. Necessary and Proper Clause To make all Laws which shall be necessary and proper for carrying into Execution the foregoing Powers, and all other Powers vested by this Constitution in the Government of the United States, or in any Department or Officer thereof.

The Elastic Clause

The framers of the Constitution wanted a national government that was strong enough to be effective. This section lists the powers given to Congress. The "necessary and proper" clause of Section 8 has become known as the elastic clause.

The Elastic Clause

The elastic clause has been stretched (like elastic) to allow Congress to meet changing circumstances.

Section 9. Powers Denied Congress

1. Slave Trade ~~The Migration or Importation of such Persons as any of the States now existing shall think proper to admit, shall not be prohibited by the Congress prior to the Year one thousand eight hundred and eight, but a Tax or duty may be imposed on such Importation, not exceeding ten dollars for each Person.~~

2. Habeas Corpus The Privilege of the **Writ of Habeas Corpus**[18] shall not be suspended, unless when in Cases of Rebellion or Invasion the public Safety may require it.

3. Illegal Punishment No **Bill of Attainder**[19] or **ex post facto Law**[20] shall be passed.

4. Direct Taxes No **Capitation**,[21] or other direct, Tax shall be laid, unless in Proportion to the Census or enumeration herein before directed to be taken.

5. Export Taxes No Tax or Duty shall be laid on Articles exported from any State.

6. No Favorites No Preference shall be given by any Regulation of Commerce or Revenue to the Ports of one State over those of another; nor shall Vessels bound to, or from, one State, be obliged to enter, clear, or pay Duties in another.

7. Public Money No Money shall be drawn from the Treasury, but in Consequence of Appropriations made by Law; and a regular Statement and Account of the Receipts and Expenditures of all public Money shall be published from time to time.

8. Titles of Nobility No Title of Nobility shall be granted by the United States: And no Person holding any Office of Profit or Trust under them, shall, without the Consent of the Congress, accept of any present, Emolument, Office, or Title, of any kind whatever, from any King, Prince, or foreign State.

Section 10. Powers Denied the States

1. Restrictions No State shall enter into any Treaty, Alliance, or Confederation; grant Letters of Marque and Reprisal; coin Money; emit Bills of Credit; make any Thing but gold and silver Coin a Tender in Payment of Debts; pass any Bill of Attainder, ex post facto Law, or Law impairing the Obligation of Contracts, or grant any Title of Nobility.

2. Import and Export Taxes No State shall, without the Consent of the Congress, lay any Imposts or Duties on Imports or Exports, except what may be absolutely necessary for executing it's inspection Laws: and the net Produce of all Duties and Imposts, laid by any State on Imports or Exports, shall be for the Use of the Treasury of the United States; and all such Laws shall be subject to the Revision and Control of the Congress.

3. Peacetime and War Restraints No State shall, without the Consent of Congress, lay any Duty of Tonnage, keep Troops, or Ships of War in time of Peace, enter into any Agreement or Compact with another State, or with a foreign Power, or engage in War, unless actually invaded, or in such imminent Danger as will not admit of delay.

EXPLORING THE DOCUMENT Although Congress has implied powers, there are also limits to its powers. Section 9 lists powers that are denied to the federal government. Several of the clauses protect the people of the United States from unjust treatment. **In what ways does the Constitution limit the powers of the federal government?**

Vocabulary

[18] **Writ of Habeas Corpus** a court order that requires the government to bring a prisoner to court and explain why he or she is being held

[19] **Bill of Attainder** a law declaring that a person is guilty of a particular crime

[20] **ex post facto Law** a law that is made effective prior to the date that it was passed and therefore punishes people for acts that were not illegal at the time

[21] **Capitation** a direct uniform tax imposed on each head, or person

Executive Branch

The president is the chief of the executive branch. It is the job of the president to enforce the laws. The framers wanted the president's and vice president's terms of office and manner of selection to be different from those of members of Congress. They decided on four-year terms, but they had a difficult time agreeing on how to select the president and vice president. The framers finally set up an electoral system, which varies greatly from our electoral process today.

Presidential Elections

In 1845 Congress set the Tuesday following the first Monday in November of every fourth year as the general election date for selecting presidential electors.

Article II The Executive

Section 1. The Presidency

1. Terms of Office The executive Power shall be vested in a President of the United States of America. He shall hold his Office during the Term of four Years, and, together with the Vice President, chosen for the same Term, be elected, as follows:

2. Electoral College Each State shall appoint, in such Manner as the Legislature thereof may direct, a Number of Electors, equal to the whole Number of Senators and Representatives to which the State may be entitled in the Congress: but no Senator or Representative, or Person holding an Office of Trust or Profit under the United States, shall be appointed an Elector.

3. Former Method of Electing President ~~The Electors shall meet in their respective States, and vote by Ballot for two Persons, of whom one at least shall not be an Inhabitant of the same State with themselves. And they shall make a List of all the Persons voted for, and of the Number of Votes for each; which List they shall sign and certify, and transmit sealed to the Seat of the Government of the United States, directed to the President of the Senate. The President of the Senate shall, in the Presence of the Senate and House of Representatives, open all the Certificates, and the Votes shall~~

The Electoral College

11 Number of Electors

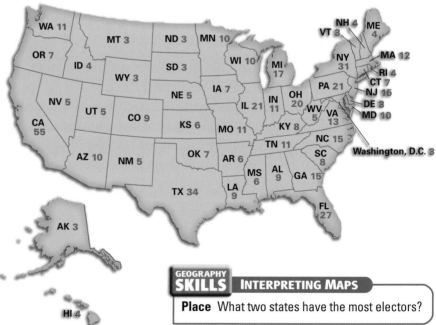

WA 11 | OR 7 | ID 4 | MT 3 | ND 3 | MN 10 | WI 10 | MI 17 | NH 4 | VT 3 | ME 4 | NY 31 | MA 12 | RI 4 | CT 7 | NJ 15 | DE 3 | MD 10 | PA 21 | OH 20 | IN 11 | WV 5 | VA 13 | NV 5 | UT 5 | CO 9 | WY 3 | SD 3 | NE 5 | IA 7 | IL 21 | KY 8 | NC 15 | CA 55 | AZ 10 | NM 5 | KS 6 | MO 11 | TN 11 | SC 8 | Washington, D.C. 3 | OK 7 | AR 6 | MS 6 | AL 9 | GA 15 | TX 34 | LA 9 | FL 27 | AK 3 | HI 4

GEOGRAPHY SKILLS INTERPRETING MAPS

Place What two states have the most electors?

then be counted. The Person having the greatest Number of Votes shall be the President, if such Number be a Majority of the whole Number of Electors appointed; and if there be more than one who have such Majority, and have an equal Number of Votes, then the House of Representatives shall immediately choose by Ballot one of them for President; and if no Person have a Majority, then from the five highest on the List the said House shall in like Manner choose the President. But in choosing the President, the Votes shall be taken by States, the Representation from each State having one Vote; A quorum for this purpose shall consist of a Member or Members from two thirds of the States, and a Majority of all the States shall be necessary to a Choice. In every Case, after the Choice of the President, the Person having the greatest Number of Votes of the Electors shall be the Vice President. But if there should remain two or more who have equal Votes, the Senate shall choose from them by Ballot the Vice President.

4. Election Day The Congress may determine the Time of choosing the Electors, and the Day on which they shall give their Votes; which Day shall be the same throughout the United States.

5. Qualifications No Person except a natural born Citizen, or a Citizen of the United States, at the time of the Adoption of this Constitution, shall be eligible to the Office of President; neither shall any Person be eligible to that Office who shall not have attained to the Age of thirty five Years, and been fourteen Years a Resident within the United States.

6. Succession In Case of the Removal of the President from Office, or of his Death, Resignation, or Inability to discharge the Powers and Duties of the said Office, the Same shall devolve on the Vice President, and the Congress may by Law provide for the Case of Removal, Death, Resignation or Inability, both of the President and Vice President, declaring what Officer shall then act as President, and such Officer shall act accordingly, until the Disability be removed, or a President shall be elected.

7. Salary The President shall, at stated Times, receive for his Services, a Compensation, which shall neither be increased nor diminished during the Period for which he shall have been elected, and he shall not receive within that Period any other Emolument from the United States, or any of them.

8. Oath of Office Before he enter on the Execution of his Office, he shall take the following Oath or Affirmation:—"I do solemnly swear (or affirm) that I will faithfully execute the Office of President of the United States, and will to the best of my Ability, preserve, protect and defend the Constitution of the United States."

EXPLORING THE DOCUMENT The youngest elected president was John F. Kennedy; he was 43 years old when he was inaugurated. (Theodore Roosevelt was 42 when he assumed office after the assassination of McKinley.) **What is the minimum required age for the office**

Presidential Salary

In 1999 Congress voted to set future presidents' salaries at $400,000 per year. The president also receives an annual expense account. The president must pay taxes only on the salary.

Commander in Chief

Today the president is in charge of the army, navy, air force, marines, and coast guard. Only Congress, however, can decide if the United States will declare war.

Appointments

Most of the president's appointments to office must be approved by the Senate.

Vocabulary

[22] **Reprieves** delays of punishment

[23] **Pardons** releases from the legal penalties associated with a crime

The State of the Union

Every year the president presents to Congress a State of the Union message. In this message, the president introduces and explains a legislative plan for the coming year.

Section 2. Powers of Presidency

1. Military Powers The President shall be Commander in Chief of the Army and Navy of the United States, and of the Militia of the several States, when called into the actual Service of the United States; he may require the Opinion, in writing, of the principal Officer in each of the executive Departments, upon any Subject relating to the Duties of their respective Offices, and he shall have Power to grant **Reprieves**[22] and **Pardons**[23] for Offences against the United States, except in Cases of Impeachment.

2. Treaties and Appointments He shall have Power, by and with the Advice and Consent of the Senate, to make Treaties, provided two thirds of the Senators present concur; and he shall nominate, and by and with the Advice and Consent of the Senate, shall appoint Ambassadors, other public Ministers and Consuls, Judges of the supreme Court, and all other Officers of the United States, whose Appointments are not herein otherwise provided for, and which shall be established by Law: but the Congress may by Law vest the Appointment of such inferior Officers, as they think proper, in the President alone, in the Courts of Law, or in the Heads of Departments.

3. Vacancies The President shall have Power to fill up all Vacancies that may happen during the Recess of the Senate, by granting Commissions which shall expire at the End of their next Session.

Section 3. Presidential Duties

He shall from time to time give to the Congress Information of the State of the Union, and recommend to their Consideration such Measures as he shall judge necessary and expedient; he may, on extraordinary Occasions, convene both Houses, or either of them, and in Case of Disagreement between them, with Respect to the Time of Adjournment, he may adjourn them to such Time as he shall think proper; he shall receive Ambassadors and other public Ministers; he shall take Care that the Laws be faithfully executed, and shall Commission all the Officers of the United States.

Section 4. Impeachment

The President, Vice President and all civil Officers of the United States, shall be removed from Office on Impeachment for, and Conviction of, Treason, Bribery, or other high Crimes and Misdemeanors.

Article III The Judiciary

Section 1. Federal Courts and Judges

The judicial Power of the United States shall be vested in one supreme Court, and in such inferior Courts as the Congress may from time to time ordain and establish. The Judges, both of the supreme and inferior Courts, shall hold their Offices during good Behavior, and shall, at stated Times, receive for their Services a Compensation, which shall not be diminished during their Continuance in Office.

Section 2. Authority of the Courts

1. General Authority The judicial Power shall extend to all Cases, in Law and Equity, arising under this Constitution, the Laws of the United States, and Treaties made, or which shall be made, under their Authority;—to all Cases affecting Ambassadors, other public Ministers and Consuls;—to all Cases of admiralty and maritime Jurisdiction;—to Controversies to which the United States shall be a Party;—to Controversies between two or more States —between a State and Citizens of another State; —between Citizens of different States;—between Citizens of the same State claiming Lands under Grants of different States, and between a State, or the Citizens thereof, and foreign States, Citizens or Subjects.

2. Supreme Authority In all Cases affecting Ambassadors, other public Ministers and Consuls, and those in which a State shall be Party, the supreme Court shall have original Jurisdiction. In all the other Cases before mentioned, the supreme Court shall have appellate Jurisdiction, both as to Law and Fact, with such Exceptions, and under such Regulations as the Congress shall make.

Federal Judicial System QUICK FACTS

Supreme Court

Reviews cases appealed from lower federal courts and highest state courts

Courts of Appeals

Review appeals from district courts

District Courts

Hold trials

Judicial Branch

The Articles of Confederation did not set up a federal court system. One of the first points that the framers of the Constitution agreed upon was to set up a national judiciary. In the Judiciary Act of 1789, Congress provided for the establishment of lower courts, such as district courts, circuit courts of appeals, and various other federal courts. The judicial system provides a check on the legislative branch: it can declare a law unconstitutional.

3. Trial by Jury The Trial of all Crimes, except in Cases of Impeachment, shall be by Jury; and such Trial shall be held in the State where the said Crimes shall have been committed; but when not committed within any State, the Trial shall be at such Place or Places as the Congress may by Law have directed.

Section 3. Treason

1. Definition Treason against the United States, shall consist only in levying War against them, or in adhering to their Enemies, giving them Aid and Comfort. No Person shall be convicted of Treason unless on the Testimony of two Witnesses to the same overt Act, or on Confession in open Court.

2. Punishment The Congress shall have Power to declare the Punishment of Treason, but no **Attainder of Treason**[24] shall work **Corruption of Blood**,[25] or Forfeiture except during the Life of the Person attainted.

Article IV Relations among States

Section 1. State Acts and Records

Full Faith and Credit shall be given in each State to the public Acts, Records, and judicial Proceedings of every other State. And the Congress may by general Laws prescribe the Manner in which such Acts, Records and Proceedings shall be proved, and the Effect thereof.

Section 2. Rights of Citizens

1. Citizenship The Citizens of each State shall be entitled to all Privileges and Immunities of Citizens in the several States.

2. Extradition A Person charged in any State with Treason, Felony, or other Crime, who shall flee from Justice, and be found in another State, shall on Demand of the executive Authority of the State from which he fled, be delivered up, to be removed to the State having Jurisdiction of the Crime.

3. Fugitive Slaves ~~No Person held to Service or Labour in one State, under the Laws thereof, escaping into another, shall, in Consequence of any Law or Regulation therein, be discharged from such Service or Labour, but shall be delivered up on Claim of the Party to whom such Service or Labour may be due.~~

The States

States must honor the laws, records, and court decisions of other states. A person cannot escape a legal obligation by moving from one state to another.

EXPLORING THE DOCUMENT The framers wanted to ensure that citizens could determine how state governments would operate. **How does the need to respect the laws of each state support the principle of popular sovereignty?**

Federalism QUICK FACTS

National
- Declare war
- Maintain armed forces
- Regulate interstate and foreign trade
- Admit new states
- Establish post offices
- Set standard weights and measures
- Coin money
- Establish foreign policy
- Make all laws necessary and proper for carrying out delegated powers

Shared
- Maintain law and order
- Levy taxes
- Borrow money
- Charter banks
- Establish courts
- Provide for public welfare

State
- Establish and maintain schools
- Establish local governments
- Regulate business within the state
- Make marriage laws
- Provide for public safety
- Assume other powers not delegated to the national government or prohibited to the states

ANALYSIS SKILL **ANALYZING INFORMATION**

Why does the power to declare war belong only to the national government?

Section 3. New States

1. Admission New States may be admitted by the Congress into this Union; but no new State shall be formed or erected within the Jurisdiction of any other State; nor any State be formed by the Junction of two or more States, or Parts of States, without the Consent of the Legislatures of the States concerned as well as of the Congress.

2. Congressional Authority The Congress shall have Power to dispose of and make all needful Rules and Regulations respecting the Territory or other Property belonging to the United States; and nothing in this Constitution shall be so construed as to Prejudice any Claims of the United States, or of any particular State.

Section 4. Guarantees to the States

The United States shall guarantee to every State in this Union a Republican Form of Government, and shall protect each of them against Invasion; and on Application of the Legislature, or of the Executive (when the Legislature cannot be convened), against domestic Violence.

 EXPLORING THE DOCUMENT In a republic, voters elect representatives to act in their best interest. **How does Article IV protect the practice of republicanism in the United States?**

Article V | Amending the Constitution

The Congress, whenever two thirds of both Houses shall deem it necessary, shall propose Amendments to this Constitution, or, on the Application of the Legislatures of two thirds of the several States, shall call a Convention for proposing Amendments, which, in either Case, shall be valid to all Intents and Purposes, as Part of this Constitution, when ratified by the Legislatures of three fourths of the several States, or by Conventions in three fourths thereof, as the one or the other Mode of Ratification may be proposed by the Congress; Provided that ~~no Amendment which may be made prior to the Year One thousand eight hundred and eight shall in any Manner affect the first and fourth Clauses in the Ninth Section of the first Article; and~~ that no State, without its Consent, shall be deprived of its equal Suffrage in the Senate.

National Supremacy

One of the biggest problems facing the delegates to the Constitutional Convention was the question of what would happen if a state law and a federal law conflicted. Which law would be followed? Who would decide? The second clause of Article VI answers those questions. When a federal law and a state law disagree, the federal law overrides the state law. The Constitution and other federal laws are the "supreme Law of the Land." This clause is often called the supremacy clause.

Article VI | Supremacy of National Government

All Debts contracted and Engagements entered into, before the Adoption of this Constitution, shall be as valid against the United States under this Constitution, as under the Confederation.

This Constitution, and the Laws of the United States which shall be made in Pursuance thereof; and all Treaties made, or which shall be made, under the Authority of the United States, shall be the supreme Law of the Land; and the Judges in every State shall be bound thereby, any Thing in the Constitution or Laws of any State to the Contrary notwithstanding.

The Senators and Representatives before mentioned, and the Members of the several State Legislatures, and all executive and judicial Officers, both of the United States and of the several States, shall be bound by Oath or Affirmation, to support this Constitution; but no religious Test shall ever be required as a Qualification to any Office or public Trust under the United States.

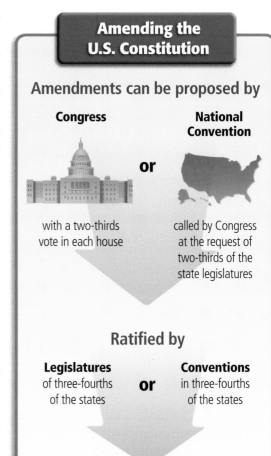

Amending the U.S. Constitution

Amendments can be proposed by

Congress with a two-thirds vote in each house

or

National Convention called by Congress at the request of two-thirds of the state legislatures

Ratified by

Legislatures of three-fourths of the states

or

Conventions in three-fourths of the states

Amendment is added to the Constitution.

Article VII | Ratification

The Ratification of the Conventions of nine States, shall be sufficient for the Establishment of this Constitution between the States so ratifying the Same.

Done in Convention by the Unanimous Consent of the States present the Seventeenth Day of September in the Year of our Lord one thousand seven hundred and Eighty seven and of the Independence of the United States of America the Twelfth In witness whereof We have hereunto subscribed our Names,

> George Washington—
> President and deputy from Virginia

Delaware

George Read
Gunning Bedford Jr.
John Dickinson
Richard Bassett
Jacob Broom

Maryland

James McHenry
Daniel of
  St. Thomas Jenifer
Daniel Carroll

Virginia

John Blair
James Madison Jr.

North Carolina

William Blount
Richard Dobbs Spaight
Hugh Williamson

South Carolina

John Rutledge
Charles Cotesworth
  Pinckney
Charles Pinckney
Pierce Butler

Georgia

William Few
Abraham Baldwin

New Hampshire

John Langdon
Nicholas Gilman

Massachusetts

Nathaniel Gorham
Rufus King

Connecticut

William Samuel Johnson
Roger Sherman

New York

Alexander Hamilton

New Jersey

William Livingston
David Brearley
William Paterson
Jonathan Dayton

Pennsylvania

Benjamin Franklin
Thomas Mifflin
Robert Morris
George Clymer
Thomas FitzSimons
Jared Ingersoll
James Wilson
Gouverneur Morris

Attest:
William Jackson,
Secretary

Constitutional Amendments

Note: The first 10 amendments to the Constitution were ratified on December 15, 1791, and form what is known as the Bill of Rights.

Amendments 1–10. The Bill of Rights

Amendment I

Congress shall make no law respecting an establishment of religion, or prohibiting the free exercise thereof; or abridging the freedom of speech, or of the press; or the right of the people peaceably to assemble, and to petition the Government for a redress of grievances.

Amendment II

A well regulated Militia, being necessary to the security of a free State, the right of the people to keep and bear Arms, shall not be infringed.

Amendment III

No Soldier shall, in time of peace be **quartered**[26] in any house, without the consent of the Owner, nor in time of war, but in a manner to be prescribed by law.

Amendment IV

The right of the people to be secure in their persons, houses, papers, and effects, against unreasonable searches and seizures, shall not be violated, and no **Warrants**[27] shall issue, but upon probable cause, supported by Oath or affirmation, and particularly describing the place to be searched, and the persons or things to be seized.

Amendment V

No person shall be held to answer for a capital, or otherwise **infamous**[28] crime, unless on a presentment or **indictment**[29] of a Grand Jury, except in

Fundamental Liberties

Freedom of Religion   Freedom of Speech

cases arising in the land or naval forces, or in the Militia, when in actual service in time of War or public danger; nor shall any person be subject for the same offence to be twice put in jeopardy of life or limb; nor shall be compelled in any criminal case to be a witness against himself, nor be deprived of life, liberty, or property, without due process of law; nor shall private property be taken for public use, without just compensation.

Amendment VI

In all criminal prosecutions, the accused shall enjoy the right to a speedy and public trial, by an impartial jury of the State and district wherein the crime shall have been committed, which district shall have been previously **ascertained**[30] by law, and to be informed of the nature and cause of the accusation; to be confronted with the witnesses against him; to have compulsory process for obtaining witnesses in his favor, and to have the Assistance of Counsel for his defence.

Amendment VII

In suits at common law, where the value in controversy shall exceed twenty dollars, the right of trial by jury shall be preserved, and no fact tried by a jury, shall be otherwise reexamined in any Court of the United States, than according to the rules of the common law.

Amendment VIII

Excessive bail shall not be required, nor excessive fines imposed, nor cruel and unusual punishments inflicted.

Amendment IX

The enumeration in the Constitution, of certain rights, shall not be construed to deny or disparage others retained by the people.

Amendment X

The powers not delegated to the United States by the Constitution, nor prohibited by it to the States, are reserved to the States respectively, or to the people.

Trials
The Sixth Amendment makes several guarantees, including a prompt trial and a trial by a jury chosen from the state and district in which the crime was committed.

Vocabulary
[30] **ascertained** found out

EXPLORING THE DOCUMENT The Ninth and Tenth Amendments were added because not every right of the people or of the states could be listed in the Constitution. **How do the Ninth and Tenth Amendments protect the rights of citizens?**

Freedom of the Press

Freedom of Assembly

Freedom to Petition the Government

ANALYSIS SKILL ANALYZING INFORMATION
Which amendment guarantees these fundamental freedoms?

The Constitution has been amended only 27 times since it was ratified more than 200 years ago. Amendments help the structure of the government change along with the values of the nation's people. Read the time line below to learn how each amendment changed the government.

1870
Amendment 15
Prohibits national and state governments from denying the vote based on race

1791
Bill of Rights
Amendments 1–10

1865
Amendment 13
Bans slavery

| 1790 | 1820 | 1870 |

1795
Amendment 11
Protects the states from lawsuits filed by citizens of other states or countries

1804
Amendment 12
Requires separate ballots for the offices of president and vice president

1868
Amendment 14
Defines citizenship and citizens' rights

Amendments 11–27

Vocabulary

[31] **construed** explained or interpreted

President and Vice President

The Twelfth Amendment changed the election procedure for president and vice president.

Amendment XI

Passed by Congress March 4, 1794. Ratified February 7, 1795.

The Judicial power of the United States shall not be **construed**[31] to extend to any suit in law or equity, commenced or prosecuted against one of the United States by Citizens of another State, or by Citizens or Subjects of any Foreign State.

Amendment XII

Passed by Congress December 9, 1803. Ratified June 15, 1804.

The Electors shall meet in their respective states and vote by ballot for President and Vice-President, one of whom, at least, shall not be an inhabitant of the same state with themselves; they shall name in their ballots the person voted for as President, and in distinct ballots the person voted for as Vice-President, and they shall make distinct lists of all persons voted for as President, and of all persons voted for as Vice-President, and of the number of votes for each, which lists they shall sign and certify, and transmit sealed to the seat of the government of the United States, directed to the President of the Senate;—the President of the Senate shall, in the presence of the

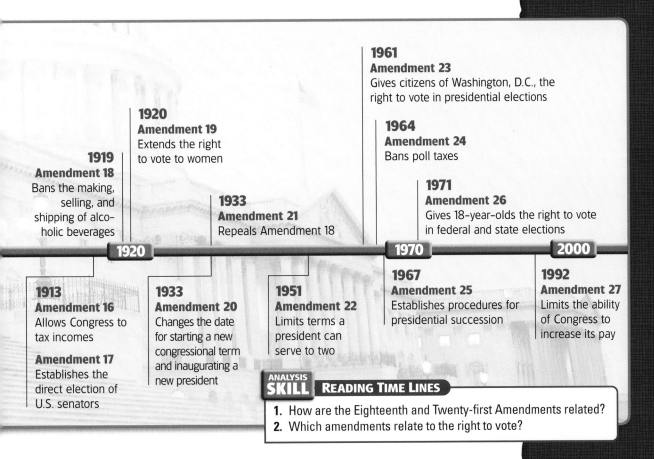

1961
Amendment 23
Gives citizens of Washington, D.C., the right to vote in presidential elections

1920
Amendment 19
Extends the right to vote to women

1964
Amendment 24
Bans poll taxes

1919
Amendment 18
Bans the making, selling, and shipping of alcoholic beverages

1933
Amendment 21
Repeals Amendment 18

1971
Amendment 26
Gives 18–year-olds the right to vote in federal and state elections

1920

1970

2000

1913
Amendment 16
Allows Congress to tax incomes

Amendment 17
Establishes the direct election of U.S. senators

1933
Amendment 20
Changes the date for starting a new congressional term and inaugurating a new president

1951
Amendment 22
Limits terms a president can serve to two

1967
Amendment 25
Establishes procedures for presidential succession

1992
Amendment 27
Limits the ability of Congress to increase its pay

ANALYSIS SKILL **READING TIME LINES**

1. How are the Eighteenth and Twenty-first Amendments related?
2. Which amendments relate to the right to vote?

Senate and House of Representatives, open all the certificates and the votes shall then be counted;—The person having the greatest number of votes for President, shall be the President, if such number be a majority of the whole number of Electors appointed; and if no person have such majority, then from the persons having the highest numbers not exceeding three on the list of those voted for as President, the House of Representatives shall choose immediately, by ballot, the President. But in choosing the President, the votes shall be taken by states, the representation from each state having one vote; a quorum for this purpose shall consist of a member or members from two-thirds of the states, and a majority of all the states shall be necessary to a choice. ~~And if the House of Representatives shall not choose a President whenever the right of choice shall devolve upon them, before the fourth day of March next following, then the Vice-President shall act as President, as in case of the death or other constitutional disability of the President.~~—The person having the greatest number of votes as Vice-President, shall be the Vice-President, if such number be a majority of the whole number of Electors appointed, and if no person have a majority, then from the two highest numbers on the list, the Senate shall choose the Vice-President; a quorum for the purpose shall consist of two-thirds of the whole number of Senators, and a majority of the whole number shall be necessary to a choice. But no person constitutionally ineligible to the office of President shall be eligible to that of Vice-President of the United States.

Amendment XIII

Passed by Congress January 31, 1865. Ratified December 6, 1865.

1. Slavery Banned Neither slavery nor **involuntary servitude,**[32] except as a punishment for crime whereof the party shall have been duly convicted, shall exist within the United States, or any place subject to their jurisdiction.

2. Enforcement Congress shall have power to enforce this article by appropriate legislation.

Amendment XIV

Passed by Congress June 13, 1866. Ratified July 9, 1868.

1. Citizenship Defined All persons born or naturalized in the United States, and subject to the jurisdiction thereof, are citizens of the United States and of the State wherein they reside. No State shall make or enforce any law which shall abridge the privileges or immunities of citizens of the United States; nor shall any State deprive any person of life, liberty, or property, without due process of law; nor deny to any person within its jurisdiction the equal protection of the laws.

2. Voting Rights Representatives shall be apportioned among the several States according to their respective numbers, counting the whole number of persons in each State, excluding Indians not taxed. But when the right to vote at any election for the choice of electors for President and Vice-President of the United States, Representatives in Congress, the Executive and Judicial officers of a State, or the members of the Legislature thereof, is denied to any of the male inhabitants of such State, being twenty-one years of age, and citizens of the United States, or in any way abridged, except for participation in rebellion, or other crime, the basis of representation therein shall be reduced in the proportion which the number of such male citizens shall bear to the whole number of male citizens twenty-one years of age in such State.

3. Rebels Banned from Government No person shall be a Senator or Representative in Congress, or elector of President and Vice-President, or hold any office, civil or military, under the United States, or under any State, who, having previously taken an oath, as a member of Congress, or as an officer of the United States, or as a member of any State legislature, or as an executive or judicial officer of any State, to support the Constitution of the United States, shall have engaged in insurrection or rebellion against the same, or given aid or comfort to the enemies thereof. But Congress may by a vote of two-thirds of each House, remove such disability.

4. Payment of Debts The validity of the public debt of the United States, authorized by law, including debts incurred for payment of pensions and

The Reconstruction Amendments

The Thirteenth, Fourteenth, and Fifteenth Amendments are often called the Reconstruction Amendments. This is because they arose during Reconstruction, the period of American history following the Civil War. The country was reconstructing itself after that terrible conflict. A key aspect of Reconstruction was extending the rights of citizenship to former slaves.

The Thirteenth Amendment banned slavery. The Fourteenth Amendment required states to respect the freedoms listed in the Bill of Rights, thus preventing states from denying rights to African Americans. The Fifteenth Amendment gave African American men the right to vote.

African Americans participate in an election.

ANALYSIS SKILL **ANALYZING INFORMATION**

Why was the Thirteenth Amendment needed?

---

bounties for services in suppressing insurrection or rebellion, shall not be questioned. But neither the United States nor any State shall assume or pay any debt or obligation incurred in aid of insurrection or rebellion against the United States, ~~or any claim for the loss or emancipation of any slave~~; but all such debts, obligations and claims shall be held illegal and void.

5. Enforcement The Congress shall have the power to enforce, by appropriate legislation, the provisions of this article.

Amendment XV

Passed by Congress February 26, 1869. Ratified February 3, 1870.

1. Voting Rights The right of citizens of the United States to vote shall not be denied or abridged by the United States or by any State on account of race, color, or previous condition of servitude.

2. Enforcement The Congress shall have the power to enforce this article by appropriate legislation.

Amendment XVI

Passed by Congress July 2, 1909. Ratified February 3, 1913.

The Congress shall have power to lay and collect taxes on incomes, from whatever source derived, without apportionment among the several States, and without regard to any census or enumeration.

Amendment XVII

Passed by Congress May 13, 1912. Ratified April 8, 1913.

1. Senators Elected by Citizens The Senate of the United States shall be composed of two Senators from each State, elected by the people thereof, for six years; and each Senator shall have one vote. The electors in each State shall have the qualifications requisite for electors of the most numerous branch of the State legislatures.

2. Vacancies When vacancies happen in the representation of any State in the Senate, the executive authority of such State shall issue writs of election to fill such vacancies: *Provided*, That the legislature of any State may empower the executive thereof to make temporary appointments until the people fill the vacancies by election as the legislature may direct.

3. Future Elections This amendment shall not be so construed as to affect the election or term of any Senator chosen before it becomes valid as part of the Constitution.

Amendment XVIII

Passed by Congress December 18, 1917. Ratified January 16, 1919. Repealed by Amendment XXI.

1. Liquor Banned After one year from the ratification of this article the manufacture, sale, or transportation of intoxicating liquors within, the importation thereof into, or the exportation thereof from the United States and all territory subject to the jurisdiction thereof for beverage purposes is hereby prohibited.

2. Enforcement The Congress and the several States shall have concurrent power to enforce this article by appropriate legislation.

3. Ratification This article shall be inoperative unless it shall have been ratified as an amendment to the Constitution by the legislatures of the several States, as provided in the Constitution, within seven years from the date of the submission hereof to the States by the Congress.

EXPLORING THE DOCUMENT The Seventeenth Amendment requires that senators be elected directly by the people instead of by the state legislatures. **What principle of our government does the Seventeenth Amendment protect?**

Prohibition

Although many people believed that the Eighteenth Amendment was good for the health and welfare of the American people, it was repealed 14 years later.

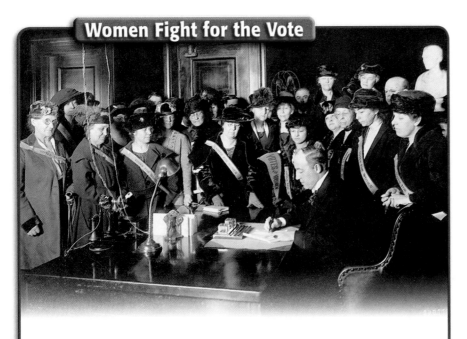

Women Fight for the Vote

To become part of the Constitution, a proposed amendment must be ratified by three-fourths of the states. Here, suffragists witness Kentucky governor Edwin P. Morrow signing the Nineteenth Amendment in January 1920. By June of that year, enough states had ratified the amendment to make it part of the Constitution. American women, after generations of struggle, had finally won the right to vote.

ANALYSIS SKILL **ANALYZING INFORMATION**

What right did the Nineteenth Amendment grant?

Amendment XIX

Passed by Congress June 4, 1919. Ratified August 18, 1920.

1. Voting Rights The right of citizens of the United States to vote shall not be denied or abridged by the United States or by any State on account of sex.

2. Enforcement Congress shall have power to enforce this article by appropriate legislation.

Amendment XX

Passed by Congress March 2, 1932. Ratified January 23, 1933.

1. Presidential Terms The terms of the President and the Vice President shall end at noon on the 20th day of January, and the terms of Senators and Representatives at noon on the 3d day of January, of the years in which such terms would have ended if this article had not been ratified; and the terms of their successors shall then begin.

Women's Suffrage

Abigail Adams and others were disappointed that the Declaration of Independence and the Constitution did not specifically include women. It took many years and much campaigning before suffrage for women was finally achieved.

2. Meeting of Congress The Congress shall assemble at least once in every year, and such meeting shall begin at noon on the 3d day of January, unless they shall by law appoint a different day.

3. Succession of Vice President If, at the time fixed for the beginning of the term of the President, the President elect shall have died, the Vice President elect shall become President. If a President shall not have been chosen before the time fixed for the beginning of his term, or if the President elect shall have failed to qualify, then the Vice President elect shall act as President until a President shall have qualified; and the Congress may by law provide for the case wherein neither a President elect nor a Vice President shall have qualified, declaring who shall then act as President, or the manner in which one who is to act shall be selected, and such person shall act accordingly until a President or Vice President shall have qualified.

4. Succession by Vote of Congress The Congress may by law provide for the case of the death of any of the persons from whom the House of Representatives may choose a President whenever the right of choice shall have devolved upon them, and for the case of the death of any of the persons from whom the Senate may choose a Vice President whenever the right of choice shall have devolved upon them.

5. Ratification ~~Sections 1 and 2 shall take effect on the 15th day of October following the ratification of this article.~~

6. Ratification ~~This article shall be inoperative unless it shall have been ratified as an amendment to the Constitution by the legislatures of three-fourths of the several States within seven years from the date of its submission.~~

Amendment XXI

Passed by Congress February 20, 1933. Ratified December 5, 1933.

1. 18th Amendment Repealed The eighteenth article of amendment to the Constitution of the United States is hereby repealed.

2. Liquor Allowed by Law The transportation or importation into any State, Territory, or Possession of the United States for delivery or use therein of intoxicating liquors, in violation of the laws thereof, is hereby prohibited.

3. Ratification ~~This article shall be inoperative unless it shall have been ratified as an amendment to the Constitution by conventions in the several States, as provided in the Constitution, within seven years from the date of the submission hereof to the States by the Congress.~~

Amendment XXII

Passed by Congress March 21, 1947. Ratified February 27, 1951.

1. Term Limits No person shall be elected to the office of the President more than twice, and no person who has held the office of President, or acted as President, for more than two years of a term to which some other person was elected President shall be elected to the office of President more than once. ~~But this Article shall not apply to any person holding the office of President when this Article was proposed by Congress, and shall not prevent any person who may be holding the office of President, or acting as President, during the term within which this Article becomes operative from holding the office of President or acting as President during the remainder of such term.~~

2. Ratification ~~This article shall be inoperative unless it shall have been ratified as an amendment to the Constitution by the legislatures of three-fourths of the several States within seven years from the date of its submission to the States by the Congress.~~

 EXPLORING THE DOCUMENT From the time of President George Washington's administration, it was a custom for presidents to serve no more than two terms in office. Franklin D. Roosevelt, however, was elected to four terms. The Twenty-second Amendment restricted presidents to no more than two terms in office. **Why do you think citizens chose to limit the power of the president in this way?**

After Franklin D. Roosevelt was elected to four consecutive terms, limits were placed on the number of terms a president could serve.

Amendment XXIII

Passed by Congress June 16, 1960. Ratified March 29, 1961.

1. District of Columbia Represented The District constituting the seat of Government of the United States shall appoint in such manner as Congress may direct:

A number of electors of President and Vice President equal to the whole number of Senators and Representatives in Congress to which the District would be entitled if it were a State, but in no event more than the least populous State; they shall be in addition to those appointed by the States, but they shall be considered, for the purposes of the election of President and Vice President, to be electors appointed by a State; and they shall meet in the District and perform such duties as provided by the twelfth article of amendment.

2. Enforcement The Congress shall have power to enforce this article by appropriate legislation.

Voting Rights

Until the ratification of the Twenty-third Amendment, the people of Washington, D.C., could not vote in presidential elections.

Poll taxes were used to deny many poor Americans, including African Americans and Hispanic Americans, their right to vote. These taxes were made unconstitutional by the Twenty-fourth Amendment.

The American GI Forum
Says: BUY YOUR
POLL TAX

1939 Poll Tax Receipt
STATE OF TEXAS · COUNTY OF

ANALYSIS SKILL **ANALYZING INFORMATION**
How did poll taxes deny poor Americans the opportunity to vote?

Presidential Disability

The illness of President Eisenhower in the 1950s and the assassination of President Kennedy in 1963 were the events behind the Twenty-fifth Amendment. The Constitution did not provide a clear-cut method for a vice president to take over for a disabled president or upon the death of a president. This amendment provides for filling the office of the vice president if a vacancy occurs, and it provides a way for the vice president—or someone else in the line of succession—to take over if the president is unable to perform the duties of that office.

Amendment XXIV

Passed by Congress August 27, 1962. Ratified January 23, 1964.

1. Voting Rights The right of citizens of the United States to vote in any primary or other election for President or Vice President, for electors for President or Vice President, or for Senator or Representative in Congress, shall not be denied or abridged by the United States or any State by reason of failure to pay poll tax or other tax.

2. Enforcement The Congress shall have power to enforce this article by appropriate legislation.

Amendment XXV

Passed by Congress July 6, 1965. Ratified February 10, 1967.

1. Sucession of Vice President In case of the removal of the President from office or of his death or resignation, the Vice President shall become President.

2. Vacancy of Vice President Whenever there is a vacancy in the office of the Vice President, the President shall nominate a Vice President who shall take office upon confirmation by a majority vote of both Houses of Congress.

3. Written Declaratrion Whenever the President transmits to the President pro tempore of the Senate and the Speaker of the House of Representatives his written declaration that he is unable to discharge the powers and duties of his office, and until he transmits to them a written declaration to the contrary, such powers and duties shall be discharged by the Vice President as Acting President.

4. Removing the President Whenever the Vice President and a majority of either the principal officers of the executive departments or of such other body as Congress may by law provide, transmit to the President pro tempore of the Senate and the Speaker of the House of Representatives their written declaration that the President is unable to discharge the powers and duties of his office, the Vice President shall immediately assume the powers and duties of the office as Acting President.

Thereafter, when the President transmits to the President pro tempore of the Senate and the Speaker of the House of Representatives his written declaration that no inability exists, he shall resume the powers and duties of his office unless the Vice President and a majority of either the principal officers of the executive department or of such other body as Congress may by law provide, transmit within four days to the President pro tempore of the Senate and the Speaker of the House of Representatives their written declaration that the President is unable to discharge the powers and duties of his office. Thereupon Congress shall decide the issue, assembling within forty-eight hours for that purpose if not in session. If the Congress, within twenty-one days after receipt of the latter written declaration, or, if Congress is not in session, within twenty-one days after Congress is required to assemble, determines by two-thirds vote of both Houses that the President is unable to discharge the powers and duties of his office, the Vice President shall continue to discharge the same as Acting President; otherwise, the President shall resume the powers and duties of his office.

Amendment XXVI

Passed by Congress March 23, 1971. Ratified July 1, 1971.

1. Voting Rights The right of citizens of the United States, who are eighteen years of age or older, to vote shall not be denied or abridged by the United States or by any State on account of age.

2. Enforcement The Congress shall have power to enforce this article by appropriate legislation.

Amendment XXVII

Originally proposed September 25, 1789. Ratified May 7, 1992.

No law, varying the compensation for the services of the Senators and Representatives, shall take effect, until an election of representatives shall have intervened.

Expanded Suffrage

The Voting Rights Act of 1970 tried to set the voting age at 18. However, the Supreme Court ruled that the act set the voting age for national elections only, not for state or local elections. The Twenty-sixth Amendment gave 18-year-old citizens the right to vote in all elections.

North Carolina State Constitution

North Carolina's first constitution was adopted in 1776. It has been substantially rewritten twice, once in 1868 (after the Civil War and during Reconstruction) and once in 1971. Most of the fundamental constitutional principles, however, have remained largely unchanged since the 1776 document. Many of these principles can be found in Article I, Declaration of Rights.

 ## North Carolina Standards

Civics and Economics Objectives

3.01 Identify the principles in the North Carolina Constitution and local charters.

3.02 Explain how the North Carolina Constitution and local charters define the framework, organization, and structure of government at the state and local level.

3.03 Explain how the state constitution grants and limits the authority of public officials and government agencies.

3.04 Describe how the state constitution and local charters may be changed, and analyze the impact of specific changes.

3.05 Analyze court cases that illustrate that the North Carolina Constitution is the law of the state.

3.06 Analyze how the Fourteenth Amendment extends the Bill of Rights' protection to citizens of a state.

3.07 Identify modern controversies related to powers of the state government.

3.08 Examine taxation and other revenue sources at the state and local level.

3.09 Describe the services provided by state and local government agencies and how funding is provided.

Preamble

The Preamble to the North Carolina Constitution explains the goals of the state government under this constitution. It is similar to the preamble to the U.S. Constitution. 3.01

We, the people of the State of North Carolina, grateful to Almighty God, the Sovereign Ruler of Nations, for the preservation of the American Union and the existence of our civil, political and religious liberties, and acknowledging our dependence upon Him for the continuance of those blessings to us and our posterity, do, for the more certain security thereof and for the better government of this State, ordain and establish this Constitution.

ARTICLE I   DECLARATION OF RIGHTS

In the U.S. Constitution, the list of rights is contained in the Bill of Rights, the first ten amendments to the Constitution. In the North Carolina Constitution, the list of rights is the first article in the document. By declaring these rights, the North Carolina Constitution limits the power of the state government. 3.01

The rights enjoyed by the citizens of North Carolina go beyond those that are guaranteed in Article I. The Fourteenth Amendment of the U.S. Constitution extends the protections in that document, such as due process and equal protection under the law, to the citizens of every state. This means that laws passed in North Carolina must apply equally to all state residents regardless of their race, color, religion, or sex. And even if North Carolina changes its constitution, the state cannot take away the rights guaranteed by the U.S. Constitution. 3.06

That the great, general, and essential principles of liberty and free government may be recognized and established, and that the relations of this State to the Union and government of the United States and those of the people of this State to the rest of the American people may be defined and affirmed, we do declare that:

Section 1. The equality and rights of persons.   We hold it to be self-evident that all persons are created equal; that they are endowed by their Creator with certain inalienable rights; that among these are life, liberty, the enjoyment of the fruits of their own labor, and the pursuit of happiness.

Section 2. Sovereignty of the people. All political power is vested in and derived from the people; all government of right originates from the people, is founded upon their will only, and is instituted solely for the good of the whole.

Section 3. Internal government of the State. The people of this State have the inherent, sole, and exclusive right of regulating the internal government and police thereof, and of altering or abolishing their Constitution and form of government whenever it may be necessary to their safety and happiness; but every such right shall be exercised in pursuance of law and consistently with the Constitution of the United States.

> The U.S. Constitution has no explicit statement that all government power comes from those who are governed, but Article I, Sections 2 and 3, of the North Carolina Constitution expressly state that the people are the source of all government power, that they retain that power, and that they may even abolish the constitution and the government if they decide it is necessary. 3.01

Section 4. Secession prohibited. This State shall ever remain a member of the American Union; the people thereof are part of the American nation; there is no right on the part of this State to secede; and all attempts, from whatever source or upon whatever pretext, to dissolve this Union or to sever this Nation, shall be resisted with the whole power of the State.

Section 5. Allegiance to the United States. Every citizen of this State owes paramount allegiance to the Constitution and government of the United States, and no law or ordinance of the State in contravention or subversion thereof can have any binding force.

Section 6. Separation of powers. The legislative, executive, and supreme judicial powers of the State government shall be forever separate and distinct from each other.

> The North Carolina Constitution states, as one of the rights guaranteed to the people, that government power will be divided among the three branches. This arrangement limits the power of any one branch of government and makes possible a system of checks and balances between the branches. Note that this section does not establish the branches; Articles II, III, and IV do that. 3.01

Section 7. Suspending laws. All power of suspending laws or the execution of laws by any authority, without the consent of the representatives of the people, is injurious to their rights and shall not be exercised.

Section 8. Representation and taxation. The people of this State shall not be taxed or made subject to the payment of any impost or duty without the consent of themselves or their representatives in the General Assembly, freely given.

> In 1628, the English Parliament presented King Charles I with the English Petition of Right, which he accepted. One section of the Petition included a demand that "no man . . . be compelled to make or yield any . . . tax . . . without common consent by act of Parliament."

Section 9. Frequent elections. For redress of grievances and for amending and strengthening the laws, elections shall be often held.

Section 10. Free elections. All elections shall be free.

In 1689, the English Parliament adopted the English Bill of Rights. Two of that document's provisions were that "election of members of Parliament ought to be free" and "it is the right of the subjects to petition the king" (Section 12, below).

Section 11. Property qualifications. As political rights and privileges are not dependent upon or modified by property, no property qualification shall affect the right to vote or hold office.

Section 12. Right of assembly and petition. The people have a right to assemble together to consult for their common good, to instruct their representatives, and to apply to the General Assembly for redress of grievances; but secret political societies are dangerous to the liberties of a free people and shall not be tolerated.

Section 13. Religious liberty. All persons have a natural and inalienable right to worship Almighty God according to the dictates of their own consciences, and no human authority shall, in any case whatever, control or interfere with the rights of conscience.

Section 14. Freedom of speech and press. Freedom of speech and of the press are two of the great bulwarks of liberty and therefore shall never be restrained, but every person shall be held responsible for their abuse.

Section 15. Education. The people have a right to the privilege of education, and it is the duty of the State to guard and maintain that right.

In 1997, in the case of *Leandro* v. *State*, the North Carolina Supreme Court ruled that the North Carolina Constitution guarantees all children in North Carolina a right to an equal opportunity to obtain a sound basic education. The Court defined a sound basic education as:
"(1) Sufficient ability to read, write and speak the English language and sufficient knowledge of fundamental mathematics and physical science to enable the student to function in a complex and rapidly changing society;
(2) sufficient fundamental knowledge of geography, history and basic economic and political systems to enable the student to make informed choices with regard to issues that affect the student personally or affect the student's community, state, and nation;
(3) sufficient academic and vocational skills to enable the student to successfully engage in post-secondary education or vocational training; and
(4) sufficient academic and vocational skills to enable the student to compete on an equal basis with others in further formal education or gainful employment in contemporary society."
3.05

Section 16. Ex post facto laws. Retrospective laws, punishing acts committed before the existence of such laws and by them only declared criminal, are oppressive, unjust, and incompatible with liberty, and therefore no ex post facto law shall be enacted. No law taxing retrospectively sales, purchases, or other acts previously done shall be enacted.

Section 17. Slavery and involuntary servitude. Slavery is forever prohibited. Involuntary servitude, except as a punishment for crime whereof the parties have been adjudged guilty, is forever prohibited.

Section 18. Court shall be open. All courts shall be open; every person for an injury done him in his lands, goods, person, or reputation shall have remedy by due course of law; and right and justice shall be administered without favor, denial, or delay.

Section 18 guarantees that North Carolina's courts are open to all citizens—every person is entitled to have his or her case heard in court. 3.01

Section 19. Law of the land; equal protection of the laws. No person shall be taken, imprisoned, or disseized of his freehold, liberties, or privileges, or outlawed, or exiled, or in any manner deprived of his life, liberty, or property, but by the law of the land. No person shall be denied the equal protection of the laws; nor shall any person be subjected to discrimination by the State because of race, color, religion, or national origin.

Swann v. *Charlotte-Mecklenburg Board of Education* (1971) was a U.S. Supreme Court case that led to the use of busing to end school segregation in the South. After the Supreme Court's decision in 1954 in *Brown* v. *Board of Education*, few states had desegregated their public schools. For example, approximately 14,000 African American students in the Charlotte-Mecklenburg, North Carolina, school system attended schools that were 99 percent or more black. Federal courts in a number of states had ordered various desegregation remedies, but none had been successful when the *Swann* case reached the Supreme Court.

In its unanimous decision, the Court held that once violations of previous orders to desegregate schools had occurred, federal district courts had broad powers to impose solutions that would be effective, including busing students across attendance zones to achieve racial balance. Such a plan would ensure that schools would be integrated and that under the Fourteenth Amendment all students would receive equal educational opportunities, regardless of their race. 3.06, 3.07

Section 20. General warrants. General warrants, whereby any officer or other person may be commanded to search suspected places without evidence of the act committed, or to seize any person or persons not named, whose offense is not particularly described and supported by evidence, are dangerous to liberty and shall not be granted.

Section 21. Inquiry into restraints on liberty. Every person restrained of his liberty is entitled to a remedy to inquire into the lawfulness thereof, and to remove the restraint if unlawful, and that remedy shall not be denied or delayed. The privilege of the writ of habeas corpus shall not be suspended.

Section 22. Modes of prosecution. Except in misdemeanor cases initiated in the District Court Division, no person shall be put to answer any criminal charge but by indictment, presentment, or impeachment. But any person, when represented by counsel, may, under such regulations as the General Assembly shall prescribe, waive indictment in noncapital cases.

Section 23. Rights of accused. In all criminal prosecutions, every person charged with crime has the right to be informed of the accusation and to confront the accusers and witnesses with other testimony, and to have counsel for defense, and not be compelled to give self-incriminating evidence, or to pay costs, jail fees, or necessary witness fees of the defense, unless found guilty.

Section 24. Right of jury trial in criminal cases. No person shall be convicted of any crime but by the unanimous verdict of a jury in open court. The General Assembly may, however, provide for other means of trial for misdemeanors, with the right of appeal for trial de novo.

Section 25. Right of jury trial in civil cases. In all controversies at law respecting property, the ancient mode of trial by jury is one of the best securities of the rights of the people, and shall remain sacred and inviolable.

Section 26. Jury service. No person shall be excluded from jury service on account of sex, race, color, religion, or national origin.

Section 27. Bail, fines, and punishments. Excessive bail shall not be required, nor excessive fines imposed, nor cruel or unusual punishments inflicted.

> The English Bill of Rights (see Section 10, above) also included a provision that "excessive bail ought not to be required, nor excessive fines imposed, nor cruel and unusual punishments inflicted."

Section 28. Imprisonment for debt. There shall be no imprisonment for debt in this State, except in cases of fraud.

Section 29. Treason against the State. Treason against the State shall consist only of levying war against it or adhering to its enemies by giving them aid and comfort. No person shall be convicted of treason unless on the testimony of two witnesses to the same overt act, or on confession in open court. No conviction of treason or attainder shall work corruption of blood or forfeiture.

Section 30. Militia and the right to bear arms. A well regulated militia being necessary to the security of a free State, the right of the people to keep and bear arms shall not be infringed; and, as standing armies in time of peace are dangerous to liberty, they shall not be maintained, and the military shall be kept under strict subordination to, and governed by, the civil power. Nothing herein shall justify the practice of carrying concealed weapons, or prevent the General Assembly from enacting penal statutes against that practice.

Section 31. Quartering of soldiers. No soldier shall in time of peace be quartered in any house without the consent of the owner, nor in time of war but in a manner prescribed by law.

Section 32. Exclusive emoluments. No person or set of persons is entitled to exclusive or separate emoluments or privileges from the community but in consideration of public services.

Section 33. Hereditary emoluments and honors. No hereditary emoluments, privileges, or honors shall be granted or conferred in this State.

Section 34. Perpetuities and monopolies. Perpetuities and monopolies are contrary to the genius of a free state and shall not be allowed.

Section 35. Recurrence to fundamental principles. A frequent recurrence to fundamental principles is absolutely necessary to preserve the blessings of liberty.

Section 36. Other rights of the people. The enumeration of rights in this Article shall not be construed to impair or deny others retained by the people.

Section 37. Rights of victims of crime.

In 1996 the North Carolina Constitution was amended to add rights for victims of crimes. This amendment created new rights, but those new rights had to be balanced against the long-standing rights of people who have been accused of crimes, such as those in Sections 18–24, above. 3.03, 3.04

(1) Basic rights. Victims of crime, as prescribed by law, shall be entitled to the following basic rights:

(a) The right as prescribed by law to be informed of and to be present at court proceedings of the accused.

(b) The right to be heard at sentencing of the accused in a manner prescribed by law, and at other times as prescribed by law or deemed appropriate by the court.

(c) The right as prescribed by law to receive restitution.

(d) The right as prescribed by law to be given information about the crime, how the criminal justice system works, the rights of victims, and the availability of services for victims.

(e) The right as prescribed by law to receive information about the conviction or final disposition and sentence of the accused.

(f) The right as prescribed by law to receive notification of escape, release, proposed parole or pardon of the accused, or notice of a reprieve or commutation of the accused's sentence.

(g) The right as prescribed by law to present their views and concerns to the Governor or agency considering any action that could result in the release of the accused, prior to such action becoming effective.

(h) The right as prescribed by law to confer with the prosecution.

(2) No money damages; other enforcement. Nothing in this section shall be construed as creating a claim for money damages against the State, a county, a municipality, or any of the agencies, instrumentalities, or employees thereof. The General Assembly may provide for other remedies to ensure adequate enforcement of this section.

(3) No ground for relief in criminal case. The failure or inability of any person to provide a right or service provided under this section may not be used by a defendant in a criminal case, an inmate, or any other accused as a ground for relief in any trial, appeal, post-conviction litigation, habeas corpus, civil action, or any similar criminal or civil proceeding. (1995, c. 438, s. 1.)

ARTICLE II   LEGISLATIVE

As in the U.S. Constitution, the first branch of government created by the North Carolina Constitution is the legislature, called the General Assembly. Article II establishes the framework, structure, and qualifications for the legislative branch. Each house of the General Assembly elects its own officers and establishes its own committees. 3.02

Section 1. Legislative power. The legislative power of the State shall be vested in the General Assembly, which shall consist of a Senate and a House of Representatives.

Section 2. Number of Senators. The Senate shall be composed of 50 Senators, biennially chosen by ballot.

Section 3. Senate districts; apportionment of Senators. The Senators shall be elected from districts. The General Assembly, at the first regular session convening after the return of every decennial census of population taken by order of Congress, shall revise the senate districts and the apportionment of Senators among those districts, subject to the following requirements:

(1) Each Senator shall represent, as nearly as may be, an equal number of inhabitants, the number of inhabitants that each Senator represents being determined for this purpose by dividing the population of the district that he represents by the number of Senators apportioned to that district;

(2) Each senate district shall at all times consist of contiguous territory;

(3) No county shall be divided in the formation of a senate district;

(4) When established, the senate districts and the apportionment of Senators shall remain unaltered until the return of another decennial census of population taken by order of Congress.

Section 4. Number of Representatives. The House of Representatives shall be composed of 120 Representatives, biennially chosen by ballot.

Section 5. Representative districts; apportionment of Representatives.
The Representatives shall be elected from districts. The General Assembly, at the first regular session convening after the return of every decennial census of population taken by order of Congress, shall revise the representative districts and the apportionment of Representatives among those districts, subject to the following requirements:

(1) Each Representative shall represent, as nearly as may be, an equal number of inhabitants, the number of inhabitants that each Representative represents being determined for this purpose by dividing the population of the district that he represents by the number of Representatives apportioned to that district;

(2) Each representative district shall at all times consist of contiguous territory;

(3) No county shall be divided in the formation of a representative district;

(4) When established, the representative districts and the apportionment of Representatives shall remain unaltered until the return of another decennial census of population taken by order of Congress.

Section 6. Qualifications for Senator. Each Senator, at the time of his election, shall be not less than 25 years of age, shall be a qualified voter of the State, and shall have resided in the State as a citizen for two years and in the district for which he is chosen for one year immediately preceding his election.

Section 7. Qualifications for Representative. Each Representative, at the time of his election, shall be a qualified voter of the State, and shall have resided in the district for which he is chosen for one year immediately preceding his election.

Section 8. Elections. The election for members of the General Assembly shall be held for the respective districts in 1972 and every two years thereafter, at the places and on the day prescribed by law.

Section 9. Term of office. The term of office of Senators and Representatives shall commence on the first day of January next after their election.

Section 10. Vacancies. Every vacancy occurring in the membership of the General Assembly by reason of death, resignation, or other cause shall be filled in the manner prescribed by law.

Section 11. Sessions.

(1) Regular Sessions. The General Assembly shall meet in regular session in 1973 and every two years thereafter on the day prescribed by law. Neither house shall proceed upon public business unless a majority of all of its members are actually present.

(2) Extra sessions on legislative call. The President of the Senate and the Speaker of the House of Representatives shall convene the General Assembly in extra session by their joint proclamation upon receipt by the President of the Senate of written requests therefor signed by three-fifths of all the members of the Senate and upon receipt by the Speaker of the House of Representatives of written requests therefor signed by three-fifths of all the members of the House of Representatives.

Section 12. Oath of members. Each member of the General Assembly, before taking his seat, shall take an oath or affirmation that he will support the Constitution and laws of the United States and the Constitution of the State of North Carolina, and will faithfully discharge his duty as a member of the Senate or House of Representatives.

Section 13. President of the Senate. The Lieutenant Governor shall be President of the Senate and shall preside over the Senate, but shall have no vote unless the Senate is equally divided.

Section 14. Other officers of the Senate.

(1) President Pro Tempore–succession to presidency. The Senate shall elect from its membership a President Pro Tempore, who shall become President of the Senate upon the failure of the Lieutenant Governor-elect to qualify, or upon succession by the Lieutenant Governor to the office of Governor,

or upon the death, resignation, or removal from office of the President of the Senate, and who shall serve until the expiration of his term of office as Senator.

(2) President Pro Tempore–temporary succession. During the physical or mental incapacity of the President of the Senate to perform the duties of his office, or during the absence of the President of the Senate, the President Pro Tempore shall preside over the Senate.

(3) Other officers. The Senate shall elect its other officers.

Section 15. Officers of the House of Representatives. The House of Representatives shall elect its Speaker and other officers.

Section 16. Compensation and allowances. The members and officers of the General Assembly shall receive for their services the compensation and allowances prescribed by law. An increase in the compensation or allowances of members shall become effective at the beginning of the next regular session of the General Assembly following the session at which it was enacted.

Section 17. Journals. Each house shall keep a journal of its proceedings, which shall be printed and made public immediately after the adjournment of the General Assembly.

Section 18. Protests. Any member of either house may dissent from and protest against any act or resolve which he may think injurious to the public or to any individual, and have the reasons of his dissent entered on the journal.

Section 19. Record votes. Upon motion made in either house and seconded by one fifth of the members present, the yeas and nays upon any question shall be taken and entered upon the journal.

Section 20. Powers of the General Assembly. Each house shall be judge of the qualifications and elections of its own members, shall sit upon its own adjournment from day to day, and shall prepare bills to be enacted into laws. The two houses may jointly adjourn to any future day or other place. Either house may, of its own motion, adjourn for a period not in excess of three days.

Section 21. Style of the acts. The style of the acts shall be: "The General Assembly of North Carolina enacts:".

Section 22. Action on bills.

(1) Bills subject to veto by Governor; override of veto. Except as provided by subsections (2) through (6) of this section, all bills shall be read three times in each house and shall be signed by the presiding officer of each house before being presented to the Governor. If the Governor approves, the Governor shall sign it and it shall become a law; but if not, the Governor shall return it with objections, together with a veto message stating the reasons for such objections, to that house in which it shall have originated, which shall enter the objections and veto message at large

Checks and Balances

One of the executive powers set out in the North Carolina Constitution is the governor's power to veto bills. The corresponding power of the legislative branch is the General Assembly's power to override the governor's veto. For more than 200 years, the governor of North Carolina did not have this veto power. Then in 1996, voters approved an amendment that gives the governor the power to veto legislation—a power that most other governors have had for a long time.

3.01, 3.03

on its journal, and proceed to reconsider it. If after such reconsideration three-fifths of the members of that house present and voting shall agree to pass the bill, it shall be sent, together with the objections and veto message, to the other house, by which it shall likewise be reconsidered; and if approved by three-fifths of the members of that house present and voting, it shall become a law notwithstanding the objections of the Governor. In all such cases the votes of both houses shall be determined by yeas and nays, and the names of the members voting shall be entered on the journal of each house respectively.

(2) Amendments to Constitution of North Carolina. Every bill proposing a new or revised Constitution or an amendment or amendments to this Constitution or calling a convention of the people of this State, and containing no other matter, shall be submitted to the qualified voters of this State after it shall have been read three times in each house and signed by the presiding officers of both houses.

(3) Amendments to Constitution of the United States. Every bill approving an amendment to the Constitution of the United States, or applying for a convention to propose amendments to the Constitution of the United States, and containing no other matter, shall be read three times in each house before it becomes law, and shall be signed by the presiding officers of both houses.

(4) Joint resolutions. Every joint resolution shall be read three times in each house before it becomes effective and shall be signed by the presiding officers of both houses.

(5) Other exceptions. Every bill: (a) In which the General Assembly makes an appointment or appointments to public office and which contains no other matter; (b) Revising the senate districts and the apportionment of Senators among those districts and containing no other matter; (c) Revising the representative districts and the apportionment of Representatives among those districts and containing no other matter; or (d) Revising the districts for the election of members of the House of Representatives of the Congress of the United States and the apportionment of Representatives among those districts and containing no other matter, shall be read three times in each house before it becomes law and shall be signed by the presiding officers of both houses.

(6) Local bills. Every bill that applies in fewer than 15 counties shall be read three times in each house before it becomes law and shall be signed by the presiding officers of both houses. The exemption from veto by the Governor provided in this subsection does not apply if the bill, at the time it is signed by the presiding officers: (a) Would extend the application of a law signed by the presiding officers during that two year term of the General Assembly so that the law would apply in more than half the counties in the State, or (b) Would enact a law identical in effect to another law or laws signed by the presiding officers during that two year term of the General Assembly that the result of those laws taken together would be a law applying in more than half the counties in the State.

Notwithstanding any other language in this subsection, the exemption from veto provided by this subsection does not apply to any bill to enact a general law classified by population or other criteria, or to any bill that contains an appropriation from the State treasury.

(7) Time for action by Governor; reconvening of session. If any bill shall not be returned by the Governor within 10 days after it shall have been presented to him, the same shall be a law in like manner as if he had signed it, unless the General Assembly shall have adjourned:

(a) For more than 30 days jointly as provided under Section 20 of Article II of this Constitution; or

(b) Sine die

in which case it shall become a law unless, within 30 days after such adjournment, it is returned by the Governor with objections and veto message to that house in which it shall have originated. When the General Assembly has adjourned sine die or for more than 30 days jointly as provided under Section 20 of Article II of this Constitution, the Governor shall reconvene that session as provided by Section 5(11) of Article III of this Constitution for reconsideration of the bill, and if the Governor does not reconvene the session, the bill shall become law on the fortieth day after such adjournment. Notwithstanding the previous sentence, if the Governor prior to reconvening the session receives written requests dated no earlier than 30 days after such adjournment, signed by a majority of the members of each house that a reconvened session to reconsider vetoed legislation is unnecessary, the Governor shall not reconvene the session for that purpose and any legislation vetoed in accordance with this section after adjournment shall not become law.

(8) Return of bills after adjournment. For purposes of return of bills not approved by the Governor, each house shall designate an officer to receive returned bills during its adjournment. (1995, c. 5, s. 1.)

Section 23. Revenue bills. No law shall be enacted to raise money on the credit of the State, or to pledge the faith of the State directly or indirectly for the payment of any debt, or to impose any tax upon the people of the State, or to allow the counties, cities, or towns to do so, unless the bill for the purpose shall have been read three several times in each house of the General Assembly and passed three several readings, which readings shall have been on three different days, and shall have been agreed to by each house respectively, and unless the yeas and nays on the second and third readings of the bill shall have been entered on the journal.

Section 24. Limitations on local, private, and special legislation.

(1) Prohibited subjects. The General Assembly shall not enact any local, private, or special act or resolution:

(a) Relating to health, sanitation, and the abatement of nuisances;

(b) Changing the names of cities, towns, and townships;

(c) Authorizing the laying out, opening, altering, maintaining, or discontinuing of highways, streets, or alleys;

(d) Relating to ferries or bridges;

(e) Relating to non-navigable streams;

(f) Relating to cemeteries;

(g) Relating to the pay of jurors;

(h) Erecting new townships, or changing township lines, or establishing or changing the lines of school districts;

(i) Remitting fines, penalties, and forfeitures, or refunding moneys legally paid into the public treasury;

(j) Regulating labor, trade, mining, or manufacturing;

(k) Extending the time for the levy or collection of taxes or otherwise relieving any collector of taxes from the due performance of his official duties or his sureties from liability;

(l) Giving effect to informal wills and deeds;

(m) Granting a divorce or securing alimony in any individual case;

(n) Altering the name of any person, or legitimating any person not born in lawful wedlock, or restoring to the rights of citizenship any person convicted of a felony.

(2) Repeals. Nor shall the General Assembly enact any such local, private, or special act by the partial repeal of a general law; but the General Assembly may at any time repeal local, private, or special laws enacted by it.

(3) Prohibited acts void. Any local, private, or special act or resolution enacted in violation of the provisions of this Section shall be void.

(4) General laws. The General Assembly may enact general laws regulating the matters set out in this Section.

ARTICLE III   EXECUTIVE

Article III of the North Carolina Constitution is similar to Article II of the U.S. Constitution. It establishes the executive branch of the state government. The governor is the chief executive officer of the state, and he or she is responsible for the proper execution of all state laws and for preparing an annual budget for the state. The executive department is responsible for running the day-to-day affairs of the state. It includes state agencies that oversee everything from education to human rights to international trade and economic development. 3.02, 3.03

Section 1. Executive power.   The executive power of the State shall be vested in the Governor.

Section 2. Governor and Lieutenant Governor: election, term, and qualifications.

(1) Election and term. The Governor and Lieutenant Governor shall be elected by the qualified voters of the State in 1972 and every four years thereafter, at the same time and places as members of the General Assembly are elected. Their term of office shall be four years and shall commence

on the first day of January next after their election and continue until their successors are elected and qualified.

(2) Qualifications. No person shall be eligible for election to the office of Governor or Lieutenant Governor unless, at the time of his election, he shall have attained the age of 30 years and shall have been a citizen of the United States for five years and a resident of this State for two years immediately preceding his election. No person elected to the office of Governor or Lieutenant Governor shall be eligible for election to more than two consecutive terms of the same office.

Section 3. Succession to office of Governor.

(1) Succession as Governor. The Lieutenant Governor-elect shall become Governor upon the failure of the Governor-elect to qualify. The Lieutenant Governor shall become Governor upon the death, resignation, or removal from office of the Governor. The further order of succession to the office of Governor shall be prescribed by law. A successor shall serve for the remainder of the term of the Governor whom he succeeds and until a new Governor is elected and qualified.

(2) Succession as Acting Governor. During the absence of the Governor from the State, or during the physical or mental incapacity of the Governor to perform the duties of his office, the Lieutenant Governor shall be Acting Governor. The further order of succession as Acting Governor shall be prescribed by law.

(3) Physical incapacity. The Governor may, by a written statement filed with the Attorney General, declare that he is physically incapable of performing the duties of his office, and may thereafter in the same manner declare that he is physically capable of performing the duties of his office.

(4) Mental incapacity. The mental incapacity of the Governor to perform the duties of his office shall be determined only by joint resolution adopted by a vote of two-thirds of all the members of each house of the General Assembly. Thereafter, the mental capacity of the Governor to perform the duties of his office shall be determined only by joint resolution adopted by a vote of a majority of all the members of each house of the General Assembly. In all cases, the General Assembly shall give the Governor such notice as it may deem proper and shall allow him an opportunity to be heard before a joint session of the General Assembly before it takes final action. When the General Assembly is not in session, the Council of State, a majority of its members concurring, may convene it in extra session for the purpose of proceeding under this paragraph.

(5) Impeachment. Removal of the Governor from office for any other cause shall be by impeachment.

Section 4. Oath of office for Governor.
The Governor, before entering upon the duties of his office, shall, before any Justice of the Supreme Court, take an oath or affirmation that he will support the Constitution and laws of the United States and of the State of North Carolina, and that he will faithfully perform the duties pertaining to the office of governor.

Section 5. Duties of Governor.

(1) Residence. The Governor shall reside at the seat of government of this State.

(2) Information to General Assembly. The Governor shall from time to time give the General Assembly information of the affairs of the State and recommend to their consideration such measures as he shall deem expedient.

(3) Budget. The Governor shall prepare and recommend to the General Assembly a comprehensive budget of the anticipated revenue and proposed expenditures of the State for the ensuing fiscal period. The budget as enacted by the General Assembly shall be administered by the Governor.

> Even though the governor is required to prepare a budget for the state, it is the General Assembly that enacts the budget, not the governor. Then, once the budget has been approved, it is up to the governor to administer it. 3.02, 3.03

The total expenditures of the State for the fiscal period covered by the budget shall not exceed the total of receipts during that fiscal period and the surplus remaining in the State Treasury at the beginning of the period. To insure that the State does not incur a deficit for any fiscal period, the Governor shall continually survey the collection of the revenue and shall effect the necessary economies in State expenditures, after first making adequate provision for the prompt payment of the principal of and interest on bonds and notes of the State according to their terms, whenever he determines that receipts during the fiscal period, when added to any surplus remaining in the State Treasury at the beginning of the period, will not be sufficient to meet budgeted expenditures. This section shall not be construed to impair the power of the State to issue its bonds and notes within the limitations imposed in Article V of this Constitution, nor to impair the obligation of bonds and notes of the State now outstanding or issued hereafter.

(4) Execution of laws. The Governor shall take care that the laws be faithfully executed.

(5) Commander in Chief. The Governor shall be Commander in Chief of the military forces of the State except when they shall be called into the service of the United States.

(6) Clemency. The Governor may grant reprieves, commutations, and pardons, after conviction, for all offenses (except in cases of impeachment), upon such conditions as he may think proper, subject to regulations prescribed by law relative to the manner of applying for pardons. The terms reprieves, commutations, and pardons shall not include paroles.

(7) Extra sessions. The Governor may, on extraordinary occasions, by and with the advice of the Council of State, convene the General Assembly in extra session by his proclamation, stating therein the purpose or purposes for which they are thus convened.

(8) Appointments. The Governor shall nominate and by and with the advice and consent of a majority of the Senators appoint all officers whose appointments are not otherwise provided for.

(9) Information. The Governor may at any time require information in writing from the head of any administrative department or agency upon any subject relating to the duties of his office.

(10) Administrative reorganization. The General Assembly shall prescribe the functions, powers, and duties of the administrative departments and agencies of the State and may alter them from time to time, but the Governor may make such changes in the allocation of offices and agencies and in the allocation of those functions, powers, and duties as he considers necessary for efficient administration. If those changes affect existing law, they shall be set forth in executive orders, which shall be submitted to the General Assembly not later than the sixtieth calendar day of its session, and shall become effective and shall have the force of law upon adjournment sine die of the session, unless specifically disapproved by resolution of either house of the General Assembly or specifically modified by joint resolution of both houses of the General Assembly.

(11) Reconvened sessions. The Governor shall, when required by Section 22 of Article II of this Constitution, reconvene a session of the General Assembly. At such reconvened session, the General Assembly may only consider such bills as were returned by the Governor to that reconvened session for reconsideration. Such reconvened session shall begin on a date set by the Governor, but no later than 40 days after the General Assembly adjourned:

> (a) For more than 30 days jointly as provided under Section 20 of Article II of this Constitution; or
>
> (b) Sine die.

If the date of reconvening the session occurs after the expiration of the terms of office of the members of the General Assembly, then the members serving for the reconvened session shall be the members for the succeeding term. (1969, c. 932, s. 1; 1977, c. 690, s. 1; 1995, c. 5, s. 2.)

Section 6. Duties of the Lieutenant Governor.

The lieutenant governor must meet the same qualifications as the governor. In addition to his or her duties listed here, the lieutenant governor becomes governor if, for any reason, the governor is unable to serve. 3.02

The Lieutenant Governor shall be President of the Senate, but shall have no vote unless the Senate is equally divided. He shall perform such additional duties as the General Assembly or the Governor may assign to him. He shall receive the compensation and allowances prescribed by law.

Section 7. Other elective officers.

(1) Officers. A Secretary of State, an Auditor, a Treasurer, a Superintendent of Public Instruction, an Attorney General, a Commissioner of Agriculture, a Commissioner of Labor, and a Commissioner of Insurance shall be elected by the qualified voters of the State in 1972 and every four years thereafter, at the same time and places as members of the General Assembly are elected. Their term of office shall be four years and shall commence on the

Checks and Balances

The North Carolina Constitution gives the governor the power to nominate and appoint certain officers of state government. The constitution also requires that a majority of the Senate consent to (approve) those nominations. 3.01

Checks and Balances

Under Article III, Section 5, paragraph 10, the General Assembly establishes administrative departments and agencies of the state, but the governor is given the power to reorganize functions, powers, and duties of those agencies as may be necessary, unless one house of the General Assembly disapproves, or both houses modify the governor's plan. 3.03

first day of January next after their election and continue until their successors are elected and qualified.

The eight elected officers named in this paragraph, plus the governor and lieutenant governor, comprise the Council of State (created by Section 8, below). These eight elected officials work with the governor—in much the same way the governor's cabinet does—to carry out the laws of the state. The difference between these officers and cabinet members is that these officers are elected by voters and cannot be replaced by the governor. In general, the duties of these eight officers are: 3.03

Elected Officer	Duties
secretary of state	keeps official state records and provides information to citizens, businesses, and government agencies
auditor	reviews the state's financial practices and promotes efficient management of state agencies
treasurer	acts as the state's banker and chief investment officer, manages state funds, advises local governments on financial matters
superintendent of public instruction	supervises the state's public education system, serves as secretary to the state board of education
attorney general	heads the state's department of justice, represents the state in civil and criminal cases, and provides official opinions on state law
commissioner of agriculture	heads the department of agriculture, which supports the production, marketing, and consumption of agricultural products, and which inspects agricultural products for quality and safety
commissioner of labor	heads the department of labor, which protects the health and safety of workers, and which promotes technical and business training
commissioner of insurance	regulates and licenses insurance companies, investigates cases of insurance fraud, and provides insurance information to citizens

(2) Duties. Their respective duties shall be prescribed by law.

(3) Vacancies. If the office of any of these officers is vacated by death, resignation, or otherwise, it shall be the duty of the Governor to appoint another to serve until his successor is elected and qualified. Every such vacancy shall be filled by election at the first election for members of the General Assembly that occurs more than 60 days after the vacancy has taken place, and the person chosen shall hold the office for the remainder of the unexpired term fixed in this Section. When a vacancy occurs in the office of any of the officers named in this Section and the term expires on the first day of January succeeding the next election for members of the General Assembly, the Governor shall appoint to fill the vacancy for the unexpired term of the office.

(4) Interim officers. Upon the occurrence of a vacancy in the office of any one of these officers for any of the causes stated in the preceding paragraph, the Governor may appoint an interim officer to perform the duties of that office until a person is appointed or elected pursuant to this Section to fill the vacancy and is qualified.

(5) Acting officers. During the physical or mental incapacity of any one of these officers to perform the duties of his office, as determined pursuant to

this Section, the duties of his office shall be performed by an acting officer who shall be appointed by the Governor.

(6) Determination of incapacity. The General Assembly shall by law prescribe with respect to those officers, other than the Governor, whose offices are created by this Article, procedures for determining the physical or mental incapacity of any officer to perform the duties of his office, and for determining whether an officer who has been temporarily incapacitated has sufficiently recovered his physical or mental capacity to perform the duties of his office. Removal of those officers from office for any other cause shall be by impeachment.

(7) Special Qualifications for Attorney General. Only persons duly authorized to practice law in the courts of this State shall be eligible for appointment or election as Attorney General.

Section 8. Council of State. The Council of State shall consist of the officers whose offices are established by this Article.

> The Council of State consists of the ten state executive branch officials elected by the people of North Carolina: the governor, lieutenant governor, attorney general, state treasurer, state auditor, superintendent of public instruction, secretary of state, and commissioners of agriculture, insurance, and labor. 3.02

Section 9. Compensation and allowances. The officers whose offices are established by this Article shall at stated periods receive the compensation and allowances prescribed by law, which shall not be diminished during the time for which they have been chosen.

Section 10. Seal of State. There shall be a seal of the State, which shall be kept by the Governor and used by him as occasion may require, and shall be called "The Great Seal of the State of North Carolina". All grants or commissions shall be issued in the name and by the authority of the State of North Carolina, sealed with "The Great Seal of the State of North Carolina", and signed by the Governor.

Section 11. Administrative departments. Not later than July 1, 1975, all administrative departments, agencies, and offices of the State and their respective functions, powers, and duties shall be allocated by law among and within not more than 25 principal administrative departments so as to group them as far as practicable according to major purposes. Regulatory, quasi-judicial, and temporary agencies may, but need not, be allocated within a principal department.

> Article III, Section 11, authorized the governor to reorganize the state government so that the executive branch would consist of fewer than 25 administrative agencies. The General Assembly approved the reorganization plans, and today there are 18 executive departments in addition to the governor and lieutenant governor. Each agency has its own functions, powers, and duties as set out in the laws of North Carolina. 3.03

ARTICLE IV   JUDICIAL

Article IV of the North Carolina Constitution establishes the third branch of North Carolina's government, the judiciary. This article establishes the state court system, sets the jurisdiction of each level of court, and prescribes the qualifications for judges. It also gives the General Assembly the power to create and organize certain parts of the judicial system, such as the superior and district courts. North Carolina's judicial system is responsible for interpreting the laws and resolving disputes in a fair, prompt, and economic manner. 3.03

Checks and Balances

The North Carolina Constitution vests all judicial power of the state in the judicial branch of the government and prohibits the General Assembly from limiting the judicial department's power or jurisdiction and from diluting that power by creating courts other than those authorized by the constitution. 3.01, 3.03

Section 1. Judicial power. The judicial power of the State shall, except as provided in Section 3 of this Article, be vested in a Court for the Trial of Impeachments and in a General Court of Justice. The General Assembly shall have no power to deprive the judicial department of any power or jurisdiction that rightfully pertains to it as a co-ordinate department of the government, nor shall it establish or authorize any courts other than as permitted by this Article.

Section 2. General Court of Justice. The General Court of Justice shall constitute a unified judicial system for purposes of jurisdiction, operation, and administration, and shall consist of an Appellate Division, a Superior Court Division, and a District Court Division.

The current North Carolina judicial system comprises the three divisions listed here, but the Appellate Division has two levels, the North Carolina Supreme Court and the North Carolina Court of Appeals (Section 5, below). So the judicial system has four levels within the three divisions. In addition to the courts described in this Article, North Carolina is using innovative courts, such as drug treatment, family, and business courts, to deal with issues where the traditional adversarial system may not be the best way to resolve a problem. 3.02

Section 3. Judicial powers of administrative agencies.

The General Assembly may vest in administrative agencies established pursuant to law such judicial powers as may be reasonably necessary as an incident to the accomplishment of the purposes for which the agencies were created. Appeals from administrative agencies shall be to the General Court of Justice.

Section 3 allows the General Assembly to give some administrative agencies, such as the Department of Crime Control and Public Safety or the Department of Environment and Natural Resources, limited judicial powers to enforce or resolve disputes over their rules and regulations. Ultimately, however, all administrative law decisions are appealable for judicial review in Superior Court. 3.02, 3.03

Section 4. Court for the Trial of Impeachments. The House of Representatives solely shall have the power of impeaching. The Court for the Trial of Impeachments shall be the Senate. When the Governor or Lieutenant Governor is impeached, the Chief Justice shall preside over the Court. A majority of the members shall be necessary to a quorum, and no person shall be convicted without the concurrence of two-thirds of the Senators present. Judgment upon conviction shall not extend beyond removal from and disqualification to hold office in this State, but the party shall be liable to indictment and punishment according to law.

Section 5. Appellate division.
The Appellate Division of the General Court of Justice shall consist of the Supreme Court and the Court of Appeals.

Section 6. Supreme Court.
(1) Membership. The Supreme Court shall consist of a Chief Justice and six Associate Justices, but the General Assembly may increase the number of Associate Justices to not more than eight. In the event the Chief Justice is unable, on account of absence or temporary incapacity, to perform any of the duties placed upon him, the senior Associate Justice available may discharge those duties.

(2) Sessions of the Supreme Court. The sessions of the Supreme Court shall be held in the City of Raleigh unless otherwise provided by the General Assembly.

> The Supreme Court is the highest court in the judicial system. It reviews appeals of decisions from lower state courts. The Court's main purpose is to decide the constitutionality of North Carolina's laws and to determine whether those laws are being properly interpreted and applied. North Carolina's Supreme Court justices are elected by the voters of the state and serve for a term of eight years. Justices may serve more than one term if voters reelect them. 3.02, 3.03

Section 7. Court of Appeals.
The structure, organization, and composition of the Court of Appeals shall be determined by the General Assembly. The Court shall have not less than five members, and may be authorized to sit in divisions, or other than en banc. Sessions of the Court shall be held at such times and places as the General Assembly may prescribe.

> Judges of the Court of Appeals are also elected by the voters for terms of eight years. The Court of Appeals handles all appeals from superior and district courts except for death penalty cases. 3.02

Section 8. Retirement of Justices and Judges.
The General Assembly shall provide by general law for the retirement of Justices and Judges of the General Court of Justice, and may provide for the temporary recall of any retired Justice or Judge to serve on the court or courts of the division from which he was retired. The General Assembly shall also prescribe maximum age limits for service as a Justice or Judge.

Section 9. Superior Courts.
(1) Superior Court districts. The General Assembly shall, from time to time, divide the State into a convenient number of Superior Court judicial districts and shall provide for the election of one or more Superior Court Judges for each district. Each regular Superior Court Judge shall reside in the district for which he is elected. The General Assembly may provide by general law for the selection or appointment of special or emergency Superior Court Judges not selected for a particular judicial district.

> Superior courts are trial courts—courts in which cases are first heard. Superior courts try all felony criminal cases and civil cases involving amounts of more than $10,000. They may also hear appeals from district courts on some issues. Cases in superior court are tried by juries of 12 citizens, although a jury trial can be waived in some civil cases. Superior court judges are elected by the voters to eight-year terms. 3.02

(2) Open at all times; sessions for trial of cases. The Superior Courts shall be open at all times for the transaction of all business except the trial of issues of fact requiring a jury. Regular trial sessions of the Superior Court shall be held at times fixed pursuant to a calendar of courts promulgated by the Supreme Court. At least two sessions for the trial of jury cases shall be held annually in each county.

(3) Clerks. A Clerk of the Superior Court for each county shall be elected for a term of four years by the qualified voters thereof, at the same time and places as members of the General Assembly are elected. If the office of Clerk of the Superior Court becomes vacant otherwise than by the expiration of the term, or if the people fail to elect, the senior regular resident Judge of the Superior Court serving the county shall appoint to fill the vacancy until an election can be regularly held.

Section 10. District Courts.

District courts are also trial courts. They hear civil cases such as divorce, child custody, and child support cases, and other civil disputes involving less than $10,000. District courts also try misdemeanor criminal cases and juvenile cases involving neglect, abuse, or delinquency. Cases are tried by a judge without a jury. District court judges are elected by voters to four-year terms. 3.02

The General Assembly shall, from time to time, divide the State into a convenient number of local court districts and shall prescribe where the District Courts shall sit, but a District Court must sit in at least one place in each county. District Judges shall be elected for each district for a term of four years, in a manner prescribed by law. When more than one District Judge is authorized and elected for a district, the Chief Justice of the Supreme Court shall designate one of the judges as Chief District Judge. Every District Judge shall reside in the district for which he is elected. For each county, the senior regular resident Judge of the Superior Court serving the county shall appoint from nominations submitted by the Clerk of the Superior Court of the county, one or more Magistrates who shall be officers of the District Court. The initial term of appointment for a magistrate shall be for two years and subsequent terms shall be for four years.

The number of District Judges and Magistrates shall, from time to time, be determined by the General Assembly. Vacancies in the office of District Judge shall be filled for the unexpired term in a manner prescribed by law. Vacancies in the office of Magistrate shall be filled for the unexpired term in the manner provided for original appointment to the office, unless otherwise provided by the General Assembly. (2004-128, s. 16.)

In addition to district court judges, there are court officers known as *magistrates*. Magistrates are judicial officers of the district court and have jurisdiction in both criminal and civil cases. For example, in criminal cases, a magistrate determines if and what further action is warranted when a police officer or a citizen claims that a crime has been committed. Magistrates also issue arrest warrants or summonses, search warrants, subpoenas, and civil warrants. Magistrates conduct hearings to set bail and conditions of release for individuals who have been charged with a criminal offense. Magistrates also have responsibilities in civil cases, including deciding evictions and cases involving up to $5,000.00 in damages in Small Claims Court and issuing important processes in cases of alleged domestic violence. 3.02

Section 11. Assignment of Judges. The Chief Justice of the Supreme Court, acting in accordance with rules of the Supreme Court, shall make assignments of Judges of the Superior Court and may transfer District Judges from one district to another for temporary or specialized duty. The principle of rotating Superior Court Judges among the various districts of a division is a salutary one and shall be observed. For this purpose the General Assembly may divide the State into a number of judicial divisions. Subject to the general supervision of the Chief Justice of the Supreme Court, assignment of District Judges within each local court district shall be made by the Chief District Judge.

Section 12. Jurisdiction of the General Court of Justice.

(1) Supreme Court. The Supreme Court shall have jurisdiction to review upon appeal any decision of the courts below, upon any matter of law or legal inference. The jurisdiction of the Supreme Court over "issues of fact" and "questions of fact" shall be the same exercised by it prior to the adoption of this Article, and the Court may issue any remedial writs necessary to give it general supervision and control over the proceedings of the other courts. The Supreme Court also has jurisdiction to review, when authorized by law, direct appeals from a final order or decision of the North Carolina Utilities Commission.

In the 1830 case of *State* v. *Mann*, defendant John Mann was accused of injuring a slave, Lydia, and was found guilty by a jury of men in his community of the crimes of assault and battery. Mann was fined $5.00 for his offense. At the time, North Carolina had no statutes relating to the treatment of slaves. Mann's conviction was based on a common-law premise that his punishment of Lydia was "cruel and unwarrantable and disproportionate to the offense." Mann appealed his conviction to the North Carolina Supreme Court. Judge Thomas Ruffin wrote, "The power of the master must be *absolute*, to render the *submission* of the slave *perfect*. It would not do to allow the rights of the master to be brought into discussion in the courts of justice. The slave, to remain a slave, must be sensible [must know] that there is no appeal from his master." Ruffin's phrase "rights of the master" referred to Article XII of the North Carolina Constitution, ". . . no freeman ought to be . . . disseized of his freehold liberties or privileges . . ." and held that the absolute power over a slave is a liberty or a privilege of a freeman. This principle meant that, unless the legislature passed a statute saying otherwise, slave owners could not be punished for injuring their own property. As a result, the supreme court overturned Mann's conviction. This case helped to establish the supremacy of the state constitution, which was based in part on common-law principles. **NC** 3.05

(2) Court of Appeals. The Court of Appeals shall have such appellate jurisdiction as the General Assembly may prescribe.

(3) Superior Court. Except as otherwise provided by the General Assembly, the Superior Court shall have original general jurisdiction throughout the State. The Clerks of the Superior Court shall have such jurisdiction and powers as the General Assembly shall prescribe by general law uniformly applicable in every county of the State.

(4) District Courts; Magistrates. The General Assembly shall, by general law uniformly applicable in every local court district of the State, prescribe the jurisdiction and powers of the District Courts and Magistrates.

(5) Waiver. The General Assembly may by general law provide that the jurisdictional limits may be waived in civil cases.

(6) Appeals. The General Assembly shall by general law provide a proper system of appeals. Appeals from Magistrates shall be heard de novo, with the right of trial by jury as defined in this Constitution and the laws of this State.

Section 13. Forms of action; rules of procedure.

(1) Forms of action. There shall be in this State but one form of action for the enforcement or protection of private rights or the redress of private wrongs, which shall be denominated a civil action, and in which there shall be a right to have issues of fact tried before a jury. Every action prosecuted by the people of the State as a party against a person charged with a public offense, for the punishment thereof, shall be termed a criminal action.

(2) Rules of procedure. The Supreme Court shall have exclusive authority to make rules of procedure and practice for the Appellate Division. The General Assembly may make rules of procedure and practice for the Superior Court and District Court Divisions, and the General Assembly may delegate this authority to the Supreme Court. No rule of procedure or practice shall abridge substantive rights or abrogate or limit the right of trial by jury. If the General Assembly should delegate to the Supreme Court the rule-making power, the General Assembly may, nevertheless, alter, amend, or repeal any rule of procedure or practice adopted by the Supreme Court for the Superior Court or District Court Divisions.

Section 14. Waiver of jury trial.
In all issues of fact joined in any court, the parties in any civil case may waive the right to have the issues determined by a jury, in which case the finding of the judge upon the facts shall have the force and effect of a verdict by a jury.

Section 15. Administration.
The General Assembly shall provide for an administrative office of the courts to carry out the provisions of this Article.

Section 16. Terms of office and election of Justices of the Supreme Court, Judges of the Court of Appeals, and Judges of the Superior Court.

Justices of the Supreme Court, Judges of the Court of Appeals, and regular Judges of the Superior Court shall be elected by the qualified voters and shall hold office for terms of eight years and until their successors are elected and qualified. Justices of the Supreme Court and Judges of the Court of Appeals shall be elected by the qualified voters of the State. Regular Judges of the Superior Court may be elected by the qualified voters of the State or by the voters of their respective districts, as the General Assembly may prescribe.

Section 17. Removal of Judges, Magistrates and Clerks.

(1) Removal of Judges by the General Assembly. Any Justice or Judge of the General Court of Justice may be removed from office for mental or physi-

cal incapacity by joint resolution of two-thirds of all the members of each house of the General Assembly. Any Justice or Judge against whom the General Assembly may be about to proceed shall receive notice thereof, accompanied by a copy of the causes alleged for his removal, at least 20 days before the day on which either house of the General Assembly shall act thereon. Removal from office by the General Assembly for any other cause shall be by impeachment.

(2) Additional method of removal of Judges. The General Assembly shall prescribe a procedure, in addition to impeachment and address set forth in this Section, for the removal of a Justice or Judge of the General Court of Justice for mental or physical incapacity interfering with the performance of his duties which is, or is likely to become, permanent, and for the censure and removal of a Justice or Judge of the General Court of Justice for willful misconduct in office, willful and persistent failure to perform his duties, habitual intemperance, conviction of a crime involving moral turpitude, or conduct prejudicial to the administration of justice that brings the judicial office into disrepute.

(3) Removal of Magistrates. The General Assembly shall provide by general law for the removal of Magistrates for misconduct or mental or physical incapacity.

(4) Removal of Clerks. Any Clerk of the Superior Court may be removed from office for misconduct or mental or physical incapacity by the senior regular resident Superior Court Judge serving the county. Any Clerk against whom proceedings are instituted shall receive written notice of the charges against him at least 10 days before the hearing upon the charges. Any Clerk so removed from office shall be entitled to an appeal as provided by law.

Section 18. District Attorney and Prosecutorial Districts.

(1) District Attorneys. The General Assembly shall, from time to time, divide the State into a convenient number of prosecutorial districts, for each of which a District Attorney shall be chosen for a term of four years by the qualified voters thereof, at the same time and places as members of the General Assembly are elected. Only persons duly authorized to practice law in the courts of this State shall be eligible for election or appointment as a District Attorney. The District Attorney shall advise the officers of justice in his district, be responsible for the prosecution on behalf of the State of all criminal actions in the Superior Courts of his district, perform such duties related to appeals therefrom as the Attorney General may require, and perform such other duties as the General Assembly may prescribe.

(2) Prosecution in District Court Division. Criminal actions in the District Court Division shall be prosecuted in such manner as the General Assembly may prescribe by general law uniformly applicable in every local court district of the State.

Section 19. Vacancies. Unless otherwise provided in this Article, all vacancies occurring in the offices provided for by this Article shall be filled by appointment of the Governor, and the appointees shall hold their places until the next election for members of the General Assembly that is held more than 60 days after the vacancy occurs, when elections shall be held to fill the offices. When the unexpired term of any of the offices named in this Article of the Constitution in which a vacancy has occurred, and in which it is herein provided that the Governor shall fill the vacancy, expires on the first day of January succeeding the next election for members of the General Assembly, the Governor shall appoint to fill that vacancy for the unexpired term of the office. If any person elected or appointed to any of these offices shall fail to qualify, the office shall be appointed to, held and filled as provided in case of vacancies occurring therein. All incumbents of these offices shall hold until their successors are qualified.

Section 20. Revenues and expenses of the judicial department. The General Assembly shall provide for the establishment of a schedule of court fees and costs which shall be uniform throughout the State within each division of the General Court of Justice. The operating expenses of the judicial department, other than compensation to process servers and other locally paid non-judicial officers, shall be paid from State funds.

Section 21. Fees, salaries, and emoluments. The General Assembly shall prescribe and regulate the fees, salaries, and emoluments of all officers provided for in this Article, but the salaries of Judges shall not be diminished during their continuance in office. In no case shall the compensation of any Judge or Magistrate be dependent upon his decision or upon the collection of costs.

Section 22. Qualification of Justices and Judges. Only persons duly authorized to practice law in the courts of this State shall be eligible for election or appointment as a Justice of the Supreme Court, Judge of the Court of Appeals, Judge of the Superior Court, or Judge of District Court. This section shall not apply to persons elected to or serving in such capacities on or before January 1, 1981.

ARTICLE V   FINANCE

Article V of the North Carolina Constitution establishes the powers of the state and local governments to tax, authorizes the creation of special taxing units, and places limits on what can be taxed and what may be exempt from taxation. It also allows the General Assembly to authorize financing of health care facilities, airport and seaport projects, higher education projects, and capital projects for industrial development and agricultural development. All government spending, at all levels, is done in accordance with budgets and appropriations approved by the relevant government body, such as the General Assembly or a city council. 3.08, 3.09

Section 1. No capitation tax to be levied. No poll or capitation tax shall be levied by the General Assembly or by any county, city or town, or other taxing unit.

Section 2. State and local taxation.

(1) Power of taxation. The power of taxation shall be exercised in a just and equitable manner, for public purposes only, and shall never be surrendered, suspended, or contracted away.

(2) Classification. Only the General Assembly shall have the power to classify property for taxation, which power shall be exercised only on a State-wide basis and shall not be delegated. No class of property shall be taxed except by uniform rule, and every classification shall be made by general law uniformly applicable in every county, city and town, and other unit of local government.

> The General Assembly determines what property will be taxed, but local governments determine the amount of the tax. In certain situations, state or local voters must approve these taxes. 3.08

(3) Exemptions. Property belonging to the State, counties, and municipal corporations shall be exempt from taxation. The General Assembly may exempt cemeteries and property held for educational, scientific, literary, cultural, charitable, or religious purposes, and, to a value not exceeding $300, any personal property. The General Assembly may exempt from taxation not exceeding $1,000 in value of property held and used as the place of residence of the owner. Every exemption shall be on a State-wide basis and shall be made by general law uniformly applicable in every county, city and town, and other unit of local government. No taxing authority other than the General Assembly may grant exemptions, and the General Assembly shall not delegate the powers accorded to it by this subsection.

(4) Special tax areas. Subject to the limitations imposed by Section 4, the General Assembly may enact general laws authorizing the governing body of any county, city, or town to define territorial areas and to levy taxes within those areas, in addition to those levied throughout the county, city, or town, in order to finance, provide, or maintain services, facilities, and functions in addition to or to a greater extent than those financed, provided, or maintained for the entire county, city, or town.

(5) Purposes of property tax. The General Assembly shall not authorize any county, city or town, special district, or other unit of local government to levy taxes on property, except for purposes authorized by general law uniformly applicable throughout the State, unless the tax is approved by a majority of the qualified voters of the unit who vote thereon.

(6) Income tax. The rate of tax on incomes shall not in any case exceed ten percent, and there shall be allowed personal exemptions and deductions so that only net incomes are taxed.

> This paragraph is an example of both the power to tax and a limitation on that power. The state can tax personal income, but the tax rate is limited to 10 percent or less, and there must be exemptions and deductions allowed. 3.03, 3.08

(7) Contracts. The General Assembly may enact laws whereby the State, any county, city or town, and any other public corporation may contract with and appropriate money to any person, association, or corporation for the accomplishment of public purposes only.

(1) Authorized purposes; two-thirds limitation. The General Assembly shall have no power to contract debts secured by a pledge of the faith and credit of the State, unless approved by a majority of the qualified voters of the State who vote thereon, except for the following purposes:

(a) to fund or refund a valid existing debt;

(b) to supply an unforeseen deficiency in the revenue;

(c) to borrow in anticipation of the collection of taxes due and payable within the current fiscal year to an amount not exceeding 50 per cent of such taxes;

(d) to suppress riots or insurrections, or to repel invasions;

(e) to meet emergencies immediately threatening the public health or safety, as conclusively determined in writing by the Governor;

(f) for any other lawful purpose, to the extent of two-thirds of the amount by which the State's outstanding indebtedness shall have been reduced during the next preceding biennium.

(2) Gift or loan of credit regulated. The General Assembly shall have no power to give or lend the credit of the State in aid of any person, association, or corporation, except a corporation in which the State has a controlling interest, unless the subject is submitted to a direct vote of the people of the State, and is approved by a majority of the qualified voters who vote thereon.

(3) Definitions. A debt is incurred within the meaning of this Section when the State borrows money. A pledge of the faith and credit within the meaning of this Section is a pledge of the taxing power. A loan of credit within the meaning of this Section occurs when the State exchanges its obligations with or in any way guarantees the debts of an individual, association, or private corporation.

(4) Certain debts barred. The General Assembly shall never assume or pay any debt or obligation, express or implied, incurred in aid of insurrection or rebellion against the United States. Neither shall the General Assembly assume or pay any debt or bond incurred or issued by authority of the Convention of 1868, the special session of the General Assembly of 1868, or the General Assemblies of 1868-69 and 1869-70, unless the subject is submitted to the people of the State and is approved by a majority of all the qualified voters at a referendum held for that sole purpose.

(5) Outstanding debt. Except as provided in subsection (4), nothing in this Section shall be construed to invalidate or impair the obligation of any bond, note, or other evidence of indebtedness outstanding or authorized for issue as of July 1, 1973.

(1) Regulation of borrowing and debt. The General Assembly shall enact general laws relating to the borrowing of money secured by a pledge of the faith and credit and the contracting of other debts by counties, cities and

towns, special districts, and other units, authorities, and agencies of local government.

(2) Authorized purposes; two-thirds limitation. The General Assembly shall have no power to authorize any county, city or town, special district, or other unit of local government to contract debts secured by a pledge of its faith and credit unless approved by a majority of the qualified voters of the unit who vote thereon, except for the following purposes:

(a) to fund or refund a valid existing debt;

(b) to supply an unforeseen deficiency in the revenue;

(c) to borrow in anticipation of the collection of taxes due and payable within the current fiscal year to an amount not exceeding 50 per cent of such taxes;

(d) to suppress riots or insurrections;

(e) to meet emergencies immediately threatening the public health or safety, as conclusively determined in writing by the Governor;

(f) for purposes authorized by general laws uniformly applicable through-out the State, to the extent of two-thirds of the amount by which the unit's outstanding indebtedness shall have been reduced during the next preceding fiscal year.

(3) Gift or loan of credit regulated. No county, city or town, special district, or other unit of local government shall give or lend its credit in aid of any person, association, or corporation, except for public purposes as authorized by general law, and unless approved by a majority of the qualified voters of the unit who vote thereon.

(4) Certain debts barred. No county, city or town, or other unit of local government shall assume or pay any debt or the interest thereon contracted directly or indirectly in aid or support of rebellion or insurrection against the United States.

(5) Definitions. A debt is incurred within the meaning of this Section when a county, city or town, special district, or other unit, authority, or agency of local government borrows money. A pledge of faith and credit within the meaning of this Section is a pledge of the taxing power. A loan of credit within the meaning of this Section occurs when a county, city or town, special district, or other unit, authority, or agency of local government exchanges its obligations with or in any way guarantees the debts of an individual, association, or private corporation.

(6) Outstanding debt. Except as provided in subsection (4), nothing in this Section shall be construed to invalidate or impair the obligation of any bond, note, or other evidence of indebtedness outstanding or authorized for issue as of July 1, 1973.

Section 5. Acts levying taxes to state objects. Every act of the General Assembly levying a tax shall state the special object to which it is to be applied, and it shall be applied to no other purpose.

Section 6. Inviolability of sinking funds and retirement funds.

(1) Sinking funds. The General Assembly shall not use or authorize to be used any part of the amount of any sinking fund for any purpose other than the retirement of the bonds for which the sinking fund has been created, except that these funds may be invested as authorized by law.

(2) Retirement funds. Neither the General Assembly nor any public officer, employee, or agency shall use or authorize to be used any part of the funds of the Teachers' and State Employees' Retirement System or the Local Governmental Employees' Retirement System for any purpose other than retirement system benefits and purposes, administrative expenses, and refunds; except that retirement system funds may be invested as authorized by law, subject to the investment limitation that the funds of the Teachers' and State Employees' Retirement System and the Local Governmental Employees' Retirement System shall not be applied, diverted, loaned to, or used by the State, any State agency, State officer, public officer, or public employee.

Section 7. Drawing public money.

(1) State treasury. No money shall be drawn from the State treasury but in consequence of appropriations made by law, and an accurate account of the receipts and expenditures of State funds shall be published annually.

(2) Local treasury. No money shall be drawn from the treasury of any county, city or town, or other unit of local government except by authority of law.

Section 8. Health care facilities.

Notwithstanding any other provisions of this Constitution, the General Assembly may enact general laws to authorize the State, counties, cities or towns, and other State and local governmental entities to issue revenue bonds to finance or refinance for any such governmental entity or any nonprofit private corporation, regardless of any church or religious relationship, the cost of acquiring, constructing, and financing health care facility projects to be operated to serve and benefit the public; provided, no cost incurred earlier than two years prior to the effective date of this section shall be refinanced.

Such bonds shall be payable from the revenues, gross or net, of any such projects and any other health care facilities of any such governmental entity or nonprofit private corporation pledged therefor; shall not be secured by a pledge of the full faith and credit, or deemed to create an indebtedness requiring voter approval of any governmental entity; and may be secured by an agreement which may provide for the conveyance of title of, with or without consideration, any such project or facilities to the governmental entity or nonprofit private corporation.

The power of eminent domain shall not be used pursuant hereto for nonprofit private corporations.

Section 9. Capital projects for industry. Notwithstanding any other provision of this Constitution, the General Assembly may enact general laws to authorize counties to create authorities to issue revenue bonds to finance, but not to refinance, the cost of capital projects consisting of industrial, manufacturing and pollution control facilities for industry and pollution control facilities for public utilities, and to refund such bonds.

In no event shall such revenue bonds be secured by or payable from any public moneys whatsoever, but such revenue bonds shall be secured by and payable only from revenues or property derived from private parties. All such capital projects and all transactions therefor shall be subject to taxation to the extent such projects and transactions would be subject to taxation if no public body were involved therewith; provided, however, that the General Assembly may provide that the interest on such revenue bonds shall be exempt from income taxes within the State.

The power of eminent domain shall not be exercised to provide any property for any such capital project.

Section 10. Joint ownership of generation and transmission facilities.

In addition to other powers conferred upon them by law, municipalities owning or operating facilities for the generation, transmission or distribution of electric power and energy and joint agencies formed by such municipalities for the purpose of owning or operating facilities for the generation and transmission of electric power and energy (each, respectively, "a unit of municipal government") may jointly or severally own, operate and maintain works, plants and facilities, within or without the State, for the generation and transmission of electric power and energy, or both, with any person, firm, association or corporation, public or private, engaged in the generation, transmission or distribution of electric power and energy for resale (each, respectively, "a co-owner") within this State or any state contiguous to this State, and may enter into and carry out agreements with respect to such jointly owned facilities.

For the purpose of financing its share of the cost of any such jointly owned electric generation or transmission facilities, a unit of municipal government may issue its revenue bonds in the manner prescribed by the General Assembly, payable as to both principal and interest solely from and secured by a lien and charge on all or any part of the revenue derived, or to be derived, by such unit of municipal government from the ownership and operation of its electric facilities; provided, however, that no unit of municipal government shall be liable, either jointly or severally, for any acts, omissions or obligations of any co-owner, nor shall any money or property of any unit of municipal government be credited or otherwise applied to the account of any co-owner or be charged with any debt, lien or mortgage as a result of any debt or obligation of any co-owner.

Section 11. Capital projects for agriculture. Notwithstanding any other provision of the Constitution the General Assembly may enact general laws to authorize the creation of an agency to issue revenue bonds to finance the cost of capital projects consisting of agricultural facilities, and to refund such bonds.

In no event shall such revenue bonds be secured by or payable from any public moneys whatsoever, but such revenue bonds shall be secured by and payable only from revenues or property derived from private parties. All such capital projects and all transactions therefor shall be subject to taxation to the extent such projects and transactions would be subject to taxation if no public body were involved therewith; provided, however, that the General Assembly may provide that the interest on such revenue bonds shall be exempt from income taxes within the State.

The power of eminent domain shall not be exercised to provide any property for any such capital project.

Section 12. Higher Education Facilities.
Notwithstanding any other provisions of this Constitution, the General Assembly may enact general laws to authorize the State or any State entity to issue revenue bonds to finance and refinance the cost of acquiring, constructing, and financing higher education facilities to be operated to serve and benefit the public for any nonprofit private corporation, regardless of any church or religious relationship provided no cost incurred earlier than five years prior to the effective date of this section shall be refinanced. Such bonds shall be payable from any revenues or assets of any such nonprofit private corporation pledged therefor, shall not be secured by a pledge of the full faith and credit of the State or such State entity or deemed to create an indebtedness requiring voter approval of the State or such entity, and, where the title to such facilities is vested in the State or any State entity, may be secured by an agreement which may provide for the conveyance of title to, with or without consideration, such facilities to the nonprofit private corporation. The power of eminent domain shall not be used pursuant hereto.

Section 13. Seaport and airport facilities.

(1) Notwithstanding any other provision of this Constitution, the General Assembly may enact general laws to grant to the State, counties, municipalities, and other State and local governmental entities all powers useful in connection with the development of new and existing seaports and airports, and to authorize such public bodies:

> (a) to acquire, construct, own, own jointly with public and private parties, lease as lessee, mortgage, sell, lease as lessor, or otherwise dispose of lands and facilities and improvements, including undivided interest therein;

> (b) to finance and refinance for public and private parties seaport and airport facilities and improvements which relate to, develop or further waterborne or airborne commerce and cargo and passenger traffic, including commercial, industrial, manufacturing, processing, mining, transportation, distribution, storage, marine, aviation and environmental facilities and improvements; and

(c) to secure any such financing or refinancing by all or any portion of their revenues, income or assets or other available monies associated with any of their seaport or airport facilities and with the facilities and improvements to be financed or refinanced, and by foreclosable liens on all or any part of their properties associated with any of their seaport or airport facilities and with the facilities and improvements to be financed or refinanced, but in no event to create a debt secured by a pledge of the faith and credit of the State or any other public body in the State.

Section 14. Project development financing. Notwithstanding Section 4 of this Article, the General Assembly may enact general laws authorizing any county, city, or town to define territorial areas in the county, city, or town and borrow money to be used to finance public improvements associated with private development projects within the territorial areas, as provided in this section. The General Assembly shall set forth by statute the method for determining the size of the territorial area and the issuing unit. This method is conclusive. When a territorial area is defined pursuant to this section, the county shall determine the current assessed value of taxable real and personal property in the territorial area. Thereafter, property in the territorial area continues to be subject to taxation to the same extent and in like manner as property not in the territorial area, but the net proceeds of taxes levied on the excess, if any, of the assessed value of taxable real and personal property in the territorial area at the time the taxes are levied over the assessed value of taxable real and personal property in the territorial area at the time the territorial area was defined may be set aside. The instruments of indebtedness authorized by this section shall be secured by these set aside proceeds. The General Assembly may authorize a county, city, or town issuing these instruments of indebtedness to pledge, as additional security, revenues available to the issuing unit from sources other than the issuing unit's exercise of its taxing power. As long as no revenues are pledged other than the set aside proceeds authorized by this section and the revenues authorized in the preceding sentence, these instruments of indebtedness may be issued without approval by referendum. The county, city, or town may not pledge as security for these instruments of indebtedness any property tax revenues other than the set aside proceeds authorized in this section, or in any other manner pledge its full faith and credit as security for these instruments of indebtedness unless a vote of the people is held as required by and in compliance with the requirements of Section 4 of this Article.

Notwithstanding the provisions of Section 2 of this Article, the General Assembly may enact general laws authorizing a county, city, or town that has defined a territorial area pursuant to this section to assess property within the territorial area at a minimum value if agreed to by the owner of the property, which agreed minimum value shall be binding on the current owner and any future owners as long as the defined territorial area is in effect. (2003 403, s.1.)

ARTICLE VI   SUFFRAGE AND ELIGIBILITY TO OFFICE

Voting is one of the key responsibilities and privileges in a democratic society. It is one of the most important ways to make your voice heard by your elected officials. To register to vote in North Carolina, you must: (1) Be a U.S. citizen, (2) Have lived in North Carolina for at least one year, (3) Be a resident of the county in which you register, (4) Be 18 years old by the date of the next general election, and (5) Have had your voting rights restored if you had been convicted of a felony or judged to be mentally incompetent. 🖃 3.01

Section 1. Who may vote. Every person born in the United States and every person who has been naturalized, 18 years of age, and possessing the qualifications set out in this Article, shall be entitled to vote at any election by the people of the State, except as herein otherwise provided.

Section 2. Qualifications of voter.

(1) Residence period for State elections. Any person who has resided in the State of North Carolina for one year and in the precinct, ward, or other election district for 30 days next preceding an election, and possesses the other qualifications set out in this Article, shall be entitled to vote at any election held in this State. Removal from one precinct, ward, or other election district to another in this State shall not operate to deprive any person of the right to vote in the precinct, ward, or other election district from which that person has removed until 30 days after the removal.

(2) Residence period for presidential elections. The General Assembly may reduce the time of residence for persons voting in presidential elections. A person made eligible by reason of a reduction in time of residence shall possess the other qualifications set out in this Article, shall only be entitled to vote for President and Vice President of the United States or for electors for President and Vice President, and shall not thereby become eligible to hold office in this State.

(3) Disqualification of felon. No person adjudged guilty of a felony against this State or the United States, or adjudged guilty of a felony in another state that also would be a felony if it had been committed in this State, shall be permitted to vote unless that person shall be first restored to the rights of citizenship in the manner prescribed by law.

Section 3. Registration. Every person offering to vote shall be at the time legally registered as a voter as herein prescribed and in the manner provided by law. The General Assembly shall enact general laws governing the registration of voters.

Even if a person qualifies to vote, he or she must still register to vote with the local board of elections in the county where he or she lives in order to become a voter. 🖃 3.03

Section 4. Qualification for registration. Every person presenting himself for registration shall be able to read and write any section of the Constitution in the English language.

Section 5. Elections by people and General Assembly. All elections by the people shall be by ballot, and all elections by the General Assembly shall be viva voce. A contested election for any office established by Article III of this Constitution shall be determined by joint ballot of both houses of the General Assembly in the manner prescribed by law.

Section 6. Eligibility to elective office. Every qualified voter in North Carolina who is 21 years of age, except as in this Constitution disqualified, shall be eligible for election by the people to office.

> Even though a person can vote at age 18, he or she is not eligible to be elected to office until the age of 21. 3.03, 3.07

Section 7. Oath. Before entering upon the duties of an office, a person elected or appointed to the office shall take and subscribe the following oath: "I, _____, do solemnly swear (or affirm) that I will support and maintain the Constitution and laws of the United States, and the Constitution and laws of North Carolina not inconsistent therewith, and that I will faithfully discharge the duties of my office as _____, so help me God."

Section 8. Disqualifications for office. The following persons shall be disqualified for office: First, any person who shall deny the being of Almighty God. Second, with respect to any office that is filled by election by the people, any person who is not qualified to vote in an election for that office. Third, any person who has been adjudged guilty of treason or any other felony against this State or the United States, or any person who has been adjudged guilty of a felony in another state that also would be a felony if it had been committed in this State, or any person who has been adjudged guilty of corruption or malpractice in any office, or any person who has been removed by impeachment from any office, and who has not been restored to the rights of citizenship in the manner prescribed by law.

Section 9. Dual office holding.

(1) Prohibitions. It is salutary that the responsibilities of self-government be widely shared among the citizens of the State and that the potential abuse of authority inherent in the holding of multiple offices by an individual be avoided. Therefore, no person who holds any office or place of trust or profit under the United States or any department thereof, or under any other state or government, shall be eligible to hold any office in this State that is filled by election by the people. No person shall hold concurrently any two offices in this State that are filled by election of the people. No person shall hold concurrently any two or more appointive offices or places of trust or profit, or any combination of elective and appointive offices or places of trust or profit, except as the General Assembly shall provide by general law.

(2) Exceptions. The provisions of this Section shall not prohibit any officer of the military forces of the State or of the United States not on active duty for an extensive period of time, any notary public, or any delegate to a Convention of the People from holding concurrently another office or place of trust or profit under this State or the United States or any department thereof.

Section 10. Continuation in office. In the absence of any contrary provision, all officers in this State, whether appointed or elected, shall hold their positions until other appointments are made or, if the offices are elective, until their successors are chosen and qualified.

ARTICLE VII   LOCAL GOVERNMENT

The North Carolina Constitution outlines the role that the state government plays in authorizing and regulating local governments within the state. For example, North Carolina has 100 counties, which vary widely in population and size. Counties are created by the General Assembly for certain public and political purposes. A county's powers, both express and implied, are given to it by statutes enacted by the General Assembly. These powers are exercised by the county's Board of Commissioners. In the exercise of some government functions, counties are simply agencies of the State. They must provide certain services, almost as if they are "branch offices of the state." These mandatory services include courthouses, law enforcement, and housing for public schools. Counties may also provide optional services, such as water and sewer and parks and recreation services. 🔷 3.02

Section 1. General Assembly to provide for local government. The General Assembly shall provide for the organization and government and the fixing of boundaries of counties, cities and towns, and other governmental subdivisions, and, except as otherwise prohibited by this Constitution, may give such powers and duties to counties, cities and towns, and other governmental subdivisions as it may deem advisable.

Each county has a board of commissioners, but no two boards are exactly alike. Boards of county commissioners vary in size, term of office, method of election, method of selecting the chairperson, and administrative structure. And these variations are not determined by the population of the county or any other objective criteria. Voters in each county also elect a sheriff (a law enforcement officer), a register of deeds (who keeps legal records such as property deeds and marriage licenses), and a clerk of court (who is really a locally elected employee of the state court system). 🔷 3.01, 3.02

The General Assembly shall not incorporate as a city or town, nor shall it authorize to be incorporated as a city or town, any territory lying within one mile of the corporate limits of any other city or town having a population of 5,000 or more according to the most recent decennial census of population taken by order of Congress, or lying within three miles of the corporate limits of any other city or town having a population of 10,000 or more according to the most recent decennial census of population taken by order of Congress, or lying within four miles of the corporate limits of any other city or town having a population of 25,000 or more according to the most recent decennial census of population taken by order of Congress, or lying within five miles of the corporate limits of any other city or town having a population of 50,000 or more according to the most recent decennial census of population taken by order of Congress. Notwithstanding the foregoing limitations, the General Assembly may incorporate a city or town by an act adopted by vote of three-fifths of all the members of each house.

The General Assembly incorporates cities or towns by granting them a charter. A charter is like a constitution for this new local government. It is the legal document that establishes a municipality and grants the new municipality certain powers, rights, and boundaries.

The legislature may require the voters to approve the incorporation, but voter approval is not required. When a city or town is incorporated, its charter designates the form of local government, such as mayor-council or council-manager, it will have. The charter also establishes the basis for other local government officials, such as the chief of police, and sets up the manner in which local ordinances—laws—will be adopted. Each municipality elects a local council—sometimes called a board of commissioners or aldermen—to run the government. The council sets the local tax rates and passes local laws, but it cannot change its charter. The legislature has the power to change or amend a municipality's charter, and the municipality has no power to prohibit the change. For example, the legislature can change a municipality's boundaries and increase or decrease the size of the city or town. Such a change would have an impact on any plans the municipality might have to annex other property adjacent to its boundaries. 3.01, 3.02, 3.04

Section 2. Sheriffs. In each county a Sheriff shall be elected by the qualified voters thereof at the same time and places as members of the General Assembly are elected and shall hold his office for a period of four years, subject to removal for cause as provided by law.

One of the local government officials specifically mentioned in the North Carolina Constitution is the sheriff. A sheriff, elected by the voters, is the chief law-enforcement officer in unincorporated areas of a county. 3.02

Section 3. Merged or consolidated counties. Any unit of local government formed by the merger or consolidation of a county or counties and the cities and towns therein shall be deemed both a county and a city for the purposes of this Constitution, and may exercise any authority conferred by law on counties, or on cities and towns, or both, as the General Assembly may provide.

ARTICLE VIII   CORPORATIONS

Section 1. Corporate charters. No corporation shall be created, nor shall its charter be extended, altered, or amended by special act, except corporations for charitable, educational, penal, or reformatory purposes that are to be and remain under the patronage and control of the State; but the General Assembly shall provide by general laws for the chartering, organization, and powers of all corporations, and for the amending, extending, and forfeiture of all charters, except those above permitted by special act. All such general acts may be altered from time to time or repealed. The General Assembly may at any time by special act repeal the charter of any corporation.

Section 2. Corporations defined. The term "corporation" as used in this Section shall be construed to include all associations and joint-stock companies having any of the powers and privileges of corporations not possessed by individuals or partnerships. All corporations shall have the right to sue and shall be subject to be sued in all courts, in like cases as natural persons.

ARTICLE IX   EDUCATION

In 1997 in the *Leandro* case, mentioned earlier with Article I, the North Carolina Supreme Court found that the North Carolina Constitution guaranteed every North Carolina child "an equal opportunity to obtain a sound basic education." The case went back to the Superior Court and went to trial in 1999. That trial was to decide whether the state was meeting its obligation to provide equal education opportunities. In 2002 Judge Howard Manning ruled that the state was not meeting that obligation. In 2004 the N.C. Supreme Court upheld Manning's ruling. The state then added $22 million to the state education budget to help certain school districts. Since 2004, Manning has held hearings and issued several letters, including one in 2006 that warned that about a dozen high schools that were not meeting standards might have to be closed if they did not improve. 3.05, 3.07

Section 1. Education encouraged. Religion, morality, and knowledge being necessary to good government and the happiness of mankind, schools, libraries, and the means of education shall forever be encouraged.

Section 2. Uniform system of schools.

(1) General and uniform system: term. The General Assembly shall provide by taxation and otherwise for a general and uniform system of free public schools, which shall be maintained at least nine months in every year, and wherein equal opportunities shall be provided for all students.

(2) Local responsibility. The General Assembly may assign to units of local government such responsibility for the financial support of the free public schools as it may deem appropriate. The governing boards of units of local government with financial responsibility for public education may use local revenues to add to or supplement any public school or post-secondary school program.

Section 3. School attendance. The General Assembly shall provide that every child of appropriate age and of sufficient mental and physical ability shall attend the public schools, unless educated by other means.

Section 4. State Board of Education.

(1) Board. The State Board of Education shall consist of the Lieutenant Governor, the Treasurer, and eleven members appointed by the Governor, subject to confirmation by the General Assembly in joint session. The General Assembly shall divide the State into eight educational districts. Of the appointive members of the Board, one shall be appointed from each of the eight educational districts and three shall be appointed from the State at large. Appointments shall be for overlapping terms of eight years. Appointments to fill vacancies shall be made by the Governor for the unexpired terms and shall not be subject to confirmation.

(2) Superintendent of Public Instruction. The Superintendent of Public Instruction shall be the secretary and chief administrative officer of the State Board of Education.

The North Carolina Constitution creates the State Board of Education to oversee the state's public school system. Article I, Section 15, guarantees the right of the people to have a free education; this article establishes the mechanism for making sure the state meets its duty to provide that education system. 3.02

Section 5. Powers and duties of Board. The State Board of Education shall supervise and administer the free public school system and the educational funds provided for its support, except the funds mentioned in Section 7 of this Article, and shall make all needed rules and regulations in relation thereto, subject to laws enacted by the General Assembly.

Section 6. State school fund. The proceeds of all lands that have been or hereafter may be granted by the United States to this State, and not otherwise appropriated by this State or the United States; all moneys, stocks, bonds, and other property belonging to the State for purposes of public education; the net proceeds of all sales of the swamp lands belonging to the State; and all other grants, gifts, and devises that have been or hereafter may be made to the State, and not otherwise appropriated by the State or by the terms of the grant, gift, or devise, shall be paid into the State Treasury and, together with so much of the revenue of the State as may be set apart for that purpose, shall be faithfully appropriated and used exclusively for establishing and maintaining a uniform system of free public schools.

In August 2005 Governor Mike Easley signed a controversial piece of legislation—the North Carolina State Lottery Act—into law. This legislation created the North Carolina Education Lottery. Under the act, 100 percent of the net proceeds—money left over after paying lottery prize money and certain expenses—of the North Carolina Education Lottery will go to help pay education expenses. These funds are to be used to pay for reduced class size in early grades, academic pre-kindergarten programs, school construction, and college and university scholarships for needy students. Some people opposed the lottery act on one or more grounds, including that the lottery is really a tax, that gambling is immoral, and that the lottery would negatively affect lower-income players more than people in other income groups. 🔲 3.07

Section 7. County school fund; State fund for certain moneys.

(a) Except as provided in subsection (b) of this section, all moneys, stocks, bonds, and other property belonging to a county school fund, and the clear proceeds of all penalties and forfeitures and of all fines collected in the several counties for any breach of the penal laws of the State, shall belong to and remain in the several counties, and shall be faithfully appropriated and used exclusively for maintaining free public schools.

(b) The General Assembly may place in a State fund the clear proceeds of all civil penalties, forfeitures, and fines which are collected by State agencies and which belong to the public schools pursuant to subsection (a) of this section. Moneys in such State fund shall be faithfully appropriated by the General Assembly, on a per pupil basis, to the counties, to be used exclusively for maintaining free public schools. (2003 423, s.1.)

Section 8. Higher education. The General Assembly shall maintain a public system of higher education, comprising The University of North Carolina and such other institutions of higher education as the General Assembly may deem wise. The General Assembly shall provide for the selection of trustees of The University of North Carolina and of the other institutions of higher education, in whom shall be vested all the privileges, rights, franchises, and endowments heretofore granted to or conferred upon the trustees of these institutions. The General Assembly may enact laws necessary and expedient for the maintenance and management of The University of North Carolina and the other public institutions of higher education.

Section 9. Benefits of public institutions of higher education.

The General Assembly shall provide that the benefits of The University of North Carolina and other public institutions of higher education, as far as practicable, be extended to the people of the State free of expense.

Section 10. Escheats.

(1) Escheats prior to July 1, 1971. All property that prior to July 1, 1971, accrued to the State from escheats, unclaimed dividends, or distributive shares of the estates of deceased persons shall be appropriated to the use of The University of North Carolina.

(2) Escheats after June 30, 1971. All property that, after June 30, 1971, shall accrue to the State from escheats, unclaimed dividends, or distributive shares of the estates of deceased persons shall be used to aid worthy and needy students who are residents of this State and are enrolled in public institutions of higher education in this State. The method, amount, and type of distribution shall be prescribed by law.

ARTICLE X   HOMESTEADS AND EXEMPTIONS

Section 1. Personal property exemptions.
The personal property of any resident of this State, to a value fixed by the General Assembly but not less than $500, to be selected by the resident, is exempted from sale under execution or other final process of any court, issued for the collection of any debt.

Section 2. Homestead exemptions.

(1) Exemption from sale; exceptions. Every homestead and the dwellings and buildings used therewith, to a value fixed by the General Assembly but not less than $1,000, to be selected by the owner thereof, or in lieu thereof, at the option of the owner, any lot in a city or town with the dwellings and buildings used thereon, and to the same value, owned and occupied by a resident of the State, shall be exempt from sale under execution or other final process obtained on any debt. But no property shall be exempt from sale for taxes, or for payment of obligations contracted for its purchase.

(2) Exemption for benefit of children. The homestead, after the death of the owner thereof, shall be exempt from the payment of any debt during the minority of the owner's children, or any of them.

(3) Exemption for benefit of surviving spouse. If the owner of a homestead dies, leaving a surviving spouse but no minor children, the homestead shall be exempt from the debts of the owner, and the rents and profits thereof shall inure to the benefit of the surviving spouse until he or she remarries, unless the surviving spouse is the owner of a separate homestead.

(4) Conveyance of homestead. Nothing contained in this Article shall operate to prevent the owner of a homestead from disposing of it by deed, but no deed made by a married owner of a homestead shall be valid without the signature and acknowledgement of his or her spouse.

Section 3. Mechanics' and laborers' liens. The General Assembly shall provide by proper legislation for giving to mechanics and laborers an adequate lien on the subject-matter of their labor. The provisions of Sections 1 and 2 of this Article shall not be so construed as to prevent a laborer's lien for work done and performed for the person claiming the exemption or a mechanic's lien for work done on the premises.

Section 4. Property of married women secured to them. The real and personal property of any female in this State acquired before marriage, and all property, real and personal, to which she may, after marriage, become in any manner entitled, shall be and remain the sole and separate estate and property of such female, and shall not be liable for any debts, obligations, or engagements of her husband, and may be devised and bequeathed and conveyed by her, subject to such regulations and limitations as the General Assembly may prescribe. Every married woman may exercise powers of attorney conferred upon her by her husband, including the power to execute and acknowledge deeds to property owned by herself and her husband or by her husband.

Section 5. Insurance. A person may insure his or her own life for the sole use and benefit of his or her spouse or children or both, and upon his or her death the proceeds from the insurance shall be paid to or for the benefit of the spouse or children or both, or to a guardian, free from all claims of the representatives or creditors of the insured or his or her estate. Any insurance policy which insures the life of a person for the sole use and benefit of that person's spouse or children or both shall not be subject to the claims of creditors of the insured during his or her lifetime, whether or not the policy reserves to the insured during his or her lifetime any or all rights provided for by the policy and whether or not the policy proceeds are payable to the estate of the insured in the event the beneficiary or beneficiaries predecease the insured.

ARTICLE XI PUNISHMENTS, CORRECTIONS, AND CHARITIES

Section 1. Punishments. The following punishments only shall be known to the laws of this State: death, imprisonment, fines, suspension of a jail or prison term with or without conditions, restitution, community service, restraints on liberty, work programs, removal from office, and disqualification to hold and enjoy any office of honor, trust, or profit under this State. (1995, c. 429, s. 2.)

Section 2. Death punishment. The object of punishments being not only to satisfy justice, but also to reform the offender and thus prevent crime, murder, arson, burglary, and rape, and these only, may be punishable with death, if the General Assembly shall so enact.

Section 3. Charitable and correctional institutions and agencies. Such charitable, benevolent, penal, and correctional institutions and agencies as the needs of humanity and the public good may require shall be established and operated by the State under such organization and in such manner as the General Assembly may prescribe.

Section 4. Welfare policy; board of public welfare. Beneficent provision for the poor, the unfortunate, and the orphan is one of the first duties of a civilized and a Christian state. Therefore the General Assembly shall provide for and define the duties of a board of public welfare.

ARTICLE XII   MILITARY FORCES

Section 1. Governor is Commander in Chief. The Governor shall be Commander in Chief of the military forces of the State and may call out those forces to execute the law, suppress riots and insurrections, and repel invasion.

ARTICLE XIII   CONVENTIONS; CONSTITUTIONAL AMENDMENT AND REVISION

Amending the North Carolina Constitution: This article sets out the two ways in which the state constitution can be amended: by a Convention of the People and by a popular vote on amendments proposed by the General Assembly and submitted to the voters. Some amendments, such as the rights given to victims of crime, make significant changes. Sometimes changes to the constitution are more limited, such as the amendment giving the governor veto power. In either case, Article XIII gives the people of North Carolina the flexibility to change government to meet new challenges. The process is not easy, but changing a constitution should not be something done lightly. 3.01, 3.04

Section 1. Convention of the People. No Convention of the People of this State shall ever be called unless by the concurrence of two-thirds of all the members of each house of the General Assembly, and unless the proposition "Convention or No Convention" is first submitted to the qualified voters of the State at the time and in the manner prescribed by the General Assembly. If a majority of the votes cast upon the proposition are in favor of a Convention, it shall assemble on the day prescribed by the General Assembly. The General Assembly shall, in the act submitting the convention proposition, propose limitations upon the authority of the Convention; and if a majority of the votes cast upon the proposition are in favor of a Convention, those limitations shall become binding upon the Convention. Delegates to the Convention shall be elected by the qualified voters at the time and in the manner prescribed in the act of submission. The

Convention shall consist of a number of delegates equal to the membership of the House of Representatives of the General Assembly that submits the convention proposition and the delegates shall be apportioned as is the House of Representatives. A Convention shall adopt no ordinance not necessary to the purpose for which the Convention has been called.

Section 2. Power to revise or amend Constitution reserved to people.

The people of this State reserve the power to amend this Constitution and to adopt a new or revised Constitution. This power may be exercised by either of the methods set out hereinafter in this Article, but in no other way.

Section 3. Revision or amendment by Convention of the People.

A Convention of the People of this State may be called pursuant to Section 1 of this Article to propose a new or revised Constitution or to propose amendments to this Constitution. Every new or revised Constitution and every constitutional amendment adopted by a Convention shall be submitted to the qualified voters of the State at the time and in the manner prescribed by the Convention. If a majority of the votes cast thereon are in favor of ratification of the new or revised Constitution or the constitutional amendment or amendments, it or they shall become effective January first next after ratification by the qualified voters unless a different effective date is prescribed by the Convention.

Section 4. Revision or amendment by legislative initiation.

A proposal of a new or revised Constitution or an amendment or amendments to this Constitution may be initiated by the General Assembly, but only if three-fifths of all the members of each house shall adopt an act submitting the proposal to the qualified voters of the State for their ratification or rejection. The proposal shall be submitted at the time and in the manner prescribed by the General Assembly. If a majority of the votes cast thereon are in favor of the proposed new or revised Constitution or constitutional amendment or amendments, it or they shall become effective January first next after ratification by the voters unless a different effective date is prescribed in the act submitting the proposal or proposals to the qualified voters.

ARTICLE XIV   MISCELLANEOUS

Section 1. Seat of government.

The permanent seat of government of this State shall be at the City of Raleigh.

Section 2. State boundaries.

The limits and boundaries of the State shall be and remain as they now are.

Section 3. General laws defined.

Whenever the General Assembly is directed or authorized by this Constitution to enact general laws, or general laws uniformly applicable throughout the State, or general laws uniformly applicable in every county, city and town, and other unit of local government, or in every local court district, no special or local act shall be enacted concerning the subject matter directed or authorized to be accomplished by general or uniformly applicable laws, and every amendment or repeal of any law relating to such subject matter shall also be general and uniform in its effect throughout the State. General laws may be enacted for classes defined by population or other criteria. General laws uniformly applicable throughout the State shall be made applicable without classification or exception in every unit of local government of like kind, such as every county, or every city and town, but need not be made applicable in every unit of local government in the State. General laws uniformly applicable in every county, city and town, and other unit of local government, or in every local court district, shall be made applicable without classification or exception in every unit of local government, or in every local court district, as the case may be. The General Assembly may at any time repeal any special, local, or private act.

Section 4. Continuity of laws; protection of office holders.

The laws of North Carolina not in conflict with this Constitution shall continue in force until lawfully altered. Except as otherwise specifically provided, the adoption of this Constitution shall not have the effect of vacating any office or term of office now filled or held by virtue of any election or appointment made under the prior Constitution of North Carolina and the laws of the State enacted pursuant thereto.

Section 5. Conservation of natural resources.

Few state constitutions have a general provision, such as Article XIV, Section 5, that requires the state to protect and preserve the lands and waters of the state for the benefit of the citizens. 3.01, 3.03

It shall be the policy of this State to conserve and protect its lands and waters for the benefit of all its citizenry, and to this end it shall be a proper function of the State of North Carolina and its political subdivisions to acquire and preserve park, recreational, and scenic areas, to control and limit the pollution of our air and water, to control excessive noise, and in every other appropriate way to preserve as a part of the common heritage of this State its forests, wetlands, estuaries, beaches, historical sites, open-lands, and places of beauty.

To accomplish the aforementioned public purposes, the State and its counties, cities and towns, and other units of local government may acquire by purchase or gift properties or interests in properties which shall, upon their special dedication to and acceptance by a law enacted by a vote of three-fifths of the members of each house of the General Assembly for those public purposes, constitute part of the 'State Nature and Historic Preserve,' and which shall not be used for other purposes except as authorized by law enacted by a vote of three-fifths of the members of each house of the General Assembly. The General Assembly shall prescribe by general law the conditions and procedures under which such properties or interests therein shall be dedicated for the aforementioned public purposes. (1971, c. 630, s. 1; S.L. 1999-268, ss 3-5; S.L. 2001 217, s. 3; S.L. 2002-3 Extra Session.)

CONSTITUTIONAL ANALYSIS QUESTIONS

1 In what ways are the preambles of the U.S. and North Carolina Constitutions similar?

2 How is the preamble of the North Carolina Constitution different from that of the U.S. Constitution?

3 How does Article I, Section 14, of the North Carolina Constitution differ from the relevant portion of the First Amendment to the U.S. Constitution?

4 Article VI, Section 7, of the North Carolina Constitution requires state officeholders to take an oath or affirmation of office. What officials in the federal government are required to take a similar oath or affirmation?

5 Article II, Section 1, of the North Carolina Constitution establishes a bicameral legislature. Which passage in the U.S. Constitution establishes a bicameral legislature? How do these two passages differ?

6 Article I, Section 2, of the U.S. Constitution establishes the length of the terms of members of the U.S. House of Representatives. Which passage in the North Carolina Constitution establishes term lengths in the North Carolina House of Representatives? How long are the terms in the U.S. and North Carolina House of Representatives?

7 How old does must a person be to serve in the U.S. House of Representatives? What is the minimum age for serving in the North Carolina House of Representatives?

8 What age requirement does the U.S. Constitution establish for U.S. Senators? Does the North Carolina Constitution set a minimum age for service in the state Senate?

9 Article I, Section 2, of the U.S. Constitution grants the House of Representatives the sole power of impeachment. Which passage of the North Carolina Constitution grants the power of impeachment, and to which house of the North Carolina General Assembly does it grant that power?

CONSTITUTIONAL ANALYSIS QUESTIONS

10 Article I, Section 3, of the U.S. Constitution requires that the U.S. Senate try all impeachments. Which passage in the North Carolina Constitution discusses impeachment trials? How are impeachments trials in North Carolina similar to those in the U.S. Senate?

11 Article I, Section 6, of the U.S. Constitution prevents members of Congress from being arrested under certain circumstances. Does the North Carolina Constitution contain a similar provision? Why might a constitution protect lawmakers from arrest at certain times? Why might a constitution lack such a provision?

12 Article I, Section 5, of the U.S. Constitution requires that a majority of members be present before a house of Congress conducts business. Which passage of the North Carolina Constitution addresses the same issue in the General Assembly? Why do the constitutions discuss this issue?

13 Article II, Section 23, of the North Carolina Constitution grants the General Assembly the exclusive power to raise revenue for the state. Which passage of the U.S. Constitution provides for the power to raise revenue?

14 Article I, Section 3, of the U.S. Constitution describes the office of the President of the Senate. Which passage(s) in the North Carolina Constitution addresses the same officer?

15 Which sections in the North Carolina Constitution discuss the proposal and passage of bills? How does that process differ from Article I, Section 7, of the U.S. Constitution?

16 Article I, Section 7, of the U.S. Constitution allows the president to veto a bill. How do the North Carolina governor's veto powers compare to those of the U.S. president?

17 Both the U.S. and North Carolina Constitutions allow a bill to become law without the signature of the chief executive. Under what circumstances does that occur?

18 Article I, Section 7, of the U.S. Constitution establishes the procedure that allows the legislature to override a veto by the executive branch. Which passage in the North Carolina Constitution details the process of overriding a veto?

19 Does the U.S. Constitution contain a provision similar to Article II, Section 19, of the North Carolina Constitution? What is it? How, if at all, does it differ from Article II, Section 19?

20 The Twentieth Amendment to the U.S. Constitution establishes the time when the U.S. Congress meets. How does this differ from the time established in the North Carolina Constitution?

21 Article II of the U.S. Constitution is devoted to the Executive Branch. Which article of the North Carolina Constitution discusses the executive branch? How do the two constitutions differ in the offices created for the executive branch?

22 The Twelfth Amendment to the U.S. Constitution requires that the president be chosen by electoral vote. How does a candidate for the governorship of North Carolina win office?

23 The Twelfth Amendment of the U.S. Constitution discusses the procedure for selecting a president if no candidate has won a majority of the electoral vote. How does that differ from the procedure that takes place if there is a tie in the North Carolina governor's race?

24 The Twentieth Amendment to the U.S. Constitution states the president-elect takes office on the 20th day of January. When does a North Carolina governor-elect take office?

25 If the president cannot fulfill the duties of office, Article II, Section 1, of the U.S. Constitution requires that the vice president assume the duties of the presidency. Who becomes Acting Governor if the North Carolina Governor cannot fulfill the duties of office?

26 Article II, Section 2, of the U.S. Constitution allows the president to make appointments to vacant offices while the Senate is in recess. Does Article III, Section 5, of the North Carolina Constitution grant the same power to the North Carolina governor to make recess appointments? How does that section differ from the U.S. Constitution?

27 How does the pardon power of the North Carolina governor discussed in Article III, Section 5, differ from the pardon power granted to the U.S. president?

28 The president's compensation for service is detailed in Article II, Section 1, of the U.S. Constitution. How are the terms of compensation for the North Carolina governor similar to those of the U.S. president?

29 In what ways are the court systems established in Article IV, Section 1, of the North Carolina Constitution and in Article III, Section 1, of the U.S. Constitution similar? In what ways are they different?

30 How do terms of office for Federal judges and North Carolina state judges differ?

31 Who is eligible to serve as a judge in North Carolina? Does the U.S. Constitution detail eligibility requirements for Federal judges?

32 Why do both the U.S. and North Carolina Constitutions prohibit reducing the salaries of a judge while the judge is serving on the court?

33 Article VI, Section 1, of the North Carolina says who may vote in North Carolina. What is the age at which a citizen of North Carolina may vote? Which amendment to the U.S. Constitution contains a similar provision?

34 Article II, Section 2, of the U.S. Constitution refers to state militias. How does Article III, Section 5, of the North Carolina Constitution compare with Article II, Section 2?

35 Article V discusses ways that amendments can be proposed for the U.S. Constitution. How does this differ from the amendment process found in Article XIII of the North Carolina Constitution?

36 The U.S. Constitution does not allow voters to directly propose constitutional amendments. According to Article XIII of the North Carolina Constitution, can voters propose an amendment to the state constitution? Explain your answer.

37 What is the process for the ratification of a proposed amendment to the U.S. Constitution? How does that process differ from ratification of a proposed amendment to the North Carolina Constitution?

38 In North Carolina, what, if any, is the procedure for enacting an entirely new or revised state constitution? Does the U.S. Constitution contain a similar provision? Why or why not?

39 How do the First Amendment of the U.S. Constitution and Article I, Section 12, of the North Carolina Constitution compare? Which provision seems to protect more freedom? Explain your answer.

40 How does Article I, Section 20, of the North Carolina Bill of Rights differ from the Fourth Amendment to the U.S. Constitution?

41 How does Article I, Section 13, of the North Carolina Bill of Rights differ from the religious freedoms protected by the First Amendment of the U.S. Constitution?

42 In what ways are the First Amendment to the U.S. Constitution and Article I, Section 14, of the North Carolina Bill of Rights similar?

43 The U.S. Bill of Rights makes no mention of the rights of crime victims. What are some of the rights crime victims have in the North Carolina Bill of Rights?

44 Under what circumstances do Article I, Section 9, of the U.S. Constitution and the North Carolina Bill of Rights allow for suspension of the writ of habeas corpus?

45 How do the guarantees of a trial by jury found in the Seventh Amendment to the U.S. Constitution and Article I, Section 25, of the North Carolina Bill of Rights differ?

46 The Fifth Amendment to the U.S. Constitution contains a provision regarding eminent domain, or the taking of private property for public use. How does that provision compare with Article I, Section 19, of the North Carolina Constitution?

47 The Fifth Amendment to the U.S. Constitution protects people against double jeopardy, or being tried twice for the same offense. The North Carolina Constitution has no explicit double jeopardy protection. What part of Article I, Section 19, might be used to create such a protection, and how would it relate to the Fifth Amendment language?

48 In what ways are the Fourteenth Amendment to the U.S. Constitution and Article I, Section 19, of the North Carolina Bill of Rights similar, and in what ways are they different?

49 Article I, Section 9, of the U.S. Constitution and Article I, Section 16, of the North Carolina Constitution prohibit passage of ex post facto laws. Why do both constitutions ban such laws?

50 The U.S. Constitution makes no reference to the right to an education. What provisions does the North Carolina Constitution include regarding the right to an education?

51 How do Article VI, Sections 1 and 2, of the North Carolina Constitution differ from the Nineteenth Amendment to the U.S. Constitution?

52 Article III, Section 8, of the North Carolina Constitution creates a Council of State. What, if any, part of Article II of the U.S. Constitution contains a parallel provision? What attitude toward the executive branch might the two different provisions reflect?

53 Article I, Section 29, of the North Carolina Bill of Rights prohibits convictions that work corruption of blood. How is this topic treated in Article III of the U.S. Constitution?

54 Many amendments to the U.S. Constitution protect the right to vote. Article VI of the North Carolina Constitution prohibits some people from voting. Who are those people?

55 What issues does Article X of the North Carolina Constitution address? Why are these matters not covered in the U.S. Constitution?

56 What topics are covered by Article XI of the North Carolina Constitution? Why do you think that these topics do not appear in the U.S. Constitution?

A

abolitionists people who campaigned to end slavery.

act a written law, also called **legislation**.

amend a word meaning "to change", used in the context of political documents, including the Constitution.

Anti-Federalists people who opposed adoption of the federal Constitution.

aristocrat a person who is born into a high-ranking class of society and receives special privileges because of the position he or she is born into; also called noble.

aristocracy the class of **aristocrats** in a country; Aristocracy is also a type of government ruled by the individuals born into a country's noble class.

atheist person who does not believe in God.

B

balanced government a government in which no single interest, group of people, or branch of government dominates.

bicameral legislature a legislature composed of two separate chambers or houses.

C

charter of incorporation a type of contract given to a company by a monarch in England, giving it the right to establish a trading colony in America;

civil of the state or government.

civil rights the term John Locke used to describe rights to such things as life, liberty, health, and property ownership; Modern civil rights include the right to vote.

civil society organizations, associations, and groups that people join voluntarily to pursue shared interests, goals, or values.

common law a body of laws based on English customs and the decisions of English courts, which is now in use in the United States.

compact an agreement.

communism a political theory that calls for the abolition of private property and common ownership of society's wealth; In practice, communist governments are ruled by a single political party and do not have free and open elections. They are typically totalitarian and suppress human rights.

conscription compulsory service in the military.

confederation a loose union of independent states; For example, the organization of states that withdrew from the Union during the Civil War was a confederation, or confederacy.

Congress the law-making or legislative body of the United States government.

constitutionalism the idea that law should limit the power of government.

D

delegate a person sent to a conference or a meeting to represent his state or nation.

democracy a form of government that allows people to participate in governing.

direct democracy a democracy in which people participate directly, by voting on laws; Compare to an **indirect democracy**.

divine right of kings a justification for rule by a **monarchy** in England; It means that God chooses a monarch and gives the monarch authority to rule. The monarch is then only answerable to God.

double jeopardy being put on trial more than once for the same crime; forbidden by the Fifth Amendment.

due process of law due process means that people must have their rights determined fairly, according to established laws.

duties taxes on the import or export of goods.

E

elastic clause name given to the last portion of Article I, section 8, of the Constitution because it gives Congress the necessary and proper powers to carry out its responsibilities and duties under the Constitution.

electors the people nominated by each state to vote for a presidential candidate; The number of electors is equal to the state's total number of senators and representatives in the U.S. Congress.

emancipation freeing someone from the control of another; Slaves who were freed were said to be emancipated.

eminent domain the government's power to take private property for public use.

Enlightenment a period of great intellectual and social change in Europe, England, and the colonies; The Enlightenment lasted from the 1650s to the 1750s.

ex post facto laws laws that seek to punish a person for something he did before the law existed; Such laws are prohibited by the Constitution.

executive the body of government that enforces the laws made by the legislature; In the United States, the executive branch includes the President and most government agencies.

F

federal national, referring to the government of the United States; For example, "federal powers" refers to the powers of the national government.

federalism a system of government in which power is divided between national and state governments.

Federalists people who supported adoption of the federal Constitution.

franchise the right to vote.

G

grand jury panels of citizens, which decide whether sufficient evidence exists to bring criminal charges against a suspect; The Fifth Amendment requires that a suspect can only be indicted by a grand jury.

H

hate speech speech that is meant to offend someone based, for example, on the person's race, gender, or religion.

House of Representatives the **lower house** of the U.S. Congress; The number of representatives of each state is proportional to its population.

human rights rights that people around the world recognize as essential to human dignity and freedom.

I

impeachment a process authorized by the Constitution to bring charges against the president and certain other officials of the federal government for misconduct while in office.

inauguration ceremony marking the start of a new Presidential term; It consists of the oath of office, an inaugural address, and other celebrations.

incorporation the process of extending the Bill of Rights to the states.

indictment a formal written accusation of a suspect.

indirect democracy a democracy in which people participate in government indirectly by electing other people to represent them and vote on laws for them; Democracy in the United States is generally indirect. Indirect democracy is also called **representative democracy**. Compare to a **direct democracy**.

J

Jim Crow laws see **segregation laws**.

judicial review the power of the judiciary to declare that laws passed by Congress are inconsistent with the Constitution; Laws that are declared to be unconstitutional cannot be enforced.

judiciary the branch of government composed of the courts, which interpret the law as applied to individual cases.

jury a group of people selected to hear a case in court and decide the truth about matters of fact presented to them.

L

legislation see act.

legislature the branch of government that makes laws; The legislature is composed of members who are elected by the people. The legislature in the United States is called Congress.

license government authorization to do a specified act.

limited government a government in which no single person holds complete governing authority.

lower house see House of Representatives.

M

member states nations that join the United Nations.

mixed government a government with the characteristics of monarchy, aristocracy, and democracy.

monarchy a government ruled by a person who inherits his or her position; The ruler of a monarchy, the monarch, rules for life. In a limited monarchy the monarch is subject to a constitution and the laws enacted under it.

N

natural laws the principles that arose to govern human behavior before society existed; Hobbes identified natural laws.

natural rights rights that all people are entitled to from the moment of birth; Locke suggested that **natural laws** gave people natural rights.

P

Parliament the representative assembly of England; It has two chambers the House of Lords and the House of Commons.

parliamentary system a parliamentary system combines the powers of the executive and the legislature; The judiciary remains separate. Most nations in Europe have a parliamentary system.

poll tax a tax that voters must pay if they want to vote.

popular sovereignty the concept that people create their government and agree or consent to be governed by it.

R

ratification the process by which the states accepted the Constitution; the process by which three-quarters of the states agree to amendments to the Constitution.

Reconstruction the period after the Civil War from 1865-1877, when the southern states were rebuilt and readmitted to the Union.

representative democracy see **indirect democracy**.

republic a republic is a **democracy** in which the head of state is elected by the people; The head of state of a republic cannot be a monarch. For example, England is a democracy, but it is not a republic because it has a Queen.

S

search warrant an order, usually issued by a judge, which allows government authorities to search for and seize certain items.

secession the act of withdrawing from a country or union.

securities a general name for stocks, bonds, and other investments.

segregation laws laws that separated people by race in transport, hotels, restaurants, theaters, parks, schools, and other public facilities; In the United States these laws were also known as Jim Crow laws.

Senate the **upper house** of the U.S. Congress; Each state has two Senators.

separation of powers under a separation of government powers each branch of government has its own specific functions and duties; no one branch can control the other branches.

social contract an agreement among people to follow laws and rules for behavior.

sovereignty the highest degree of political authority.

state a word used by Plato meaning government.

suffrage the right to vote; See also **franchise**.

T

totalitarian government a government that claims total authority over its subjects in their public and private lives.

U

upper house see Senate.

V

veto power the president's ability to block legislation that has been passed by both houses.

Index

A

abolition, 72–74
absolute monarchy, 8–9
Act Concerning Religion (Maryland), 49
Adams, John, 29
adverse witnesses, 58
advisory council, 15
affirmation, 56
Africa, 93
African Americans, 88–89
    Black Codes, 76, 80
    Civil Rights Act, 77, 80
    education of, 80, 99
    Fourteenth Amendment and, 78–80
    Plessy v. *Ferguson,* 79, 99
    voting rights for, 3, 78, 83–84, 83, 84
Age of Absolutism, 9
amend, 27, 39
American Women Suffrage Association, 86
ancien régime, 63
Anthony, Susan B., 85
Antifederalist Papers, 40–41
Antifederalists, 40–41
Areopagitica (Milton), 49, 68
Argentina, 93
aristocracy, 5, 14, 18
    during Enlightenment, 8–9
Aristotle, 3–4, 5
arms, right to bear, 55, 55p
Article I, 33–35, 72
Article II, 35–37
Article III, 38, 38p
Article IV, 39, 39m, 72
Article V, 39
Article VI, 40
Article VII, 40
articles, 33
Articles of Confederation, 24, 25–27
assassinations, 35, 76
assembly, elected 15
assembly, right to, 54, 54p
atheists, 48
Athens, 2
Atlantic Charter, 97
Axis powers, 96, 97

B

bail, 50, 57, 57p, 58
balance of powers, 33
balanced government, 5, 6, 12
banks, 43
barons, 47
Belgium, 92
bicameral legislature, 25, 33
Bill of Rights (English), 9, 48, 50
Bill of Rights (U.S.), 46–67, 52–60, 79
    Declaration of Rights of Man and, 62–66
Black Codes, 76, 80
Booth, John Wilkes, 76
border states, 74
Brazil, 93
Brown, Linda, 80
Brown v. *Board of Education* (1954), 80, 99
Brutus, 40
Burr, Aaron, 36
Bush v. *Gore* (2000), 59

C

cabinet members, 37
California, 33
Cato, 4, 40
Central America, 93
Charles I, king of England, 48
Charles II, king of England, 48
charter of incorporation, 14, 15
checks and balances, 101
Chile, 93
China, 96
Church of England, 54
Churchill, Winston, 97
Cicero, 5
citizenship
    in ancient Greece, 2
    of Native Americans, 83
    in Roman republic, 5
    states and, 26, 39
city-states, 2
civil government, 15
civil rights, 49, 99
Civil Rights Act (1866), 77
Civil Rights Act (1875), 80
Civil Rights Cases, 81
civil society, 103, 104, 105
Civil War, 18, 73–74
Clinton, Bill, 37
Coercive Acts (1774), 16
Coke, Sir Edward, 48
colonial government, 14–18, 93
    Articles of Confederation and, 25–27
commander in chief, 37
commerce, 27, 29, 34
common good, 3, 10, 17
common law, 47
Common Sense (Paine), 17
commonwealth, 11
communism, 93, 103
compact, 14, 15
competitive elections, 94
compulsory process, 59
compulsory voting, 95
Confederate States of America, 73–74
confederation, 26
congress, 16
Congress, U.S.
    admitting new states, 39
    under Articles of Confederation, 26–27
    development of, 30
    limits on, 35
    powers of, 31, 34
Connecticut, 30, 41
Connecticut Compromise, 30
conscription, 86
Consitution, North Carolina, 138–180
Constitution, U.S.
    amending the, 39, 90
    ancient sources of, 2–6
    Article I, 33–35, 33p, 34p, 72
    Article II, 35–37, 35p, 37p
    Article III, 38, 38p
    Article IV, 39, 39m, 72
    Article V, 39
    Article VI, 40
    Article VII, 40
    Bill of Rights, 52–60
    Constitutional Convention, 29–31
    democracy in the, 6
    division of, 33
    human rights and, 98–99
    ratification of, 40, 41
    signing the, 31
    slavery and the, 72–74
    written, 18
    See also individual amendments
Constitutional Convention, 29–31, 72
constitutionalism, 92–94
constitutions, 3–4
    state, 24–25, 50, 78
consul, 5
consul of plebes, 5
Continental Army, 17
Continental Congress, First, 16, 20–21
Continental Congress, Second, 17
Cosby, William, 50
cotton, 72
courts, federal, 34
cruel or unusual punishment, 50, 59
currency. See money
Czech Republic, 103, 103p

D

damages, 50
death penalty, 59
Declaration and Resolves of the First Continental Congress, 20–21
Declaration of Independence, 17–18, 18p, 25, 64, 65
Declaration of Resolves of the First Continental Congress, 16
Declaration of Rights of Man, 62–66
Delaware, 41, 74
democracy
    ancient, 2–4
    limited powers and, 101
    mixed government and, 5
    See also direct democracy; indirect democracy; representative democracy
Democracy's Century, 94, 96
direct democracy, 2
discrimination, 80–81, 84
divine right of kings, 10
double jeopardy, 59
due process of law, 47, 50, 79

E

education, 80–81, 99, 104
effects, 55
Eighth Amendment, 53, 57, 58, 59
elastic clause, 34
elections, 25
    of 1800, 36
    of 1866, 77
    competitive, 94
    multiparty, 94
electoral system, 36
Emancipation Proclamation, 74, 88–89
eminent domain, 56
emperor, 5
England
    colonies of, 14–18, 16, 17
    French and Indian War, 16, 18
    individual rights, 47–49
    Magna Carta, 47–48, 47p, 50
    monarchy in, 8–9
    Petition of Right, 48